Praise for *HTML & CSS: The Good Parts*

"Ben has an encyclopedic knowledge of web development and makes even the most obtuse-sounding concepts seem eminently approachable. All while writing a book filled with charm, wit, and aplomb. (Yeah, I hate him, too. Great book, though.)"

—Ethan Marcotte, coauthor of *Designing with Web Standards*, Third Edition

"*HTML & CSS: The Good Parts* is essential for those who work building web pages and need to take their understanding and knowledge to the next level. Web developers and designers of all types need to have solid depth of understanding of how HTML and CSS work as well as how they interact with the browser. The difference I find between an okay web designer and developer (including those who work with tools that create and manage sites) and a really good one is the depth of understanding they have and use of HTML and CSS. This book provides that depth and understanding.

"In my opinion one of the best pieces for me in this book is the inclusion of the proper structuring of pages, sites, and the depth of the discussion for integration is essential for the maintenance, use, and even SEO considerations. This is something that far too often gets missed and is not understood well. Having this knowledge and these skills in your tool belt will only lead to much improved outcomes that are easier to build out, manage, and use."

—Thomas Vander Wal, founder and senior consultant at InfoCloud Solutions

"I've always said that the beauty (and the frustration) in CSS is that there are so many ways to do things. Ben has done a fantastic job of homing in on the good, the bad, and the ugly in the broad CSS realm. His useful real-world approach not only gives you a great reference to the most commonly used elements, properties, and values, but it also addresses the advantages (and pitfalls) of various techniques. Whether you're working on small or large sites, Ben clearly presents the principles you need to crank your skills up to the next level."

—Stephanie Sullivan, author, *Mastering CSS with Dreamweaver CS4*

D1534558

HTML & CSS: The Good Parts

Ben Henick

O'REILLY®

Beijing · Cambridge · Farnham · Köln · Sebastopol · Taipei · Tokyo

HTML & CSS: The Good Parts
by Ben Henick

Published by O'Reilly Media, Inc., 1005 Gravenstein Highway North, Sebastopol, CA 95472.

O'Reilly books may be purchased for educational, business, or sales promotional use. Online editions are also available for most titles (*http://my.safaribooksonline.com*). For more information, contact our corporate/institutional sales department: 800-998-9938 or *corporate@oreilly.com*.

Editor: Simon St.Laurent
Production Editor: Loranah Dimant
Copyeditor: Emily Quill
Proofreader: Sada Preisch

Indexer: Lucie Haskins
Cover Designer: Karen Montgomery
Interior Designer: David Futato
Illustrator: Robert Romano

Printing History:
February 2010:   First Edition.

ISBN: 978-0-596-15760-9

[SB]

1265650326

To the memory of my mother and the patience of my father—each a wellspring of love, hope, and knowledge.

Table of Contents

Preface xvii

1. **Hypertext at the Core** 1
   The Web Without Links   1
   URIs   2
      Managing Links   3
      Improving the User Experience with Linking   3
      Hypertext Implementation Challenges   4

2. **Working with HTML Markup** 7
   HTML Syntax   7
      Tags, Elements, and Attributes   8
      Page Structure   10
   Rendering Modes, Flavors of HTML, and Document Type Declarations 10
      HTML or XHTML?   11
      Strict, Transitional, or Frameset?   12
      A Tale of Two Box Models   12
      Choosing the Right Document Type for Your Project   13
   Beautiful Parts: Universal Attributes   14
      Providing Stylesheet Hooks with class and id   14
      Describing Content with title and lang   15
      The contenteditable Attribute in HTML5   17
   Separating Content, Structure, Presentation, and Behavior   18
      Making Your Sites "Safe As Houses"   18
      Separation in Practice   18
      Working with Document Trees   19
   Browsers, Parsing, and Rendering   20
      Dynamic HTML, Ajax, and Rendering   21

3. **CSS Overview** 23
   Connecting Stylesheets to HTML Documents   23

Referencing a Stylesheet with link   23
Targeting Internet Explorer Versions with Conditional Comments   24
Replacing link with style   25
Using @import   25
Beware of style Attributes!   25
Targeting Rules to Specific Media   26
Choosing the Elements You Want to Style: Writing Selectors   27
Parents, Children, and Siblings: Element/Node Relationships   28
Simple Selectors   29
Multiple and Descendant Selectors   29
Selecting Direct Child Elements   30
Rule Conflicts, Priority, and Precedence   31
Selector Priority   31
Avoiding Rule Conflicts   32
Value Inheritance   33
CSS Property and Value Survey   33
CSS Units   33
Cross-Media Length and Size Units   34
Pitch and the Value of a Pixel   34
Print-Friendly Length Units   36
font-size Keywords   36
Color Units   37
Key CSS Layout Properties   37

4. Developing a Healthy Relationship with Standards **41**
The Broad Landscape of Web-Related Standards   41
Why Web Standards?   42
Interoperability   42
Market Forces   43
Forward Compatibility   43
Accessibility   43
Vendor Priorities   44
Legacy Asset Inertia   44
Best Practices (and Lack Thereof)   44
Strict Constructionism   45
Taking the Middle Road: Standards-Friendliness   45
Benefits of Standards-Friendliness   46
Rules of Standards-Friendly Development   46

5. Effective Style and Structure **49**
The Four Habits of Effective Stylists   49
Habit #1: Keeping It Simple   50
Habit #2: Keeping It Flexible   52

Habit #3: Keeping to Consistency   55
Habit #4: Keeping Your Bearings   57
CSS Zen and the Stylist's Experience   59
The Functional Principles of CSS Zen   60
Information Architecture and Web Usability   61
Multidimensionality   62
Navigation: Orientation and Wayfinding   63
Visit Strategies   64
Guideposts for Creating Usable Interfaces   66
Predicting Visitor Behavior with Scenarios and User Testing   67
Taxonomy and Nomenclature   68
Applying Taxonomy Through the Cascade   70
New Structural Elements (HTML5)   72

6. Solving the Puzzle of CSS Layout **73**
The CSS Box Model and Element Size Control   73
Quirks Mode and Strict Mode   73
auto Values   74
The overflow Property   75
Limiting But Not Fixing Element Dimensions   77
Handling the Unpredictable   77
Margins, Borders, and Padding   78
Negative Margins   79
Collapsed Margins   80
Borders   81
Padding   82
The Box Behavior of the Document Root Elements   82
Box Property Dimensions and the % Value   82
Element Flow   83
Inline Elements   83
Block Elements   83
Inline-Block Elements   84
Using the display Property to Change an Element's Flow   84
The display Property   85
The float and clear Properties   86
The Rules of the float Property   86
Canceling float Values with Corresponding clear Values   87
float Context   88
Implementing Multicolumn Layouts   88
Converting the Two-Column Layout from Markup Tables to CSS   89
How the Two-Column Styles Work   90
Benefits of Confining Layout Specifications to Stylesheets   92
Moving from Two Columns to Three   93

Dealing with More Than Three Columns   95
Semantically Empty Containers for Multicolumn Layouts   95
Advanced Layout in CSS3   96
CSS Positioning Properties   96
How Positioning Works   96
Bounding Positioned Elements   99
The visibility and z-index Properties   99
Altering Visibility Without Affecting Document Flow   100
Stacking   101
Obtaining Precise Navigation Source Order and Layout   102
Orienting the List   102
Forcing the Navigation List into the Desired Coordinates   104
Layout Types and Canvas Grids   106
Fixed, Proportional, and Flexible Layouts   106
Defining Grids   108
The Rule of Thirds, the Golden Ratio, and the Fibonacci Sequence 110
Implementing a Flexible Page Grid   111

7. Working with Lists **115**
Ordered and Unordered Lists   115
User Agent Default Styles for Ordered and Unordered Lists   115
Creating Valid Ordered and Unordered Lists   116
The list-style-type Property and the type Attribute   116
The nav Element (HTML5)   117
Changing the Range of an Ordered List   119
Other Uses for Lists   120
Outlines   120
Inline Serial Lists   120
Altering the Layout of Footer Links   121
Bullets in Backgrounds?   121
Styling Navigation Elements   121
Placing the Primary Site Navigation Within the Source Order   122
The Primary Navigation Layout Recipe   122
The Footer Navigation Recipe   123
Definition Lists   124
Styling Definition Lists   124
Dictionary Example   125
Dialogue Example   127

8. Headings, Hyperlinks, Inline Elements, and Quotations **129**
Headings and Good Writing   129
Headings in Print   129
Optimal Heading Insertion   131

Styling Heading Elements 131
   Heading Sizes and Type Treatments 132
   Normalizing Heading Dimensions 132
   Heading Accents 133
Link Markup 133
   Link Attributes 134
   Virtuous Use of the href Attribute 134
   Linking to Specific Passages Within Documents 135
   Creating Effective Link Content and title Values 136
Styling Links 137
   Link Pseudoclasses 137
   Using display: block to Increase the Footprint of a Link .. 138
   The text-decoration Property 139
   The cursor Property 140
Adding Semantic Value with Inline Elements 140
Quotations 142

9. Colors and Backgrounds **143**
Color Theory and Web Color Practice 143
   Usability, Accessibility, and Color 144
   The Additive Color Model 144
   The HSB Color Model 145
   The Subtractive Color Model 145
   Design, Contrast, and Complements 146
   Identifying Colors, in Brief 147
   Display Environments and the Web-Safe Palette 148
   Creating Your Own Palettes 149
CSS Backgrounds 150
   Setting background-position Values 151
   The CSS background Shorthand Property 152
Composing Background Images 152
   "Faux Columns" 154
   Tiled Background Textures and Patterns 155
   Large Background Textures and Nonrepeating Devices ... 156
   Drop Shadows, Gel Effects, and Rounded Corners 157
Bitmapped Copy and Fahrner Image Replacement 157
   The FIR Stylesheet Rules 159
   Drawbacks of FIR 159
Reducing Server Load with Sprites 160

10. (Data) Tables **163**
The Disadvantages of Layout Tables 163
   Source Order: Square Peg, Round Hole 163

CSS Zen Becomes a Myth	164
Template Slavery Is Unavoidable	164
Positioning Is Rendered Useless	164
The Parts of a Data Table	165
Example: The Full Smash of Table Markup	166
Composing Cells	168
Table and Data Composition	170
Table Headers, Footers, and Heading Cells	172
Attribute and Child Selectors	173
Reducing Header and Footer Contrast	173
Adding Rollover Accents to a Table	175

11. Images and Multimedia **177**

Replaced Elements	177
Preparing Images for Production	178
The alt Attribute Explained	179
Image Dimensions and Borders	179
Image Production	180
Cropping	180
Matting: Creating a Virtual "Frame"	181
Resampling: Altering the Absolute Size of an Image	182
Level Changes: Optimizing the Contrast of Photographs	183
Applying Multiple Adjustments	185
Working with Color Profiles	185
Image Optimization	186
Choosing the Right Image Format	186
Finding the Happy Medium Between Size and Quality	187
Publishing Images	188
Keeping Images Organized	188
Image Publishing and Management in a CMS	189
Image Publication Etiquette	190
Styling Images and Plug-in Content	190
Composing Image Layout Within a Column	190
Captioning Images	191
Working with Previews (Thumbnail Images) in a Gallery or Slideshow Setting	192
Lightbox: Previews, Galleries, and Slideshows	194
SlideShowPro	194
Adding Motion and Sound: Using SWFObject to Insert Flash Videos and Presentations	195
Inserting Unwrapped Multimedia	196
A Tale of Three Companies	197
Enter Flash	197

Using Bare Markup to Publish Multimedia Content	198
A Caveat of Plug-in Content Styling	198
Sidestepping Plug-ins with the HTTP Content-Disposition Header Field	199
Keeping an Open Mind	199
The video and audio Elements (HTML5)	199
The canvas Element (HTML5)	201
12. Web Typography	**203**
A Brief History of Letterforms	203
Origins of Modern Western Letterforms	204
Gutenberg's Press and the Art of Typography	204
The Emergence of Digital Typesetting	205
Different Limitations Without Changed Expectations	205
A Visual Glossary of Typography	206
Aliasing and Anti-Aliasing	210
Type Styles, Readability, and Legibility	212
Styling for Readability	212
Styling for Legibility	213
"The Fold" and Tiny Type	213
Sizing Type	215
Choosing the Right Units for Sizing Type	216
Em/Percentage Size Telescoping	216
Size Keywords	217
Working with Typefaces and Fonts	217
The Challenge of Limited Choices	217
Applying Type Choices: the font-family Property	220
Finding Canonical Typeface Names	222
Accessing System Default Type with the font Property	222
Character Encoding in Brief	224
What Is Character Encoding?	224
ASCII, ISO 8859-1, Unicode, and UTF-8	225
Choosing an Encoding Scheme	225
Inserting Entities to Provide Non-ASCII Characters	226
Creating Balanced Type Treatments	228
Predictability, Preference, and Panic	228
Assessing Content Scope	229
Distinguishing Type: Face, Size, Weight, Style, Color	230
Setting Type Around Blowouts	232
Styling Passages of Similar Priority	232
Enter Type Treatments	233
Typographical Miscellany in CSS	234
The line-height Property	234

The font-variant and text-transform Properties 235
The letter-spacing and word-spacing Properties 236
The white-space Property 236
The Practice of Good Web Typography 236

13. Clean and Accessible Forms **237**
Building Effective Forms 237
Web Applications, User Perspective, and Design Choices 237
Organizing User Interfaces by Function 238
Ten Rules for Effective Web Forms and Applications 239
Assessment and Structure 241
Establishing Requirements 241
Markup and Structure 243
Basic Form Structure, Presentation, and Behavior 246
Form-Originated get Requests 247
The post Method and File Uploads 249
Manipulating the Size and Appearance of Individual Controls 249
Prototyping and Layout 251
Prototyping 101 251
Design Patterns, Style Resets, and Form Layout 252
Grouping Controls by Appearance 254
Required Fields and Other Submission Constraints 255
Identifying Required Fields 255
Discovering and Identifying User Input Errors 256
The disabled and readonly Attributes 257
Creating Accessible Forms 258
Implementing Forms for Accessibility 259
Supporting Keyboard Navigation of Forms 260
Form Features in HTML5 261
New Input Types 262
The required Attribute 262

14. The Bad Parts **265**
The Numbing Nature of Internet Explorer (Especially IE 6) 265
Browser Wars 2.0 266
Absent or Poor Selector Support 267
hasLayout 268
Margin Doubling 268
expression() Values 269
ActiveX Filters and Transitions 269
PNG Support (or Lack Thereof) 270
Poor Property Support 270
Issues with XHTML and XML 271

Systemic Ugliness   271
  Template Fragility and Third-Party Content   272
  Markup Validation As a Prerequisite to Proper Style Implementation   272
  "Best Viewed with"   272
  Graded Support   273
  embed Versus object   274
  Form Controls, Plug-in Instances, and Element Stacking   275
  Invalid Markup for Stupid Reasons   276
HTML's Bad Neighborhoods and Cul-de-Sacs   276
  Frames   277
  The strike Element   278
  The name Attribute   279
  The noscript and noframes Elements   279
  Semantic Contortions and the Limited Vocabulary of HTML   280
  Inline Presentation Elements   280
  Manipulating Vertical Space: hr and br   281
  The pre Element Versus the white-space Property   281
CSS Travesties   282
  @-Rules   282
  Computed Values and Rounding Differences   282
  Vendor-Specific -moz and -webkit Property Prefixes   283
  The inherit Value   283
  Hiding Stuff: z-index and clip   284
  Counters   284
  Element Flow Rules   285
  Unicode Code Position Values and the content Property   285
The Awful Parts   286
  The marquee and blink Elements   286
  MSIE User Interface Properties   287
  The align Attribute   287
  The style Attribute   287
  div-itis   288
  Event Handler Attributes   288
  Gratuitous Underlining   289
  The http-equiv Attribute   289
Picking Up the Pieces   290

Appendix: URIs, Client-Server Architecture, and HTTP 291

Glossary 297

Index 303

Preface

HTML and CSS are old technologies that have seen over a decade of use and continue to evolve. Web developers celebrating their fifteenth year of work have seen all kinds of projects built across a wide variety of browsers, experimented with different features, and noted their successes and failures.

Despite their best efforts, the people who created HTML and CSS didn't always get it right. Some experiments didn't work out very well. At the same time, some pieces proved even more useful than expected. Mastering these technologies requires figuring out which pieces of the specs are cruft, in urgent need of abandonment, and which are gold, deserving maximum use. Focusing on HTML and CSS best practices does more than help you create sites that work: it lets you build more effective sites more efficiently, with much lighter long-term maintenance costs.

The Who and What of This Book

Hopefully you're holding this book because you read a glowing review on one of your favorite websites, or because somebody you know said that you *absolutely need* to read it. (An author can dream.)

Still, you need more information than that. Is this book for you?

If you and your priorities are described in the paragraphs that follow, then you should walk out of the store with this book under your arm, or at least sit down in the nearest available chair and start reading.

What Are the Good Parts?

There's no getting around the fact that long stretches of HTML and CSS are boring. I mean *sleep-through-it* boring. In this way, web technologies are like a certain class of movies: viewers find themselves wanting to skip the exposition so they can watch the good parts.

This book attempts to cater to that sentiment. All of the exposition—which I *do* invite the reader to tackle—is tucked away into Chapters 2 and 3, available for a quick "rewind" if you realize that you might have missed something.

The nonexpository parts are about making cool stuff happen: nailing down faithfulness to composites, getting the upper hand over bugs, building template markup that can survive redesigns, and manifold other topics.

What You Should Know Before You Read This Book

This book makes one basic assumption: that you're familiar with the scope of HTML 4.01 elements, CSS selectors, and CSS property/value pairs. The companion website (*http://www.htmlcssgoodparts.net*) for this book includes reference tables that link to exhaustive descriptions of HTML and CSS on third-party sites, but it will be far easier to follow along if you're already familiar with the capabilities of HTML and CSS.

In addition, this book will be easier to digest if you've gained an understanding of the separation of behavior, presentation, content, and structure into separate layers within a site or application.

If you feel uneasy about any of this, O'Reilly's *Definitive Guides* and *Pocket References* for HTML and CSS come highly recommended.

For the benefit of readers who may have overestimated their knowledge, the basics of page, stylesheet, and element structure *are* covered as briefly as possible.

The Ideal Reader

You might be an ideal reader of this book if:

- You're confident when the time comes to start building the server side of an application, but redesigns get on your nerves because you're forced to dive back into the code and revise the bits of markup that are interspersed within it. The most effective solution to this problem is called the "CSS Zen" technique, exemplified by Dave Shea's CSS Zen Garden (*http://www.csszengarden.com/*). This book explains CSS Zen—structuring production of markup so that redesign efforts can be confined to stylesheets—from a perspective suited to engineers.

- You're skilled at the use of a web-centric Integrated Development Environment (IDE) such as Adobe Dreamweaver or Microsoft Visual Studio, but your expectations routinely collide with its limitations. Left unattended, an IDE typically inserts all manner of cruft (i.e., "excess; superfluous junk") into web materials, egregiously violating the KISS (Keep It Simple, Stupid) Principle. This occurs because IDEs are one-size-fits-all solutions. This book explains HTML and CSS in enough detail that you can start configuring your tools of choice to handle the specific cases you work with every day.

- You have—for whatever reason—a lot of bad habits that need to be superseded by good ones. Some of you probably still use HTML to manage presentation as well as structure, and CSS meanwhile is terse to the point of impenetrability. This book's perspective places CSS in a useful light.

- You're a print-trained graphic designer who needs to understand the strengths and limitations of the web medium in order to avoid career stagnation. You've looked at HTML, you've looked at CSS, and you believe they fit together—but you just don't understand *how*. This book takes a close look at the connection between the two, so that you can get the hang of putting design elements exactly where you want them.

- Your professional role encourages or perhaps even requires you to develop to statutory accessibility requirements, or internally mandated cross-media usability requirements. Without CSS-ready markup, there's little hope of developing cross-media-friendly sites, much less sites accessible to impaired users. This book explains how to develop a site so that accessibility requirements can be met without needing to build multiple sites in parallel.

- You're already a specialist in some skill set outside of the presentation layer, and you want to make your job easier. Put simply, narrower specialization leads to reduced skill overlap, which in turn poses barriers to intrateam communication. This book lays out the priorities of the developers whose work lies closest to site visitors, and in so doing gives you the information you need to communicate more effectively with your teammates.

- You're tired of beating your head against the brick wall more commonly known as Internet Explorer 6. Several sites, particularly Position Is Everything (*http://www.positioniseverything.net/*), delve into solutions for the nightmare that is stylesheet authoring for legacy versions of Internet Explorer. However, most online resources are tuned to specific bugs and behaviors. In Chapter 14, you'll find condensed explanations of the quirks "under the hood" that cause unwanted collisions and blowouts, as well as a cookbook of practices and techniques that will help you avoid many such problems altogether.

A Warning About Familiarity (or Lack Thereof)

Chances are that you are already familiar with some of the contents of this book. Because its audience comprises a wide range of specialists, there may be times when material meant for engineers is painfully obvious to designers, and vice versa. There may also be times when the discussion begins to remind you of a contentious argument. Creative and implementation decisions are too often made from a position of political strength instead of merit, and it's my hope that this book can be used to support merit-based arguments against Bad Ideas.

If instead everything in this book is new, it's possible that you've gotten a bit ahead of yourself. The book's companion website is built in large part to meet the needs of folks like you, by way of ensuring that *all* purchasers of this book will be able to get some value from it. However, if the material does seem a bit advanced, you can expect some difficulty. The best way of dealing with *that* is to be patient, and ask lots of questions of colleagues and associates.

Objectives of This Book

This book is meant to translate into plain English the quirks of HTML, CSS, and the document tree that are hard to grasp without guidance or experience:

- Choosing and using the ideal version of HTML for your project
- Removing the obstacles between your current practice and consistently valid markup
- Using HTML to implement for structure, rather than presentation, in ways that get the best out of CSS
- Obscure-yet-useful HTML elements
- Getting-plug-in-content-to-work-dammit
- Using tables properly, and getting the most out of them
- The method behind the madness of CSS selectors, particularly descendant selectors
- CSS selector precedence
- The CSS block layout context
- CSS margin collapsing
- Bugs and other oddities imposed by Internet Explorer 6
- Wrangling form presentation
- The history behind the bugginess of web browsers
- What HTTP does when your back is turned (and why it's important)

This book tries to cover what all presentation layer developers *should* know. It aims to describe the many *relationships* between layers of the web technology stack that are touched by designers and presentation layer developers, and also to present the strengths of HTML and CSS.

This book will also introduce the less experienced reader to a long list of CSS layout "tricks" essential to the demands of presentation, accessibility, and Search Engine Optimization (SEO). These include:

- Centering content
- Using enhanced Fahrner Image Replacement to implement bitmapped heading type
- Creating well-aligned columns of equal (or apparently equal) height

- Using the CSS `float` property to get the best of both column presentation and markup source order
- Building versatile, visually rich navigation interfaces
- Developing work habits that will make your sites Ajax-ready
- Getting the most out of the CSS `position` property
- Creating versatile grid systems for your sites

A full reading of this book should imbue the reader with the majority of the knowledge needed to transform nearly any consistent set of composites—no matter how far-out their apparent requirements—into the presentation and content layers of an accessible, usable, and "crawl"-able website.

What Is Not In This Book

This book focuses tightly on practices that maximize the effectiveness of markup and stylesheets. For that reason, a number of things are not included in this book:

Sparsely supported bits of advanced and platform-specific CSS
> You can do a lot of fun stuff with CSS...but unfortunately, some of it relies on unevenly supported CSS selectors and properties. Such cases will be handled in terms of *desired results*: if an ActiveX filter supported in Internet Explorer has an analog in Firefox, it might be mentioned, or vice versa for `-moz-*` properties that have analogs in the IE runtime environment. The *minimum* requirement for discussion of implementation techniques in this book is reliable support in both Firefox 3 and Internet Explorer 8, and broader platform support for techniques that render obscure accents.

CSS properties targeted at comparatively obscure media types
> This book will cover production techniques well suited to the creation of highly accessible sites, but it is only intended as an *introduction* to implementing sites that are accessible to impaired visitors.

JavaScript and the Document Object Model (DOM)
> While this book will mention JavaScript at times and even occasionally show a bit of code, its focus on HTML and CSS means that it doesn't cover how to manipulate HTML and CSS with JavaScript or the DOM.

Integration with frameworks such as jQuery and YUI
> Many people have many beautiful things to say about JavaScript frameworks, but you won't find any mention of them in this book. Despite their usefulness in a variety of environments, JavaScript frameworks are neglected here for reasons of scope. The best resources for learning about the interaction of JavaScript frameworks, styles, and markup are to be found in web resources and books that focus on frameworks specifically.

Comprehensive discussion of CSS frameworks such as YUI Grids and Blueprint

The goal of this book is to help you burnish your skills in good faith so that the results on your résumé are pleasing not only to Human Resources evaluators, but to hiring managers as well. Therefore, reading this book should help you to better understand any CSS framework that you might be called upon to use, instead of instructing you on the use of any framework in particular.

Web server configuration techniques

Typical web server runtime configurations neglect a number of settings that can ease the achievement of usability, accessibility, and standards compliance objectives. However, these oversights fall more into the domain of system administrators. A number of other O'Reilly titles, particularly *Webmaster in a Nutshell (http: //oreilly.com/catalog/9780596003579/)* and *Website Optimization (http://oreilly .com/catalog/9780596515089/)*, address this area of interest. A number of online communities and blogs also explore this topic from time to time.

Developing for the mobile web

This book has the misfortune of being written by a lifetime resident of the U.S., where the feature set and reliability of mobile web access has plenty of room for improvement. The iPhone's popularity has improved the situation, but still has not made it entirely tolerable. As it stands, only a minority of the mobile device users in the U.S. can hold any realistic expectation of using the same Web as personal computer users. Meanwhile, the expense of prepaid device connectivity found in the U.S., and the wildly uneven availability of unencumbered emulators for mobile device platforms, further exacerbates the problems faced when developing mobile content for U.S. visitors. It is my hope that the *next* edition of this book will be able to include development techniques intended to benefit site visitors who use mobile devices.

Any mention of the Opera desktop browser

If there is one omission from this book over which I agonize, it's the omission of the Opera desktop browser from all discussions of browser behavior. Unfortunately, when I weighed Opera's market share against the amount of testing its inclusion in the book would require, the results of the comparison were superlatively discouraging. Since I owe Chris Mills of Opera *direct* thanks for his role in helping me to secure the contract for this book, rest assured that I did not make my decision lightly. Given any more than the barest amount of reader interest, I won't hesitate to discuss the Opera desktop browser at length on this book's companion website.

About Web Standards

Last but not least, there is the question of compliance with World Wide Web Consortium (W3C) Recommendations in commercial settings, particularly those environments that are nurtured in large enterprises.

I've always made it a point to distinguish between "standards friendliness" and "standards compliance." The first obeys the *spirit* of so-called web standards and is easy to achieve with practice, while the second focuses on obeying the *letter* of the Recommendations and can prove impossible to achieve.

The effectiveness of a website is enhanced far more by standards friendliness than by standards compliance, with the greatest enhancements coming from adherence to both objectives. This book embraces the compromises and fallbacks that preserve standards friendliness in spite of adverse development conditions, with only the occasional twisted grimace.

You may have noticed that I referred to "so-called" web standards earlier. The underlying irony is that web standards...aren't, at least not literally.

Standardization requires conscientious use of a formally defined system across an entire industry, typically (if not always) by standards bodies whose work contributes directly or indirectly to policies and publications of the International Organization for Standardization (ISO).

Another hallmark of true standards is an objective set of criteria and processes by which claims of compliance can be *enforced*—an asset that the W3C's products very much lack.

For these reasons the popular definition of W3C Recommendations as *standards* is reasonable in spirit, but has no basis in literal fact.

That said, the practice of web standards development has evolved tremendously since the go-go era of the 1990s, a point that's explored in greater detail on this book's companion website.

About Photoshop

Chapters 9 and 11 discuss image production techniques in some detail, and the procedures described there are based on the Adobe Photoshop user interface. I took this approach because in any moderately sized group of web professionals, you'll find a wide diversity of preferred tools and implementation techniques...*until* you get to the question of working with graphics. Alternatives to Photoshop (particularly Fireworks, another Adobe product) claim their devotees, but even those operators will agree that a working knowledge of Photoshop's toolset and user interface is immensely useful.

My choice was also based on slanted experience; I haven't used anything other than Photoshop to manipulate web images since I was a full-on novice. My hope is that visitors to this book's companion site will submit their own alternative-title cookbooks for the image manipulation techniques discussed in the book.

The matter of relying on Photoshop also illuminates the importance of tool choice with respect to team effectiveness. Chapter 4 introduces the value of production standards and code libraries, but the benefits of tool uniformity also extend to off-the-shelf software choices.

What You'll Find on the Companion Website

The companion website to this book, *www.htmlcssgoodparts.net*, contains a wealth of information. Among the goodies you'll find are:

- Errata and corrections
- Blog entries about reader questions, current technical developments, and best practices
- Staged demonstrations of techniques discussed in the book, complete with source markup and stylesheet rules and indexed to page numbers
- Boilerplate and/or templates for multicolumn layouts and other widgets
- HTML and CSS reference tables that link to multiple third-party documentation sources
- Visitor-submitted reviews of books and software of interest to this book's audience

Nomenclature

Names for the various pieces of web technology sometimes vary from shop to shop and from place to place. To minimize the potential for confusion, the terms spelled out below in *emphasis* are used consistently throughout the book.

Files are discrete nodes on a server host's native filesystem, while *resources* are documents or document fragments referenced by discrete Uniform Resource Identifier (URIs). Not all files are URIs, and not all URIs are files; a URI might contain several files, database query results, or data streams, while a file might amount to nothing more than the logic that determines the content of multiple URIs.

Pages or *documents* contain one or more resources of arbitrary classification and are the visitor-facing output of a request for a single URI (or perhaps multiple URIs, on sites where Ajax has been deployed). Finally, this book treats the differences between the terms "URI" and "URL" as minor to the point of insignificance, in part because the term "resource" itself has been so muddled it's become functionally meaningless in the face of rapid evolution.

Content is the matter around which websites are built.

HTML, XHTML, and XML tags are referred to in sum as *markup*.

Stylesheets are the content of CSS files or `style` elements. Stylesheet *rules* assign presentation to one or several elements within a page. A stylesheet rule contains a *selector*, which defines the element(s) on the page to which one or more *property/value pairs* are to be applied.

Browsers are also known as *user agents*, *UAs*, or *clients*.

HTML and CSS are *parsed* in serial fashion, and according to the results of that process the browser *renders* a page.

JavaScript is a registered trademark of Sun Microsystems that refers here to the programming language used to script data processing and interactivity within browsers. Different vendors refer to it by different names to avoid court trouble, but where there's a browser, there's usually a JavaScript interpreter.

The *Document Object Model* (or *DOM*) is both the representation of a web document's structure, and the definition of how that structure ought to be organized, queried, and altered programmatically. Several DOM specifications for web documents exist, though only one is developed and sanctioned by the World Wide Web Consortium as a body.

The stack of web-related services is colloquially and commonly understood to include an operating system, a web service, a relational database service, a server-side scripting language, HTML, CSS, and JavaScript. The platforms used in the first four layers of the stack vary from shop to shop. Of the layers on this notional stack, the first four layers refer to the *server-side* environment, and the latter three to the *client-side* environment.

The client-side environment is artificially divided into four sublayers: *structure* (defined by markup), *content* (enclosed by markup), *presentation* (defined by CSS), and *behavior* (defined by JavaScript). Together these form a second Model-View-Controller (MVC) architecture that mirrors and interacts with the MVC architecture on the server side.

Ajax is an acronym representing *Asynchronous JavaScript And XML*, an implementation approach made convenient by the ubiquity of the `GetXMLHttpRequest` Application Programming Interface (API).

HTML *elements* are the principal items in the HTML namespace; *tags* are literal markup, which might well contain *attributes* with *values*, and most often enclose content.

Copy and *illustrations* are to content what *text* and *images* are to data.

A *doctype declaration* can (and usually should) appear at the beginning of a given web document and identifies the version of HTML against which that document should validate. The *document type definition* (also called a *DTD*) is a machine-readable series of statements that defines validity for the applicable version of HTML. The values contained in a doctype declaration directly reference a specific DTD.

W3C *Recommendations* are official documents that serve as specifications for web technology platforms and best practices associated with the use of those platforms.

Project managers minimize the obstacles standing between a project team and the completion of their deliverables. *Designers* create the look, feel, and user experience of sites. *Engineers* and *application developers* design and write the code that makes sites go. *Presentation layer developers* as a group deliver everything that directly faces site visitors; of these, *stylists* create templates and stylesheets, and *producers* ensure that content gets placed into production. Most other roles commonly found in web project teams are titled here as they would be in an advertising/marketing environment.

Current browsers or user agents refer to the mass-market browser versions current when this book went to press: Internet Explorer 6–8, Firefox 3.x, and Safari 3.x–4.x.

Several of the terms listed here point to obscure processes with an impact on the web user experience; these processes will be discussed in more detail throughout this book.

"Read the Source, Luke!"

When I first started working with the web platform in 1995, "Read the Source, Luke!" was easily the most popular advice given to the greenest newbies on mailing lists. This hearkens back to the climactic moments of *Star Wars: A New Hope*, and exhorts the petitioner to read through the source markup (and now, 13 years later, the stylesheet rules) of results they find admirable.

There's more to this advice than sci-fi nerd humor. The best understanding of effective passages of markup and styles comes from reading through them without filters—in much the same way that "Force-sensitives" of the *Star Wars* milieu get the most out of *their* talents by letting go of their prejudicial thoughts.

If you try to puzzle out how somebody accomplished a presentation goal *before* you read his source, you might be badly disappointed...and if you *never* read his source, you might never figure it out for yourself.

However, before we can get into the finer points of learning from source markup and CSS, it's best to look at the Web as a system—the relationships between the underlying conventions and technologies that make it go.

Conventions Used in This Book

The following font conventions are used in this book:

Italic
> Indicates pathnames, filenames, and program names; also Internet addresses, such as domain names and URLs

`Constant width`
> Indicates command lines and options that should be typed verbatim; names and keywords in programs, including method names, variable names, and class names; and HTML element tags

Constant width bold
> Indicates emphasis in program code lines

Constant width italic
> Indicates text that should be replaced with user-supplied values

This icon signifies a tip, suggestion, or general note.

This icon indicates a warning or caution.

Using Code Examples

This book is here to help you get your job done. In general, you may use the code in this book in your programs and documentation. You do not need to contact us for permission unless you're reproducing a significant portion of the code. For example, writing a program that uses several chunks of code from this book does not require permission. Selling or distributing a CD-ROM of examples from O'Reilly books does require permission. Answering a question by citing this book and quoting example code does not require permission. Incorporating a significant amount of example code from this book into your product's documentation does require permission.

We appreciate, but do not require, attribution. An attribution usually includes the title, author, publisher, and ISBN. For example: "*HTML & CSS: The Good Parts*, by Ben Henick. Copyright 2010 Ben Henick, 978-059615760-9."

If you feel your use of code examples falls outside fair use or the permission given above, feel free to contact us at *permissions@oreilly.com*.

Safari® Books Online

 Safari Books Online is an on-demand digital library that lets you easily search over 7,500 technology and creative reference books and videos to find the answers you need quickly.

With a subscription, you can read any page and watch any video from our library online. Read books on your cell phone and mobile devices. Access new titles before they are available for print, and get exclusive access to manuscripts in development and post feedback for the authors. Copy and paste code samples, organize your favorites, download chapters, bookmark key sections, create notes, print out pages, and benefit from tons of other time-saving features.

O'Reilly Media has uploaded this book to the Safari Books Online service. To have full digital access to this book and others on similar topics from O'Reilly and other publishers, sign up for free at *http://my.safaribooksonline.com*.

How to Contact O'Reilly

We have tested and verified the information in this book to the best of our ability, but you may find that features have changed (or even that we have made a few mistakes!). Please let us know about any errors you find, as well as your suggestions for future editions, by writing to:

O'Reilly Media, Inc.
1005 Gravenstein Highway North
Sebastopol, CA 95472
800-998-9938 (in the U.S. or Canada)
707-829-0515 (international/local)
707-829-0104 (fax)

O'Reilly's catalog page for this book, which lists errata, examples, and any additional information, is at:

http://www.oreilly.com/catalog/9780596157609/

The author has a companion website for this book at:

http://www.htmlcssgoodparts.net

To comment or ask technical questions about this book, send email to the following, quoting the book's ISBN (9780596157609):

bookquestions@oreilly.com

For more information about our books, conferences, Resource Centers, and the O'Reilly Network, see our website at:

http://www.oreilly.com

Acknowledgments

When I reflect upon my experiences of 15 years as a site builder, the quality that impresses me most is ignorance. There's plenty of it to go around, and like many site builders, I often take opportunities to castigate the ignorance of others less skilled...but not in this book.

Why?

Of greater concern still is my own ignorance, which is no less deserving of criticism. Close on the heels of ignorance are trepidation and obstinacy, both of which were regular contributors to my internal dialogue during the year that I took to write this book.

Given that attitude, this book attempts to exemplify the belief that one should light a candle for others to find their way, instead of cursing the darkness. I give fair due to the comfort engendered by continued reliance upon legacy production techniques, and where best practices are mentioned, I make a point of selling them as softly as I can without muddling my message.

In sum, I tried to fill this book with the advice that would have stood me in good stead eight or nine years ago, that instead many people (including myself) sorted out only by trial, error, and accident, and thence shared one iota at a time as they became able.

I hope that this book will be as useful to you now, as it would've been to me when I was working toward CSS mastery.

There are a number of people whose involvement in my life brought me far enough to achieve that state of mastery and to write this book. Since this is my first chance to call them out fully in public, I feel that I ought to mention them by name. Apart from my family, these benefactors include Christian Cepel, Steven Champeon, Sumin Chou, Teddi Deppner, Nick Finck, David Hemphill, Molly Holzschlag, Brenda Houston, Ethan Marcotte, Doug Petersen, Lance Taylor, Thomas Vander Wal, Peter Zale, and Jeffrey Zeldman. These individuals have each made significant contributions to my life, and without *all* of them, it's likely that this book would never have been written.

There are also several people named in the book itself. Of these, Chris Mills of Opera Software has my special thanks. Chris has never been far from this project—he's the one who suggested me to O'Reilly Media as an author candidate. In fact, Chris started me down this road in the first place, by inviting me to contribute to the Opera Web Standards Curriculum (*http://www.opera.com/company/education/curriculum*).

The contents and quality of this book are not owed to my work alone. In fact, it was kept from the precipice of failure by the indefatigable patience of Simon St.Laurent, my editor at O'Reilly Media. My words might be on these pages and my name might be on the cover, but Simon's constant support of this project bridged the long gap between my effort and a successful conclusion.

Michael Smith is ultimately responsible for this book's contents on the subject of HTML5, and the absence of his name from its cover makes poor thanks for his willingness to rescue me from lurching through that proverbial minefield.

I had the opportunity to handpick three technical reviewers: Kimberly Blessing, Gez Lemon, and Chris Van Domelen. Each of them made categorically critical contributions to the accuracy and currency of this book, any remaining lack of which is my responsibility alone.

Kimberly and Chris have also been stalwart associates and sources of technical advice for several years, and I find myself unable (as in so many other cases) to thank them in adequate measure for their help.

O'Reilly Media was gracious enough to provide three additional technical reviewers: Edd Dumbill, Elaine Nelson, and Shelley Powers. Their contributions helped find many more glitches and improve the structure of the book.

While I might've written this book someday, you wouldn't be reading it now without the outstanding work of Douglas Crockford, which proved that a "Good Parts" series would find enthusiastic readers.

I believe strongly that things *really* work on account of the work done by "backstage" folks, and this project confirmed that belief. Especially high praise goes to Emily Quill, who untangled the unwieldy parts of this book's draft, and in doing so, ensured that you will get your money's worth for this book. Loranah Dimant tirelessly addressed my last-minute edits and ensured a bright polish for the book.

My final thanks here go to Eric Meyer, who sets the bar high for the rest of us who take a hand at developer education.

In closing, I hope that the knowledge you gain from this book will lead you to achievements that are no less impressive in degree than those of the people mentioned here.

CHAPTER 1

Hypertext at the Core

A properly built website is far more than the sum of its markup, stylesheets, scripting, and multimedia resources. Well-built websites take full advantage of their hypertext medium, making a once obscure technology central to the way we consume information. Without easily activated *links*, the Web wouldn't be the Web; it would be just a rigidly organized heap of documents.

While hypertext offers tremendous flexibility, it also requires developers to help visitors find their way. Visitors will take unexpected paths even within a site, and will arrive from sites or bookmarks that you don't control. The power that hypertext provides also comes with the responsibility to structure your site in ways that visitors will be able to comprehend and navigate.

The Web Without Links

The Web's use of links to connect information makes it different from previous media. Today, when the Web is so familiar, it's easy to forget those differences, but they pave the way to developing successful websites. So what happens when you remove hyperlinks from a site?

- The first and most significant result of excising hypertext from a networked information system is that *content becomes strictly linea*r: one must first read through a given amount of content before reaching the object of his interest. Take the links out of hypermedia and the result is nearly useless without a concerted attempt at imposing internal order and structure.

- Linear resources are *designed and structured on different assumptions*, expecting that a reader has examined (or at least referred to) previous passages of content. Take this book as an example. You can jump around within it, but chapters are still ordered by the descending importance of the subjects that they cover. Also, if the companion website for this book (*http://www.htmlcssgoodparts.net*) did not exist, there would be plenty of verbose markup examples between its covers.

- *The visitor's sense of location is informed by standard cues.* Most books and other linear information resources have some sort of header or footer content on every page (or on the title bar of the reader application), and a visitor's state of progress through a networked information resource, like a large Portable Document Format (PDF) file, is cued by a vertical scroll bar.

These distinctions illustrate how *hyperlinks* add new dimensions to documents. While this gives the Web tremendous flexibility, it also creates challenges. The added navigational possibilities result in systems that make it difficult to maintain a sense of place. While the consumer of a linear resource can count on traditional cues and her own critical thinking skills to enforce her sense of place, the consumer of hyperlinked resources needs the help of designers and implementers to maintain her sense of location.

Notions of "beginning" and "end" are artificial if not entirely absent from web media. This is a marked departure from the fundamental nature of nonhyperlinked resources, which are bounded by definition.

URIs

In a perfect system, Uniform Resource Identifiers, or URIs (formerly Uniform Resource Locators, or URLs) would be hidden from the site visitor. They aren't especially human-readable, comprised as they are of a protocol token, a host alias, and something that looks like a filesystem reference but isn't. URIs often end in token/value pairs that are deliberately designed to be computer-readable, as opposed to visitor-friendly.

We're all familiar with simple URIs like `http://www.example.com/` that point to the home page of a site. These appear in advertisements and on business cards, and the `http://` has come to mean "type this in to find the website." However, well-crafted URIs can contain a lot of information—look at commonly encountered URIs at your favorite search site or news site, and you'll see a lot more going on. Google search result URIs, for example, can contain a parameter named `start` that specifies the number of results ranked higher than those displayed, as in `http://www.google.com/?q=hyper text&hl=en&start=10`. In a similar vein, popular Content Management System (CMS) platforms and e-commerce catalog platforms allow the same resource to be associated with *multiple* URIs, where the longer URIs enhance a resource's searchability or specify that additional content be served along with the core resource (e.g., a product listing or the summary of a weblog entry).

 Browsers and other tools use the HTTP protocol to process URIs and retrieve information. If you want to know more about how this processing works, and how its features and limitations might affect your pages, see the appendix.

Managing Links

Hypertext as we understand it today was first implemented at Stanford University in the 1960s, but didn't become an everyday tool until the advent of affordable commercial Internet access three decades later. The "explosion" of the Internet not only provided a way for hyperlinks to connect across a broad network, but it also nurtured an understanding that web hyperlinks should be simple and tolerant of failure.

HTML link conventions assume that the person creating a link knows what will be at the URI at the end of it. That doesn't necessarily mean that link creators *control* what is at the end of the link, however. In fact, the ability to link to any content without having to ask its creator beforehand is a critical aspect of the Web's success. If it has a URI, you can link to it. If a URI doesn't work, a well-built site will report an error (like the ubiquitous "404 Not Found") and present a page that can help the lost visitors find their way again.

The power and immediacy of web links raised all kinds of cultural (and in some cases legal) questions about what it means to be able to link directly to someone else's material, but over time a simpler and probably more intractable issue arose: *link rot*. Creating links to information you don't control eventually means that over time those links break, as information and even sites change or disappear. It also means that you may have visitors arriving at your site who are confused and frustrated because they didn't find what they wanted immediately.

To some degree, link rot is inevitable, and even automated systems (like search engines) have a difficult time keeping up with it. Even if links still point to useful pages, they may evolve over time into something very different. Within your own sites, you have somewhat more control, though major site redesigns can make this difficult. Caution, well-built error pages, and clear navigation can help minimize these problems.

 While visitors can usually deal with regular links that send them to the wrong place, it may be more difficult for your pages to recover from missing images, code, stylesheets, or other components that are supposed to be inserted via accurate `href` and `src` values. The more important the component to your page, the more you will want to link to it at a stable location under your control.

Improving the User Experience with Linking

Links are part of HTML, the means by which URIs are most commonly exposed within the Web's application layer, at the point where HTML and HTTP intersect. At the application level, there isn't much difference between following a link and accessing a given URI through the Location bar of a browser.

Links provide infinite opportunities to site builders—opportunities that are usually passed over. Anything can link to anything else. Hyperlinks in documents aren't constrained to site navigation, stylesheet references, and syndication references; they can also point to an unlimited number of related documents and all kinds of alternative content. Hyperlinks that respond to user interaction can be placed anywhere, point to anything, and trigger behavior limited only by platform constraints, good sense, and a site builder's imagination. Well-implemented hypertext enhances information with the following benefits, among many:

Broadened accessibility to and control of information
> Hyperlinks can always reference every part of the Web that is not access-controlled. Rather than delivering long chunks of exposition out of necessity (as this book does) or referring to other matters that must then be physically obtained, hyperlinks allow the users to decide for themselves which information resources they will access and how.

Creation of multiple narratives from a single body of content
> Hyperlinks make it possible for a visitor's "journey" to take any and all forms that he desires...within reason.

Community-driven attention flow
> Incoming hyperlinks lend credibility to destination content without the need for subject matter–expert intervention—a fact that defines a number of systems already in use, especially Google's PageRank algorithm. It remains possible for the "wisdom of crowds" to be qualitatively poor, but accuracy tends to increase over time since subject matter experts remain closely involved with the process.

Hypertext Implementation Challenges

Web technology allows users to direct their own experience in ways that until 1992 had been the stuff of science fiction. No single person or entity has unqualified control over a given user's web experience (although not for lack of trying). A single user session can result in requests for content from multiple unaffiliated authors, on tangential or unrelated subjects, and require an arbitrary amount of user interaction.

This seeming anarchy places new demands on implementers:

1. Context (i.e., steady "You Are Here" and "That's Over There" signaling) is the most important part of an effective site, apart from the actual site content.

2. Untested assumptions about a visitor's goals and knowledge create a short, straight path to folly and disaster.

3. Duplication of content adds needless burdens to the user experience (and to the site building process).

4. The Web's lack of bounds, assumptions, and context can create user impairments out of thin air, and often these impairments *must* be addressed. The Web's tremendous openness creates the need for specialist disciplines in web information architecture and usability.

Because the Web *breaks* the linear structure of traditional media outright, implementers must never forget that their tools define *context*, first and foremost.

CHAPTER 2

Working with HTML Markup

When building a site, one of the most important tasks that you perform is link creation, but HyperText Markup Language (HTML) offers a heap of features beyond links. HTML documents describe the hypertext and contain much of the content users explore while visiting the Web, connecting them to other resources including presentation style, scripts, images, video, sound, and much more. As you'll see, a key part of working with HTML is knowing when to let other technologies (and sometimes people) do their work.

HTML has been in constant development since its invention in 1992, and web software (like browsers and web-focused IDEs) have evolved apace. As HTML nears its third decade, clear best practices for markup have emerged both from HTML markup itself and from the technical and business ecosystems that interact with it. Clear HTML syntax lets you build a reliable document tree to hold your content and support additional layers of style and behavior. Chapter 5 is devoted to the features of CSS that interact with the document tree.

HTML Syntax

HTML and its stricter sibling XHTML define a set of rules for marking up documents, as well as rules for how that markup should be structured. HTML parsers (but not XHTML parsers) usually follow a principle referred to as "Postel's Law," stated as follows:

> Be conservative in what you send, and liberal in what you accept.

Where XHTML requires the creator of the document to write very precise markup, HTML parsers will liberally repair omissions and remove empty elements that are present in markup. This makes the document valid from the visitor's perspective, though not necessarily using the structure originally intended by the stylist. (HTML5 is defining this behavior formally, but in the past it has varied from browser to browser.)

Tags, Elements, and Attributes

HTML defines a number of *elements*, each of which falls within a particular semantic domain and takes a name derived or borrowed whole from English. Elements define the structure of the document and lay the foundation for its presentation and manipulation.

Each element reference in a document is contained within one or two *tags*—tokens enclosed by angle brackets (< and >) containing the name of the element being used. *Opening tags* always begin with < immediately followed by the element name, and reference all attributes and values associated with the element; *closing tags* are feature-less apart from the element name, which is preceded by a forward slash.

Elements without discrete closing tags are handled in different ways:

- HTML elements with *optional* closing tags—most notably li (list item) and p (paragraph) elements—allow for complete omission of the closing tag.
- HTML elements that *forbid* a closing tag are indistinguishable from opening tags of other elements.
- XHTML elements always either forbid or require closing tags; "optional" doesn't get much traction in XHTML.
- Tags referencing XHTML elements that forbid closing tags terminate not with >, but with />. This token is usually preceded by a space, to prevent parsing failures at the hands of legacy user agents.

Tags can contain an arbitrary amount of whitespace, and attributes can be listed in any order within an opening tag.

All element instances can be modified through the use of *attributes*, most of which should in turn be followed by *values*. In plain HTML, elements and attributes are case insensitive, but in XHTML, they should be written entirely in lowercase characters. As a dialect of XML, XHTML poses two additional rules:

- XHTML is *broadly* case sensitive, which can matter with respect to values, while HTML enforces the case sensitivity of values only for the class and id attributes.
- Where an attribute is applied within an XHTML tag, it *must* be followed with a value. In the case of attributes that are typically deprived of a value in HTML, the common practice is to duplicate the name of the attribute in the value (e.g., checked="checked" instead of simply checked).

Example 2-1 shows some valid XHTML 1.0 Transitional markup.

Example 2-1. XHTML 1.0 snippet

```
<div id="header"><h1><a href="/">AcmeStore.com</a></h1></div>

<img src="/images/portrait.gif" width="144" height="180" alt="This is a random portrait
of somebody." />
```

The first line of Example 2-1 contains three elements, one inside another, not unlike a matryoshka doll. It's important to remember that when elements are nested, they should be closed in the *reverse* order in which they were opened, to create the nesting shown in Figure 2-1. Inadvertent failure to follow this rule is a common cause of blowouts.

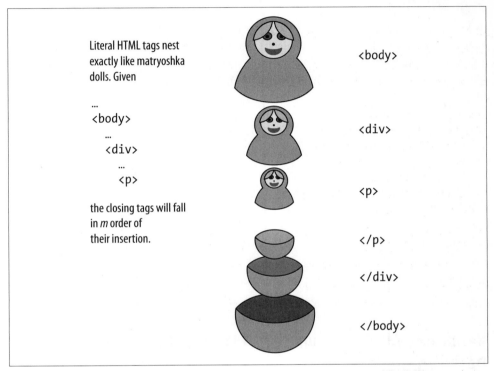

Figure 2-1. Well-formed HTML tags nest in exactly the same way as matryoshka dolls

Example 2-1 also treats attribute values according to XHTML rules. XHTML values are *always* quoted. HTML values follow a different rule:

> In certain cases, authors may specify the value of an attribute without any quotation marks. The attribute value may only contain letters (a–z and A–Z), digits (0–9), hyphens (ASCII decimal 45), periods (ASCII decimal 46), underscores (ASCII decimal 95), and colons (ASCII decimal 58). *We recommend using quotation marks even when it is possible to eliminate them* [emphasis].
>
> —*HTML 4.01 specification*, World Wide Web Consortium

Character references within attribute values are discussed in "Inserting Entities to Provide Non-ASCII Characters" on page 226 and "The Fine Print of URL Encoding: ASCII Entities" on page 248.

Page Structure

When a browser receives content it believes to be HTML, it will attempt to process the content based on what it can figure out from the markup contained in the document. Even if that markup has missing parts, is structured strangely, or is otherwise not standards-compliant, the browser can usually display something resembling what its creator had in mind.

If a web document is to be *valid*, however, it *must* contain a number of properly structured elements with appropriate content. A valid HTML document contains the following components, in order:

1. The document type declaration
2. The document's html element
3. Within the html element, the document's head element
4. Within the head element, a title element and any necessary link, script, base, and meta elements
5. Within the html element and after the head element, the document's body element, which represents everything on the page that might be directly user-facing
6. Within the document's body element, at least one block element

Rendering Modes, Flavors of HTML, and Document Type Declarations

As of this writing, HTML has been steadily evolving for 17 years. Five versions have been developed, and HTML5, the most recent of these, is steadily making its way to popular use though it is not yet complete. The World Wide Web Consortium (W3C) has also published a Recommendation for XHTML, the XML-conformant version of HTML 4.01.

While it is still too early to know what the "good parts" of HTML5 will be, throughout this book we will cover new HTML5 functionality where it might change best practices.

Since version 1.0, HTML has included something called the *document type declaration* at the very beginning of the document. This identifies the version of HTML used

---

in a document to a user agent, but was generally ignored by web browsers until 2001. For example, the document type declaration for HTML 4.01 Strict would look like the following:

```
<!DOCTYPE HTML PUBLIC "-//W3C//DTD HTML 4.01//EN"
"http://www.w3.org/TR/html4/strict.dtd">
```

The most significant impact of the document type declaration is its influence on the way that element footprints are rendered. Different DOCTYPEs lead to different rendering modes. (They also set expectations for HTML validators.)

> You've probably seen the acronym "DTD," which expands to "Document Type Definition." The DTD is the machine-readable definition that the document type declaration is intended to reference. At any rate, the declaration and definition are different matters; the former ideally points to the latter, and only the latter is referred to as a DTD. This book's companion website (*http://www.htmlcssgoodparts.net*) examines the finer points of DTDs and document type declarations in greater detail.

HTML or XHTML?

The currently popular "flavors" of HTML are variants of HTML 4.01. The widest divide lies between those variants that follow traditional HTML syntax, and those redefined to meet XML's requirements for well formedness. When served with the correct MIME type (see Table A-1 in the appendix), XHTML is also parsed according to the stricter syntactical requirements of XML.

Normal HTML enforces somewhat looser rules, allowing things like the omission of closing tags, and is case insensitive. XHTML, meanwhile, requires all elements to be properly closed with a complete tag or /> as needed, and named entirely in lowercase characters.

XHTML suffers one substantial disadvantage—its canonical MIME type isn't supported by Internet Explorer, a problem discussed in greater detail in Chapter 14.

However, carefully formatted XHTML (or HTML written under the constraints of XHTML) offers an even greater advantage that has led to its selection for markup examples in this book and its related materials. Because XHTML's required syntax is more rigid, XHTML source fragments are measurably easier to read than their HTML analogs, and the rules defining valid XHTML are less confusing.

> HTML5 includes support for an XML syntax, but does not require its use.

Strict, Transitional, or Frameset?

As HTML has evolved, a number of elements have been *deprecated*: that is, officially designated as obsolescent or out of scope. In addition, many elements have circumscribed scope—they must appear within certain elements or contain certain elements.

In brief, the differences between the Strict, Transitional, and Frameset subtypes of HTML can be defined in terms of permissiveness and rigidity. Strict variants have the narrowest requirements with respect to the contents or containers of certain elements, and are less relaxed about the use of deprecated elements.

The Frameset subtype, meanwhile, is meant to be used in one circumstance: for documents that define a series of `frame` elements. Framesets and frames will be discussed in more detail in Chapter 14.

Finally, note that `iframe` elements fall within the scope of the Transitional document types, *not* the Frameset document types.

 HTML5 offers only one choice for document type, which is effectively Strict plus new HTML5 features.

CSS3 allows those definitions to be made independently of the document type with the `box-sizing` property, which has two values: `content-box` and `border-box`. The layout behaviors associated with these values are given close attention in Chapter 6.

A Tale of Two Box Models

Current web browsers use document type declarations as a "switch" that can determine the "box model" used to define the underlying measurements that will inform the page layout.

The dimensions of an element box defined by HTML can be modified with various CSS properties that control its content footprint, gutters (`padding`, etc.), borders, and margins as separate components. Older browsers calculate these dimensions *subtractively*: custom footprint dimensions *include* associated gutters and borders. Margins are also treated differently with respect to containing elements.

However, the CSS 2.1 specification requires that footprint calculations be handled *additively*, so that gutters, borders, and margins are rendered as an addition to any custom footprint dimensions. Of course, there is still a lot of content on the Web that was styled to accommodate the older layout approach.

By including a document type declaration in a document, a page author sets a switch that defines the layout model that will be applied to a page's block elements by default. Some declarations cause rendering engines to behave according to the technical standard set in the CSS 2.1 specification, while others cause rendering engines to behave according to the legacy approach (frequently referred to as "quirks mode"). Where a document type declaration is omitted, the legacy box model is applied.

In cases where the distinction might be important, source examples in this book and its companion materials will be framed in terms of the box model defined in the CSS 2.1 specification.

 For a thorough list of DOCTYPEs and the modes that various browsers use to render them, see *http://hsivonen.iki.fi/doctype/*.

Choosing the Right Document Type for Your Project

In the hands of experienced developers, document type choices are a question of personal preference. I always use XHTML 1.0 Transitional for new projects and redesigns-from-scratch—thanks to the consistency of XML's rules, I find that the resulting markup is easier to comprehend during the production and quality assurance phases of a project.

However, my needs are not yours. In order to address your most important needs, you should ask the following questions before choosing the document type to be used on a particular project:

What "flavor" of HTML does the project sponsor use on its other online properties, or use as a matter of course?
> Generally speaking, it's best to stick with conventions established by materials already in production.

Does anyone hold the expectation that content will be stored in a datastore meant to be accessed by multiple systems?
> In this case, XHTML—which is a dialect of XML—might well be a better choice, since portability is perhaps the greatest strength of XML.

How likely is it that your work product will be processed by transformation algorithms such as search-and-replace functions?
> Strict document types will hold up better in the face of transformation algorithms.

Finally, on a somewhat different note, there is the question of how you use your tools. It's generally best to hang onto the tools you're already using, unless you have an obvious need to change.

Beautiful Parts: Universal Attributes

You'll be seeing a lot of the `class` and `id` attributes throughout this book. These are *universal attributes*—they can be used by *any* element in the HTML vocabulary that's valid as well as `body` itself.

In addition to `class` and `id`, there are four other attributes that are similarly versatile:

- `title`
- `lang/xml:lang`
- `dir`
- `style`

`dir` specifies which direction type should run. `style` will be described in Chapter 14.

Providing Stylesheet Hooks with class and id

Two attributes that can be assigned to *all* elements are `class` and `id`. Several `class` values but only one `id` value can be assigned to a given element. Multiple `class` values are separated by spaces, e.g., `class="alternate callToAction"`.

Valid `class` and `id` values should contain only letters, numbers, hyphens, and underscores. These values should begin only with letters and numbers. However, Internet Explorer 6 parses and applies stylesheet values that are associated with `class` values, `id` values, and property names that begin with underscores—an oversight that provides stylists with a low-pass filtering technique.

A more important question is *where* to put `class`es and `id`s. As a rule, `class`es should be assigned to those frequently encountered elements that share both design purpose and presentation peculiarities, but aren't used predictably. On many sites, `class`es are also assigned to the `body` elements of pages that fall within a single section of the site's architecture, such as the common "About" and "Contact" sections.

The overall structure of site templates tends to inform where and how `id` and `class` values are assigned. I typically assign the following `id`s to the appropriate elements of every site template that I build:

- `main`
- `header`
- `primaryNav`
- `bodyCopy`
- `sidebar`
- `footer`
- `secondaryNav`

If you look carefully at that list, you'll note the total absence of page- or site-specific values that refer to page coordinates (e.g., left or right columns), color, or specific sizes. A similar reliance upon context is used for class values as well; section values and hints to purpose such as error make frequent appearances, but references to absolute dimensions or colors do not. The closest thing to an exception in this regard is made for form styles, where minimally subjective class values like short, medium, and long turn up with regularity in order to avoid styling label/field pairs one by one.

Describing Content with title and lang

In addition to id and class, HTML 4.x and XHTML 1.x added two other universal attributes that are used to provide metadata about the language and general nature of the content related to the elements to which they are applied.

Of these, title is more commonly used. Its value is an arbitrary string that provides a brief description of an element's content. It can also include the title of a link's destination, a technique used extensively on Wikipedia. Finally, browsers can put aside title values and display them as document metadata. If implemented and used well, title values can be a tremendous help to visitors trying to find needle-sized bits of information in haystack-sized information stores.

The title attribute is comparable to the alt attribute used for images, but is distinguished from alt by the fact that alt is meant to be displayed as a *substitute* for an image that cannot be displayed, whereas title *describes* content instead of serving as a fallback for it.

In current desktop browsers, the value of the title attribute is displayed in a tool tip when the associated element is moused over, as shown in Figure 2-2. These tool tips are truncated by some browsers when they run long, though the truncation point varies from one browser to the next.

		to the next
superscript	[none]	best assigned an infinitesimal line-
subscript	[none]	A survey of HTML 4 inline elements.
insertion	[none]	styled with an underline, by default

Figure 2-2. A title tool tip, as displayed by Internet Explorer 8 on Vista/Aero

The lang attribute, meanwhile, is a meaningful nod to the "World Wide" part of the Web. In much the same way that the title attribute can be used to supply supplemental information about the content of an element or the destination of a link, lang does exactly the same for foreign-language content.

You are supremely polite when you use the `lang` attribute, because it aids visitors in the task of understanding the context of foreign-language content even when they cannot make out its exact meaning. Furthermore, screen readers need an accurate `lang` or `Content-Language` response header value to pronounce foreign-language content accurately.

The `hreflang` attribute exists as a counterpart to the `lang` attribute and is used to signal that a hyperlink points to content written in a language other than that specified for the current document.

Finally, note that XHTML served with the `application/xhtml+xml` MIME type should use the `xml:lang` attribute in place of the `lang` attribute.

When the the `lang` or `xml:lang` attributes are used to describe an entire document, they should be attached to the `html` element, instead of the `html` element.

The value that you provide for the `lang` attribute (and the `Content-Language` HTTP response header field) is chosen from a list composed from various ISO-sanctioned codes and structured according to rules maintained by the IETF.

Table 2-1. Frequently encountered Content-Language values

Language	lang/Content-language value
English	en
English (American)	en-US
English (British)	en-GB
Chinese (Simplified)	zh-Hans
Chinese (Traditional)	zh-Hant
Chinese (Taiwanese, no script specified)	zh-TW
Spanish	es
Japanese	ja
French	fr
Portuguese	pt
Portuguese (Brazilian)	pt-BR
German	de
Arabic	ar
Russian	ru
Korean	ko

To learn more about effectively using the `title` attribute in links, read "Creating Effective Link Content and title Values" on page 136. `lang` values of interest are listed in Table 2-1.

The contenteditable Attribute in HTML5

The HTML5 specification adds a number of new global attributes to HTML, including `contenteditable`, which is already supported by most modern browsers. It's mainly intended for providing in-browser rich-text/WYSIWYG editors—the kind of editing interfaces you might find in browser-based blog-authoring tools, for example.

The `contenteditable` attribute essentially enables you as an author to specify that particular parts of a page (the contents of particular elements) are editable. Within those editable parts of the page, users can potentially perform actions like selecting text, cutting and pasting, and moving text (including by dragging and dropping it), as well as changing the character formatting of text to appear bold or italic, or in a different color, or even actions like adding hyperlinks.

Just setting the `contenteditable` attribute on a particular element won't cause a browser to actually expose any obvious editing controls to the users. However, it generally *will* enable users to at least perform actions that have common, familiar keyboard shortcuts (for example, Ctrl-X to cut, Ctrl-V to paste, or Ctrl-B and Ctrl-I for bold and italic). Some browsers even provide a text-editing context menu that's available by right-clicking in a `contenteditable` area; this may add a few additional character-formatting actions that don't have common keyboard shortcuts, such as changing the font size or color of selected text.

It's possible that other browsers will follow suit and expose more `contenteditable` text-editing actions (such as, say, an action for easily adding hyperlinks) through a related context menu. However, all that being said, if you want to provide an in-browser user interface for performing editing actions in `contenteditable` content, you'll also need to write some programming (scripting) in JavaScript. For example, you can easily add a button to a page allowing users to make selected text bold (rather than forcing them to use a keyboard shortcut), but to make it work, you'll need to add some scripting that associates your button with the action you expect it to perform. (The HTML5 specification provides a number of APIs to facilitate scripting in combination with the `contenteditable` attribute, but I won't go into the details here.)

Another limitation of `contenteditable` is that, on its own, it provides no means for users to actually save the contents of any pages they've edited. That's something else for which you, as an author, will need to provide an interface.

Separating Content, Structure, Presentation, and Behavior

Making Your Sites "Safe As Houses"

Imagine a dwelling. The simplest such structure meant to stand for any length of time will have some kind of durable structural frame anchored to the ground and covered with some kind of paneling.

For the client side of a website, that frame and cover are the structural layer, the markup: it defines the overall form of the result.

When you start getting fancy with your house, you can add things like siding, paint, trim, and shingles. This is like the presentation layer of your website, driven on the whole by CSS. In the same way that the walls and roof will fall off of a poorly framed house, CSS will be difficult to use if the markup is not properly assembled.

A good house has things like climate-control hardware, doors, windows, electricity, and plumbing. In many cases, things like this are what make the house truly enjoyable to live in. Likewise, the behavior layer of a website is the part that most clearly responds to user activity. However, without the other parts of the architecture and engineering properly installed, the behavior layer will most likely be ineffective.

And what about the content? Well, as the point of a house is to shelter people and their stuff, so the point of a website is to serve as the ideal vessel of a heap of content. Each HTML page holds a markup structure wrapped around content.

Separation in Practice

When a developer works under the principle of separation, the likely result is that each client-side layer of the site enjoys tremendous independence from the particulars of the other layers. That independence will never be *complete*; at best, it will enable in new properties the reuse of assets that already exist. At any rate, the principle of separation assumes the following dependencies:

1. A site's behavior loses its punch without the presence of an effective presentation.
2. A site's presentation is dependent upon the underlying quality of its structure.
3. Without thoughtfully assembled content, creating a solid site structure becomes a fool's errand.

However, it's easy to achieve a level of "layer independence" that will minimize the impact of changes—so that, by defining a `class` that is only assigned to an element when a visitor interacts with it, you can make unlimited changes to the presentation of an element without also needing to alter any JavaScript that defines its behavior. Likewise, you can give yourself free rein to fiddle with a stylesheet and completely revise a site's presentation without being forced to dig into any of the site's structure or content—the "CSS Zen" approach (see the section "The Functional Principles of CSS Zen" on page 60).

Working with Document Trees

Much of the work at the beginning of a website development project revolves around developing a simple HTML structure that CSS and perhaps eventually JavaScript can use as a framework for their presentation and behavior activity. This work focuses on creating a basic structure that many documents can use as their foundation and possibly as their template. At this point in the process, the focus is less on content and more on common structures that wrap that content. Example 2-2 shows the body element of a simple HTML document structure.

Example 2-2. A simple HTML document structure

```
<body>
 <h1>...</h1>
 <div id="main">
   <div id="priorityContent">
    <div id="bodyCopy">

      <h2>...</h2>
      <div class="section">
        ...
      </div>

      <h2>...</h2>
      <div class="section">
        ...
      </div>
    </div>

    <div id="sidebar">


      ...
    </div>

    <ul id="primaryNav">
      ...
    </ul>
    <div id="footer"
      <ul id="secondaryNav">
      ...
      </ul>
    <p id="colophon">...</p>
    </div>

  </div>
 </div>
</body>
```

This sample provides more than just a template. Its nested and labeled elements also define a structure that CSS (and JavaScript) can build on, creating a tree (labeled using # for ids and . for classes) that looks something like:

 The production standards enforced at many workplaces generally rely on class values in templates more heavily than suggested in Example 2-2 and the document tree outline below.

- body
  - h1
  - div#main
    - div#priorityContent
      - div#bodyCopy
        - h2
        - div.section
          - ...
      - div#sidebar
        - ...
    - ul#primaryNav
    - div#footer
      - ul#secondaryNav
      - p#colophon

Sketching your document tree as a nested list and then creating markup from the structure you've defined may make it easier to see and manipulate the tree structure you'll need. The tree shown here is relatively simple, and doesn't reach down into individual paragraphs or other forms of content. As you fill documents with additional content, you will be constantly extending the document tree, and expanding the amount of material that your stylesheets and perhaps your JavaScript code can modify.

Browsers, Parsing, and Rendering

Current web browsers typically parse and render content piecemeal, quite often starting the process before a page has been received in full by the browser. HTML browsers—or more generically, user agents—will process an HTML or XHTML document serially from the beginning of a document's source, working out the relationships between the various elements it contains and filling in gaps if necessary to create a document tree. Meanwhile, they read any CSS specified by the HTML in a similar fashion, matching up stylesheet selectors to the elements contained in the page as described in the next chapter.

The serial nature of these processes is important for three reasons:

The only way in which user intervention can affect parsing is to halt it
> The markup, CSS, JavaScript, session data, and user data received by the browser in the scope of a single page set the stage for everything that happens until the page is completely rendered.

Until a page and its related media are completely received, parsed, and rendered, their appearance is subject to change at the hands of the browser's rendering engine
> In high-latency environments, slow arrivals can create visually disconcerting results as the page shifts over time to accommodate recently arrived components. This behavior can lead to the dreaded "Flash of Unstyled Content," which is explored briefly on this book's companion website.

There is no strict rule as to what a web browser should or should not parse, as long as the data in question can be interpreted
> Browsers are permissive about what they attempt to download and parse. This permissiveness leaves it to the discretion of a site's developers to conserve resources, a task best accomplished by ensuring that stylesheet data is matched with care to the requirements of the current document. This is a potential cause for concern to those who need to account for performance in marginal environments.

Because Ajax uses the W3C Document Object Model Application Programming Interface (DOM API) to update the contents of arbitrary elements within a page, it's absolutely vital that markup within any page intended to contain the output of Ajax calls be syntactically correct. This is particularly true with respect to sibling elements of those meant to be updated.

Markup syntax errors alter the document tree and element boundaries into a configuration different than what's intended, which can make it unnecessarily difficult to find the cause of JavaScript errors in Ajax-oriented code.

Dynamic HTML, Ajax, and Rendering

First- and second-generation desktop browsers only ran a single set of rendering passes per page request, so that additional rendering would only take place after another page request had been sent to a server. All subsequent desktop browsing platforms have made it possible to insert additional content after the initial "page load," a feature that was called "Dynamic HTML" until the XMLHttpRequest API became popular. The ability of this new API to asynchronously request and insert new content without loading an entirely new page eventually led to the adoption of the term "Ajax."

CHAPTER 3

CSS Overview

Like in a cinematic or musical work, the "Good Parts" of CSS are easier to find if you have a basic understanding of what's going on. This chapter lays the foundation for what's to come in the rest of this book—it explores the role of CSS in creating successful websites, and provides a survey of its basic components.

If you're in a hurry to get to the Good Parts, you can skip ahead. There are some mentions of Bad Parts and Awful Parts here worth noting, though, and CSS is complicated enough that a quick review can be helpful.

Connecting Stylesheets to HTML Documents

HTML documents can specify the stylesheets that are applied to them, using the `link` element, the `style` element, or the `@import` declaration.

Go to *http://www.htmlcssgoodparts.net/* for an interactive demonstration of the relationships between stylesheet rules and elements in a typical page.

Referencing a Stylesheet with link

The most common method of associating styles with your document is to use a `link` element within the `head` of a document. The source of `link` elements usually looks something like this:

```
<link rel="stylesheet" href="/styles.css" media="screen" title="Primary Stylesheet" />
```

This approach also supports stylesheet *choices*: a stylist can create multiple stylesheets, assign a `title` to each, and assign a second `rel` (relation) value of `alternate` to all but one of the referenced stylesheets. (Multiple `rel` values should be separated by spaces.)

Users will then be able to choose which stylesheet they want to associate with your site. This feature is supported by Firefox, recent versions of Safari, and Internet Explorer 8.

Targeting Internet Explorer Versions with Conditional Comments

Internet Explorer's partial support for CSS has created a variety of problems for developers. However, one of Internet Explorer's other nonstandard features makes it possible to specify stylesheets *only* for Internet Explorer, even to the degree of specifying particular versions of that browser.

 Updates made to Windows in late 2009 disabled Internet Explorer 8's support for conditional comments when operating in "IE8 Standards" mode.

Internet Explorer defines HTML comments differently than other browsers, which allows you to include source that only Internet Explorer will parse as proper markup.

One possible example that references a stylesheet is:

```
<!-- [if lt IE 8]><link rel="stylesheet"
href="/styles.ie.css" media="screen" /><![endif]-->
```

The `<![endif]-->` closing "tag" is a constant feature of such markup. The opening matter is written in the following format, with user-supplied values in emphasis:

```
<!-- [if version_constraint IE version]>
```

The user-supplied values work as follows:

`version_constraint`
    This item is optional, but where present can take one of four forms:

- `gt`: greater than [>]
- `gte`: greater than or equal to [≥]
- `lt`: less than [<]
- `lte`: less than or equal to [≤]

`version`
    This item is also optional, and where used corresponds to a major release: 5, 5.5, 6, 7, or 8.

The Internet Explorer conditional comment syntax also supports Boolean AND, OR, and NOT operators, which are explained in more detail at the Microsoft Developer Network site (*http://msdn.microsoft.com/en-us/library/ms537512.aspx*).

Low-pass and high-pass rule filters can serve as fit alternatives to stylesheets conditionally targeted to legacy versions of Internet Explorer. These rule filters are discussed in more detail in Chapter 14.

Replacing link with style

When the `style` element is used, it can contain any quantity of valid CSS. One effective use of `style` blocks is to serve CSS rules that are specific to a single page; I make a regular habit of using this technique. Many developers use `style` elements to reference stylesheets requested via the `@import` rule, which is discussed in more detail next.

The conditional comments described earlier can also enclose a `style` element or its content.

It's generally best to keep `style` blocks short, as their presence affects the proportion of keyword-rich content in a page, thus having the potential for a slightly negative impact on Search Engine Optimization (SEO) efforts.

When a page marked up in XHTML is served with the correct MIME type (`application/xhtml+xml`), `style` content must be placed inside a `<![CDATA[ ... ]]>` (character data) block.

Using @import

The `@import` statement first became popular in the late 1990s, when developers discovered that Netscape 4 wouldn't parse it. This made it easy to include more advanced stylesheets that would work with other browsers, while leaving Netscape 4 alone.

In contemporary use, `@import` declarations are reduced to their original intended function, which is to serve as an analog to an `include` function that is applied specifically to stylesheets.

`@import` declarations must always appear at the top of a stylesheet's source order, valid `@import` declarations can only be preceded by an `@charset` declaration. The browser parses and applies the styles in an `@imported` stylesheet as though they were in the place of the `@import` declaration that referenced them, a fact that can affect rule priority.

For the sake of consistency with other bits of CSS syntax, only the parenthetical method of reference will be demonstrated:

```
@import url(/form_styles.css);
```

It is also possible to apply stylesheets called `@import` to specific media, which is discussed shortly.

Beware of style Attributes!

The first rule of standards-friendly development (see "Rules of Standards-Friendly Development" on page 46) demands that you keep presentation details out of your markup, so avoid the `style` attribute however and whenever possible. In those (extremely) rare instances where it *must* be used (for example, Content Management Systems that lock out stylesheets), it should contain the desired series of valid property/ value pairs, just as if those same pairs were being included in a stylesheet rule applying only to that element.

The `style` attribute is further discussed (and subjected to passionate abuse) in "The Awful Parts" on page 286.

Targeting Rules to Specific Media

HTML and CSS allow you to create different stylesheets for different media, most commonly `screen` and `print`. A single document might have several stylesheets, each targeted at one or more media. There are three approaches to applying styles to specific media:

Add an optional `media` attribute/value pair to an appropriate `link` or `style` element
Adding a `media` attribute to one of these elements will cause the valid rules contained within that element's scope to apply only to the desired media. Therefore, if you want a `link`ed stylesheet to apply only to printed pages, you would include `media="print"` in the applicable `link` tag.

Add an `@media` block to a style block that hasn't already been assigned a mutually exclusive `media` value
For example, `@media print { body { font-size: 12pt; } }` will cause the default type size of a given page or site to be changed to 12 points.

Add a media value to an `@import` declaration that isn't already placed within a mutually exclusive media scope
In the same way that the `@media` selector trails with the names of one or more recognized media, the file reference in an `@import` declaration can be followed with the names of one or more recognized media, for example, `@import(/styles.print.css) print;`. This approach targets all of the rules in that stylesheet to the desired medium or media.

Note that `@import` declarations placed *inside* `@media` blocks are invalid.

Where multiple media are named, they should be comma-separated.

The following media type values are described in the CSS 2.1 specification and claim greater-than-insignificant support from browser and other user agent vendors:

`all`
All devices

screen
> Monitor-type displays attached to personal computers, typically cathode ray tube (CRT; "TV-type") or liquid crystal diode (LCD; "flat panel") displays; often applicable mobile device displays as well, at vendors' discretion

print
> Paper sheets of arbitrary number and area, coated with ink, pigment, or toner

handheld
> Mobile devices and personal digital assistants (PDAs); poorly supported by all but very recently marketed devices, as of 2009

projection
> Tabletop projectors; poorly supported by nearly all vendors

speech
> Screen reader and text-to-phone platforms; poorly supported

The remaining media types described in the CSS 2.1 specification are functionally unsupported:

braille
> Braille terminals

embossed
> Braille printers

tty
> Two-dimensional fixed pitch display environments (usually a monochrome CRT display or command-line client software); accurately cognate to the traditional Unix designation for dumb terminals

tv
> Television browsers, like the erstwhile WebTV

Choosing the Elements You Want to Style: Writing Selectors

A typical stylesheet, regardless of its scope, is a series of rules structured as follows:

```
selector { property: value; property: value; [ ... ] }
```

The bad news—and the bane of many newcomers to CSS—is that this structure is terse to the point of impenetrability.

The steep learning curve of CSS syntax is rewarded with the ability to affect a page's presentation with a superlative degree of granularity. Any selector can point to any arbitrary set of elements within a page, and CSS properties can accomplish anything within the limits of an implementer's experience and imagination, when put to thoughtful use.

The concepts explained briefly here are taken up in much greater detail in "Applying Taxonomy Through the Cascade" on page 70.

Parents, Children, and Siblings: Element/Node Relationships

The section "Tags, Elements, and Attributes" on page 8 introduced the idea of element *nesting* for the purpose of explaining how tags-inside-tags need to be written. Element nesting opens to door to one of the most important aspects of applied HTML and CSS:

> It is not only allowed but actually encouraged to "wrap" stretches of clearly related content in elements set aside for just that purpose, and to assign descriptive ids and/or classes to such wrappers.

When such "semantically appropriate" elements are used to enclose content, new relationships are created in the document tree, thereby increasing the number of CSS selectors that can be used in the course of implementing a design.

Multiple nested elements have what are referred to as *parent*, *child*, and *sibling* relationships:

Document tree
> The notional branching structure of all elements in a document. Synonymous with "Document Object Model" as applied to a specific document.

Parent
> The element that directly contains the element at the focus of concern.

Ancestor
> An element higher in the document tree, possibly many levels higher, that contains the element in question.

Child
> The element that is directly contained by the element at the focus of concern.

Descendant
> An element contained by the element in question which is deeper in the document tree.

Sibling
> An element that shares a common *immediate* parent with the element at the focus of concern.

CSS makes a clear distinction made between generic parent and child elements, and those that are *immediate* or *direct*. For example, an li element in a valid document claims some ul or ol element as its direct parent, but will also have at least one—if not two—other parent elements within its document tree: body (which is required by the DTD for the various flavors of HTML 4.x) and quite likely another block element.

Simple Selectors

Typically, selectors interface with markup at three main points: element names, `class` attribute values, and `id` attribute values.

Elements
```
p { ... }
```
classes
```
.about { ... }
```
ids
```
#corporatehistory { ... }
```

The following fragment of markup includes hooks for all of the example selectors just shown:

```
<body class="about" ... >
...
    <div id="corporatehistory" ... >
    ...
        <p>The 1990s were a time of drastic change throughout the industry.<p>
    ...
    </div>
...
</body>
```

The `p { ... }` selector will apply to the `p` element in code fragment just shown. The `.about { ... }` selector will apply to the `body` element, whose `class` value is "about". And finally, the `#corporatehistory { ... }` selector will apply to the `div` element with an `id` of "corporatehistory".

Beyond these three foundations, CSS 2.1 specifies other selector types, including universal selectors (`*`), child selectors (`div > p`), descendant selectors (`div p`), adjacent selectors (`ol + p`), and attribute selectors (`p[lang]`, `p[lang="en"]` or a number of other variants). It also includes the `:first-line`, `:first-letter`, `:before`, and `:after` pseudoelements, as well as a variety of pseudoclasses: `:first-child`, `:link`, `:visited`, `:active`, `:hover`, `:focus`, and `:lang`. CSS3 adds even more pseudoclasses and pseudoelements, but is still in development.

Multiple and Descendant Selectors

The capacity to combine multiple selectors in a single rule is by far the greatest contributor to the versatility of CSS. Selectors can be combined and comma-separated to apply the same characteristics to multiple arbitrary elements, whitespace-separated to reference child elements, and concatenated to enforce a high degree of granularity. There is no limit on the number or type of selectors that can be associated with a single stylesheet rule.

The examples shown in Table 3-1 are assumed to be in a stylesheet that applies to an entire site.

Table 3-1. CSS selectors scoped in plain English

Selector	Applies to
p	All paragraphs in the document
.about	All elements in the document with a class value of about
#corporatehistory	The element in the document with an id value of corporatehistory (if present)
h1,h2,h3	All first-, second-, and third-level headings in the document
.privacy,.copyright	All elements with a class of privacy or copyright
#header,#footer	The element assigned an id of header, and the element assigned an id of footer
p.footnote	All paragraphs assigned a class of footnote
#bodycopy.usergenerated	An element that has been assigned both an id of bodycopy *and* a class of usergenerated
.navigation a	All links with an ancestor parent assigned a class of navigation
#primarynavigation li.current	All list items with a class of current and an ancestor parent with an id of primarynavigation
.about #bodycopy	Any element on the site with an id of bodycopy and an ancestor parent assigned a class of about
body#personalproducts, body#proproducts, body#enterpriseproducts	The body elements within the site assigned the ids personalproducts, proproducts, and enterpriseproducts
body#personalproducts #bodycopy, body#proproducts #bodycopy, body#enterpriseproducts #bodycopy	The elements assigned an id of bodycopy, within the documents suggested by the previous example
ol li ol li ol li	A list item in the third level of a nested ordered list (such as an outline)

Selecting Direct Child Elements

CSS provides the > selector to create selectors for elements with an immediate child relationship, so that:

```
#bodycopy>p { ... }
```

refers to the paragraph element in:

```
<div id="bodycopy"><p>...</p></div>
```

but *not* the paragraph element in:

```
<div id="bodycopy"> ... <blockquote><p> ... </p></blockquote> ... </div>
```

The > selector is discussed as one of the Bad Parts—not because there's anything wrong with it, but rather because it's not supported by Internet Explorer 6.

Rule Conflicts, Priority, and Precedence

The *cascade* allows well-written selectors to target *any* range of elements in the document, without respect to the level of the document tree in which that range of elements lies.

A close look at the selector examples presented so far reveals that conflicts seem inevitable. A rule such as p { ... } would apply to the preceding source example, but presumably so would #bodycopy p { ... }. When there is a conflict, which value gets applied?

Selector Priority

The types of selectors used in a rule dictate that rule's priority. In *ascending* order of weight, they are:

1. User agent stylesheet selectors
2. User stylesheet selectors
3. The universal selector (*)
4. Elements and pseudoelements (e.g., first-letter)
5. Classes, pseudoclasses (e.g., :hover), and attributes ([selected="selected"])
6. ids
7. Values of inline style attributes, as explained in "The Awful Parts" on page 286

Given any two rules, the one with the highest-priority selector will automatically take precedence. In cases where two rules contain selectors of equal priority, it then becomes necessary to count the number of selectors in each rule—a rule with two id selectors takes priority over a rule with one id selector and four (or eighteen) class selectors, for example.

When any two selectors claim identical priority and weight, it then becomes necessary to consider the presence of any !important values that they contain, as well as their relative position in the source order of the styles applied to a document. The importance of rule source order is explained in the following section, and taken up directly in the explanation of link pseudoclasses (see "Link Pseudoclasses" on page 137).

Avoiding Rule Conflicts

Where two conflicting rules claim an *identical* priority, the browser applies the *latter* of those two rules, considered in terms of style source order. Style source order is determined by the order in which external stylesheets and `style` element content are inserted into a document, so that given the following fragment of markup:

```
<link rel="stylesheet" type="text/css" href="/styles.css" media="all" />
<style type="text/css">@import (/styles.signup.css);</style>
```

The contents of `/styles.signup.css` are assigned a later source order than the contents of `/styles.css`. Placing the `@import` declaration in `/styles.css` would instead give the contents of `/styles.signup.css` an *earlier* source order.

There are two other methods of increasing the priority of property/value declarations: the `!important` value and overloaded selectors. The former is best applied to general cases, while the latter is best applied to edge cases.

The `!important` value follows a normal property/value pair, like so:

```
color: #f00 !important;
```

In practice the values supplanted with `!important` are given absolute priority in all stylesheet rule conflicts, unless a user stylesheet also addresses the same conflict with an `!important` value of its own.

In its turn, selector overloading relies on the fact that *all* selectors attached to a rule contribute to that rule's priority, even if the elements they specify are completely absent from the document to which the styles are being applied.

Consider the following two rules in the context of the same page and stylesheet:

```
a:visited { color: rgb(128,0,128); }
.sidebar a { color: rgb(0,0,255); }
```

Given the requirements of the specification, both rules acquire the same priority. To have any hope of being applied, the second of the two rules just given *must* be inserted later in the stylesheet. However, if project requirements deny that outcome, it might be practical to overload the rule with an additional *bogus* selector.

This scenario is fairly unlikely. Instead, selector overloading demonstrates its greatest value when a rule assigns style values to several sections of a site or page at once, and in so doing makes it otherwise impossible to give priority to values in even narrower contexts.

Overloaded selectors should be embellished by accompanying comments whenever possible, in order to make them more accessible to automated search/replace functions.

Value Inheritance

Only font/text and foreground color values are preserved within an element's descendants. Background properties often *appear* to be inherited, and this illusion works because where two elements share a context and overlap in the layout—as is always the case with descendant elements that share a stacking context. The latter element in the source order is always stacked *above* its immediate parent or other ancestor.

 Element stacking contexts are discussed in greater detail in Chapter 6.

Meanwhile, there are two types of elements that do *not* inherit the font/text and foreground color values of their parent elements:

Form controls
> The type in form controls is set in the fonts and colors specified by the operating system defaults, unless it is deliberately reset in the stylesheet.

`iframes`
> Since an `iframe` is populated by its own separate document, its font/text and foreground color properties are defined by stylesheet rules associated with that document.

CSS Property and Value Survey

Figuring out how to specify the element you want to style is probably the hardest part of learning CSS and writing production stylesheets. However, climbing that learning curve doesn't lead to results until you know how to supply style properties and values to the elements that you've carefully chosen.

CSS Units

While CSS supports a seemingly endless list of properties, the scheme for setting values is fairly predictable. Table 3-2 describes the most frequently used values.

Table 3-2. Commonly encountered CSS length/size, keyword, and color units

Unit	Type	Example
px (pixels)	length	`width: 744px;`
em (ems)	length	`margin-left; 1.25em;`
% (percent)	length	`left: 34%;`
pt (points)	length	`font-size: 12pt;`

Unit	Type	Example
in (inches)	length	margin-top: .75in;
cm (centimeters)	length	margin-top: 1.905cm;
xx-small ... xx-large	font size	font-size: large;
rgb(r,g,b)	color (decimal)	background-color: rgb(221,204,187);
#rrggbb	color (hexadecimal)	background-color: #ddccbb;
#rgb	color (hexadecimal, reduced depth)	background-color: #dcb;

Cross-Media Length and Size Units

There are three commonly used units in stylesheets intended for **screen** display:

px *(pixels)*
> Pixels are absolute units, equal to one pixel on the user's screen display; always expressed as an integer.

em *(ems)*
> In digital typesetting environments (including CSS), an em is equivalent to the greatest possible height of a glyph (letter) in the applicable font and size combination. The contemporary definition contrasts with the *historical* definition: the width of a capital "M" in the font and size of the type to which it is applied as a measurement. This unit is usually expressed with a floating-point value.

% *(percent)*
> Percentage units are computed relative to some baseline measurement, which varies according to property and context. Floating-point percentage values are allowed.

em and % units are discussed in "Layout Types and Canvas Grids" on page 106.

Pitch and the Value of a Pixel

The **screen, handheld,** and **projection** media types all support the **px** unit, but CSS provides no standard mechanism for defining display pitch.

Since the pixel is the atomic unit of screen displays, all page elements must be computed in terms of pixels before rendering can take place. Because of this requirement, display pitch will determine the literal size of everything presented by the browser. The smaller the display pitch, the smaller everything will be when a page is rendered and displayed.

Table 3-3 shows the approximate arithmetic behind common display resolutions and pitches, as found on both contemporary backlit LCD and older CRT displays. Commonly encountered form factors are shown in bold.

Table 3-3. Commonly encountered screen display form factors, resolutions, and display pitches

Size (viewable)	Resolution	Aspect ratio	Width (mm)	Height (mm)	Pitch (mm)	px/in
10.2″	**1024×600**	**≈17:10**	**224**	**130**	**0.218**	**116**
12″ (CRT)	640×480	4:3	244	183	0.381	66
12″	1024×768	4:3	244	183	0.238	106
13″	**1280×800**	**16:10**	**280**	**175**	**0.219**	**116**
14″ (CRT)	800×600	4:3	284	213	0.355	71
15″	1024×768	4:3	305	229	0.298	85
16″ (CRT)	**1024×768**	**4:3**	**325**	**245**	**0.318**	**80**
17″	1280×1024	5:4	337	270	0.263	96
17″	1366×768	≈16:9	376	212	0.276	92
17″	1440×900	16:10	366	229	0.254	100
19″	**1440×900**	**16:10**	**409**	**256**	**0.284**	**89**
22″	1680×1050	16:10	474	296	0.282	90
23″ (CRT)	1600×1200	4:3	447	335	0.279	91

As of this writing, two types of displays (19″, 1440×900; and 22″, 1680×1050) are particularly high sellers on Amazon.com (though both types are outsold by netbooks). Going by this table, the pitches of these two types of displays differ by only 2μm (less than 1%), averaging out at nearly 90 pixels per inch.

Considering that Windows assumes a display pitch of 96 pixels per inch for the purpose of displaying print documents onscreen, it would appear at first that stylists have little to worry about when it comes to predicting the literal size of their product on the screen display of the typical user.

In most cases, default assumptions offer few caveats to trouble the conscientious stylist. However, consider the fact that a pixel on a netbook contains less than two-thirds of the area of a pixel on one of the high-selling displays mentioned earlier. This means that the physical dimensions of a layout will decrease by one quarter on each axis when viewed on a netbook, as compared to the most popular types of desktop monitors.

The physically variable nature of pixels leads to a concept that every web developer would do well to keep in mind:

> Designers who fail to account for the range of conditions under which their sites are visited will likely experience shock when exposed to their work in an unexpected setting. Stylists are among the reviewers who can prevent such surprises.

Print-Friendly Length Units

Chapter 1 pointed out that unlike its predecessors, the Web is an unbounded medium. That lack of constraints applies not only to the Web's domain of information, but also to its interface—when viewed on most hardware platforms, web documents can be scrolled, minimized, maximized, and otherwise manipulated within browser windows to the limits of the designer's imagination and the visitor's patience.

The print medium yields with greater ease to assumptions about environment, since readers of printed pages typically read from sheets of US Letter (8½″ × 11″) or ISO A4 paper, which are similar in size.

Print stylesheets can make good use of additional units, all of which can be specified in floating-point values:

pt

Type is traditionally measured in *points*; there are 72 in an inch. Expressed in Système International (SI) units, a point is roughly equivalent to 353 μm, yielding slightly less than 28.35 points per centimeter.

in

One inch is defined by international treaty as being equal to 2.54 cm. By way of comparison, a row of four hexagonal wooden pencils laid side by side and flush will measure nine-eighths of an inch (1.125″) across.

cm

Centimeters. One sheet of A4 paper measures 21 cm × 29.7 cm.

This list is not comprehensive; additional units are described on this book's companion website. Also, note that `line-height` values can be specified with floating-point numbers and without a unit. In such cases, a value of `1` is equivalent to `1em`.

font-size Keywords

In situations where the priority of accessibility outweighs the need to express design composites precisely, `font-size` keywords can be used to surrender presentation control to the visitor. The domain of `font-size` keywords contains seven values, listed below from largest to smallest:

- `xx-large`
- `x-large`
- `large`
- `medium` (default)
- `small`
- `x-small`
- `xx-small`

`font-size` keyword values are also discussed in "Size Keywords" on page 217.

Color Units

CSS supports a three-channel (red, green, blue) color space with eight bits of color depth per channel. Such a space yields 16.7 million (2^{24}) possible colors.

Wherever there's a need to reference a color, stylists have at their disposal three styles of notation:

`rgb(r,g,b)`
> Three channels, decimal; each channel takes a range of 0–255.

`#rrggbb`
> Three channels, hexadecimal; each channel takes a range of 00–ff.

`#rgb`
> Three channels, hexadecimal, reduced depth; each channel takes a range of 0–f. The equivalent color in full-depth notation is found by doubling each hexadecimal digit, so that `#6cf` and `#66ccff` are identical.

When creating stylesheets, it's important to choose the most appropriate color notation and use it with ironbound consistency for the sake of stylesheet legibility. The advantages and disadvantages of each are described in Table 3-4.

Table 3-4. Advantages and disadvantages of the three styles of CSS color notation

Style	Advantages	Disadvantages
Six-digit hex	• Precision	• Difficulty of visualization
	• Ease of migration from legacy markup	• Illegibility
24-bit decimal	• Human readability	• Vulnerability to input errors
	• Accessibility to scripted transitions	• Lack of copy+paste functionality in third-party tools
Truncated hex	• Simplicity	• Lack of depth
	• Suitability for prototyping	

Chapter 9 goes into greater detail about working with color.

Key CSS Layout Properties

In order to implement all but the simplest layouts, it becomes necessary to use a number of layout properties that alter the flow of elements within a document. The most functionally useful properties and values are described in Table 3-5 (defaults are in bold). These properties and values will be explained in greater detail in Chapter 6.

Table 3-5. Commonly supported CSS layout properties and values

Property	Values
display	• block
	• inline
	• inline-block
	• none
width/height	• [length]
	• **auto**
float	• left
	• **none**
	• right
clear	• **both**
	• left
	• none
	• right
position	• absolute
	• fixed
	• relative
	• **static**
top/right/bottom/left	• [length]

The *functions* of the properties listed in Table 3-5 are described next and shown in Figure 3-1.

display
> HTML specifies that elements exhibit one of several kinds of layout behavior. Normally this behavior is set by the element's definition in the DTD, but that behavior will correspond to and may be overridden by the value of the CSS display property. inline describes elements that flow without deliberate linebreaks on a (usually) common baseline, and have limited interaction with CSS layout and box properties. block describes elements that are followed and preceded by linebreaks, and expand to fill the entire width of the containing element (unless otherwise specified). inline-block describes elements that flow like inline elements, but interact with the full range of CSS layout and block properties, like block elements. The none value is cognate to elements that are hidden by default, and supplying this value will remove the affected element from the document flow entirely.

width *and* height
> Describes the dimensions of block and inline-block elements. A width value of auto causes the affected element to expand to the full width of its containing

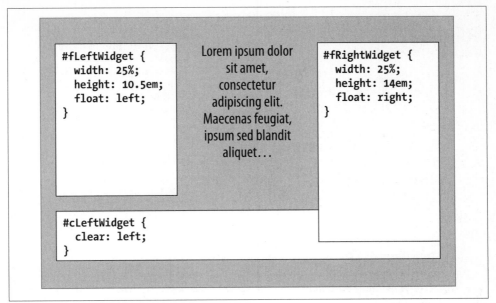

Figure 3-1. The use of the float and clear properties changes the relationship between the affected element and the element(s) that follow it

element, while a `height` value of auto causes the affected element to expand to the full height of its *nonfloated* content.

float
> When changed, specifies that an element should hew to the specified margin of its containing element, and allow following elements to flow around it. A `float` property/value pair must always appear in tandem with an explicit `width` property/value pair, unless it's assigned to an element (such as an image) that has an *intrinsic* width.

clear
> Describes the containing element margin(s) to which an element should be anchored, thus ensuring that it will be placed *below* any nearby preceding elements that have a comparable `float` value.

position, top, right, bottom, *and* left
> Alters the location of the specified content border(s) of the affected element, when a `position` value other than `static` is supplied. As layout tools go, these properties are spectacularly powerful—powerful enough that they're explained at exhaustive length in "CSS Positioning Properties" on page 96. Figure 3-2 describes the relationships between various types of positioned elements.

The layout properties described here are a small subset of the full body of CSS layout properties. The others are described throughout the rest of this book.

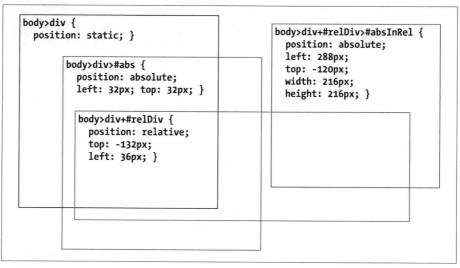

Figure 3-2. A position value other than static changes the positioning context, as shown here

CHAPTER 4

Developing a Healthy Relationship with Standards

The Web as practiced is not the same as the Web as specified. While the Web is built on standards and specifications, adherence to the rules is sporadic at best. Software developers often extend functionality, leave out functionality, or implement things incorrectly. Web developers often create sites that more or less conform to the specifications, but they may also tune their work to run on a particular browser, with all of its idiosyncrasies, or leave their slightly broken markup at the mercy of a browser's rendering engine.

Ignoring or abandoning standards to focus exclusively on browser results leads to a maze of constant testing on every imaginable browser, and possibly a powerless sense of resignation when you recognize the inevitability of alienated site visitors. On the other hand, sticking to the spirit, the letter, and the fine details of specifications may limit your ability to reach visitors through the tools they have, rather than the tools you wish they had. Fortunately, there is a middle way.

The Broad Landscape of Web-Related Standards

While HTML and CSS are the focus of this book, there are a number of significant standards that relate directly to web development. These include:

HTTP 1.x
> Hypertext Transfer Protocol—already explained in brief earlier—claims both the W3C and the IETF as custodians. This partnership is appropriate, as the IETF is the body responsible for the ongoing development of the protocols used on the Internet as a whole. The appendix outlines aspects of HTTP that HTML and CSS developers should understand.

Web Content Accessibility Guidelines (WCAG)
> Two versions of the Web Content Accessibility Guidelines have been published. The first became a W3C Recommendation in May 1999, and is referenced directly

in the United States Government regulations that define websites that are accessible to the functionally impaired. The latest version achieved Recommendation status in December 2008, and applies not only to traditionally designed websites, but web platforms in general.

ECMA-262
The syntax, grammar, and core objects of the language usually referred to as JavaScript are defined in a standard endorsed by Ecma International (originally chartered as the European Computer Manufacturers Association).

Document Object Model (DOM) Levels 1–3
Valid web documents have a coherent, tree-like structure, and the DOM specifications define the programmatic interfaces to that structure.

The vendor-specific DOM APIs used when Dynamic HTML was first supported are sometimes referred to as "DOM Level 0." Levels 1 through 3 are defined in a number of W3C Recommendations and Drafts.

ISO 639, 8859, and 10646
The W3C and vendors currently rely on these standards for implementing character encodings and language references. The last of these is called Unicode, and is encoded using one of the Unicode Transformation Format (UTF) schemes. Nonlogographic writing is often encoded using UTF-8. For more information about character encoding, consult "Character Encoding in Brief" on page 224.

The Web also relies on standards for things like image formats (JPEG, GIF, PNG, SVG) and other content that might be included in pages.

Why Web Standards?

Since the publication of the first IETF draft specification for HTML, browser vendors and site developers have made a frequent bad habit of disregarding published web standards. At the same time, the community of developers who make a point of respecting those standards (of which this author considers himself a devoted if usually quiet member) has never been anything but vocal and predictable, if not actually disciplined. There are a number of issues at work behind the scenes of the ongoing debate.

 This section addresses web standards as they are typically promoted.

Interoperability

Untested assumptions about visitors are a big mistake. Common adherence to standards would reduce the number of assumptions. Developers could build their sites and deploy them with a minimum of platform testing. And who doesn't want that?

Market Forces

The virtues of interoperability do not, however, harmonize easily with the hot desire for bells, whistles, and pretty things often felt by artists and marketers. Browser vendors cannot ignore the imperative to innovate, and the market usually works on a shorter life cycle than the standards acceptance process.

Market forces are what drove the prospect of common standards compliance off the rails in the first place. In early 1995, `table` support was introduced in Netscape 1.1, while codification of earlier enhancements brought to market by Mosaic 2.0 was still awaiting acceptance. In effect, Netscape—then still deserving of the "startup" label and two years from its groundbreaking entry into the equity markets—was capable of running circles around the standards adoption process, and the market responded. The resulting conditions nurtured a diffident attitude toward web standards that persists more than a decade later.

Forward Compatibility

It is often argued that standards compliance ensures the longevity of sites that respect it; while features are often added to user agent platforms, they are rarely removed or disabled (the `blink` element being a notable but absurd exception). Older standards, meanwhile, tend to lie within the lowest common denominator of features supported by all user agents. The upshot of these two facts is that standards compliance allows sites to better survive across browser versions.

Accessibility

Standards compliance tends to make materials more accessible to impaired users, many of whom rely on various forms of third-party assistive technology to ensure a meaningful experience. The standards are a useful guide in this respect for a number of reasons:

- While not enforced by an impartial body, W3C Recommendations *are* authoritative and as such are incorporated into requirements of statute law relating to accessibility, especially in the United States.

- The published Recommendations provide vendors of assistive technology with baseline expectations for their customers' browsing environments, even when that baseline follows lowest common denominators.

- From the beginning, one of the principal design goals of HTML has been cross-media compatibility, which makes it easier to create technology.

Vendor Priorities

After the release of Internet Explorer 6 in 2001, Microsoft's attention to the web user experience entered an era of somnolence that has only just definitively ended with the release of Internet Explorer 8, a substantial upgrade.

IE6 was released at a time when market shares of competing user agent platforms were on the wane, and the public understanding is that Microsoft made a strategic decision to rest on its laurels until developer community outcry—driven by an official United States Government recommendation to stop using Internet Explorer altogether, among other factors—encouraged it to resume significant ongoing development of Internet Explorer.

A similar incident illuminates Netscape 4's poor support for CSS. When CSS 1.0 was in development, Netscape and Microsoft offered competing proposals to the W3C, and Netscape's proposal was rejected outright. It's apocryphally understood that because Netscape 4 was about to pass its RTM (release to manufacturing) milestone, frantic last-minute engineering of Netscape 4's rendering engine was required in order to provide any support whatsoever for the W3C-mandated CSS—a necessarily slapdash effort that had long-term consequences for the quality of the browser, to say nothing of Netscape's viability.

Legacy Asset Inertia

During the era of the Web's fastest growth, standards were barely on the proverbial radar, and the cost of putting sites into production was high because the tools available at the time were quite primitive.

As a result of those adverse conditions, tremendous investments were made in poorly built web properties and the software that made them go. These properties continue to be nurtured because the cost of replacing them—measured in terms of institutional politics and capital investment—is seen as too high.

This phenomenon most strongly affects typical web developers in the area of third-party content and solutions, particularly news publishing and advertising platforms.

Best Practices (and Lack Thereof)

Web shops and solo web developers can be found under a wide variety of institutional umbrellas: solo freelancers, specialist boutiques, large advertising agencies, mass media outlets, online businesses, medium-size businesses, information technology and information services departments of every imaginable size, and departments that have one or two developers fully responsible for the breadth of that unit's web presence. In addition, there are legions of do-it-yourself-ers, who can be undercapitalized, bloody-minded, or both. Websites are built by all kinds of people, and everyone has different notions of what makes a website good or bad. That difference in judgment of quality and choice of tools, which in large enterprises is compounded by interdepartmental confusion and infighting, results in widely varying ideas of best practices.

An individual's most valuable web development qualification is neither her level of skill nor her degree of talent, but instead her ability to interact agreeably with teammates and others in order to be effective at her job, a quality frequently called "team fit." That dynamic is made still more complex by the fact that there is a high incidence of introvert personality traits amongst the population of professional web developers. Finally, the reluctance of many employers to take responsibility for their employees' ongoing skill development puts considerable drag on the momentum of median skills growth—sometimes to the point of eliminating that momentum completely.

As you can imagine, such an environment can result in wildly differing opinions regarding good and bad.

Strict Constructionism

The most passionate dispute that many developers have with the prospect of standards compliance is that it's an all-or-nothing affair. The most visible requirement of standards compliance is valid markup, which is too often impossible to publish because of the many challenges explained earlier.

In addition to meeting the extreme challenge of genuine standards compliance, well-intentioned development teams must tolerate the rather shrill and morally superior attitude of many self-styled standards advocates, and the result is a large cadre of professionals who couldn't possibly care less about standards compliance.

Taking the Middle Road: Standards-Friendliness

Even when work product can't stand up perfectly to the test of validation, the good intentions that underlie web standards remain relevant.

The primary goal of standards-friendliness is to allow iterative enhancement of work product, a significant aspect of which is forward compatibility. Standards-friendliness leads to syntactically correct markup in good source order that strictly enforces separation of structure from presentation, while minimizing the amount of time spent struggling with the minutiae of validation. While this practice concedes more to adverse circumstances than many web standards advocates feel is appropriate—since after all, the project sponsor is the one who signs the paychecks—it still yields many benefits.

Benefits of Standards-Friendliness

What do you get in return for the extra effort of a standards-friendly approach?

Standards-friendly deliverables follow the Pareto (80/20) Rule, creating optimal benefit for the amount of time invested

> The alternatives are unmaintainable assets, lack of scalability, and inflexibility. Such outcomes increase delivery times over the long term, since there's little in standards-ignorant work product on which to base modular assets.

Accessible assets become much easier to create

> When the source order of content is easily human-readable and developers use appropriate elements—especially lists, in the case of navigation functionality—the result presents few if any challenges for users of assistive technology.

Users of alternative media also benefit from these accessibility improvements

> Standards-friendly development offers the best opportunities to apply separate presentation layers to content on a per-media (e.g., screen, print, mobile) basis without being forced to create multiple instances of the same content, saving huge amounts of time and other resources.

Data becomes more portable

> When datastores are designed in the spirit of standards-friendliness, their contents can be transformed for use in other information systems, perhaps even systems that aren't web-based. Microformats advocates are especially ebullient about this benefit.

Rules of Standards-Friendly Development

Following some basic rules of standards-friendly development can simplify creating and developing your sites in the long run:

1. Avoid presentation-oriented markup (especially inline `style` attributes) at all reasonable cost.
2. Keep the source order of page content easily human-readable at all times.
3. Overbuild markup relating to overall document structure, but otherwise keep markup to the minimum required by the circumstances.
4. Relegate the use of table markup to data presentation *only*.
5. Ensure that all elements are properly closed, nested, populated, and supplied with required attributes; relegate all other validity concerns to a lower priority.
6. If possible, assign a distinctive `id` or `class` (or even one of each) to each `body` element within a site's scope, to account for edge cases.
7. Give all `id`s and `class`es names that are driven by context, rather than presentation. If you find yourself unable to follow this rule, you're probably breaking Rule #1;

if you're able to follow it, you're probably doing a good job of following Rules #2 and #3.

8. Always use lists and headings where called for, even though it can be challenging to put the latter inside the former.

9. Relegate all images intended to provide design accents to the CSS `background-image` property.

10. Draft separate stylesheets for Internet Explorer, limited to the scope of addressing layout bugs.

Like all rules, these have their exceptions—and because it de-emphasizes the value of *completely* valid markup, Rule #5 breaks a few broader rules itself.

The guiding principle of these practices is not *perfection* but *practicality*: it's often impossible to maintain perfect control over the entirety of a complex site, once poor third-party content and other flaws are taken into account.

CHAPTER 5

Effective Style and Structure

One can read markup like music and gain an appreciation for a document as a complete product—but when the presentation is completely removed into its own dedicated scope, the only way to make sense of the result is to ride *two* trains of thought in parallel. For most people, that kind of perfectly balanced multitasking takes practice.

However, there are tools and habits that make it easier. Among the tools are the developer interfaces provided with every major browser, all designed to display related markup and stylesheet rules *in context*.

Habits are a different matter. Remember that the Web is a multidimensional space: if you see markup or CSS and your thought process is still constrained to only two (or even three) dimensions, *you're not seeing the whole picture*.

 Most of this section deals with presentation-layer development practice on a theoretical level. If you want to skip to the "climax" of this material, you should read "Taxonomy and Nomenclature" on page 68.

The Four Habits of Effective Stylists

The Web has no beginning and no end. Individual *pages* might be bounded, but even those usually contain links to other sources of information, and visitors could have arrived from any context. Even when a document ends, the user experience doesn't.

Working in this unbounded environment requires a tight focus on *information* in preference to any notion of the finished site. Everything else takes lower priority: designers' hangups, branding guidelines, even release schedules don't matter when you're in the early stages of a project. A stylist who keeps an effective focus on the information is able to accommodate most of his team's priorities as a matter of course.

Successful stylists need to adopt four habits to give information its due:

1. Keep It Simple, Stupid.
2. Keep it flexible.
3. Keep to consistency.
4. Keep your bearings.

These four habits enhance *process* and *product*, making it possible to create better work product in less time than is possible without a thoughtfully disciplined approach. Developers of large sites especially have need of the resource savings implied by these habits.

The perspective that complements and aids these habits leads eventually to the concept of "CSS Zen." For more information about this concept, see "The Functional Principles of CSS Zen" on page 60.

Habit #1: Keeping It Simple

Simplicity of design—otherwise known as "the KISS Principle" (Keep It Simple, Stupid)—can take several forms in a developer's work product: less markup, shorter pipelines, less-ornate application objects, and fewer features are all results of a push for simplicity.

More parts means more things that move, more things that interact, more dependencies, more things that can break, and more ways in which things can break.

> Successful practitioners of simplicity remove *everything* that doesn't need to be there.

The first challenge, then, is to set criteria of necessity. Most excess markup serves one of two objectives: futureproofing or precision of layout. In the latter case, its presence should be considered necessary only if your workplace culture is tuned to give the clueless what they want. This even goes for optional-yet-desirable accents like rounded corners, for which simple and complex implementations are shown below:

```
/* *** simple styles *** */

.someElementWithCorners { padding: 1em; background-color: #ccc; -moz-border-radius:
.75em;  -webkit-border-radius: .75em; }
.someElementWithCorners b { display: none; }

/* *** ...but if EVERYBODY MUST have the same presentation, these rules will go in
the IE conditional stylesheets... *** */

.someElementWithCorners { position: relative; }

.someElementWithCorners b.trc,
.someElementWithCorners b.brc,
.someElementWithCorners b.blc,
.someElementWithCorners b.tlc { display: block; position: absolute; z-index: 0; width:
.75em;  height: .75em; overflow: hidden; background-image:
```

```
url(/images/corner_circle.png); }

.someElementWithCorners b.trc { top: 0; right: 0; background-position: 100% 0; }
.someElementWithCorners b.brc { bottom: 0; right: 0; background-position: 100% 100%; }
.someElementWithCorners b.blc { bottom: 0; left: 0; background-position: 0 100%; }
.someElementWithCorners b.tlc { top: 0; left: 0; }

.someElementWithCorners p,
.someElementWithCorners h4 { position: relative; z-index: 1; }

...

<!-- ...And now for the markup: -->

<div class="someElementWithCorners">
  <h4>Lorem Ipsum Dolor Sit Amet</h4>
  <p>This is filler content for a source example. In it the quick red fox jumps over
    the lazy brown dog.</p><b class="trc"> </b><b class="brc"> </b><b
    class="blc"> </b><b class="tlc"> </b>
</div>
```

In the *simple* implementation, only the first stylesheet rule is used, the four b elements
are omitted, there's no need for an extra background image, and on account of Internet
Explorer's absent support for rounded corners, its users just don't see them. (Although
yes, it does rely on the nonstandard `-webkit-border-radius` and `-moz-border-radius`
properties.)

The more complex, rounded-corners implementation works, but with experience its
problems become glaring:

- The markup is irrevocably tied to presentation; removing the rounded corners from
  the design will suggest (if not require) work to remove the presentation-specific
  matter.

- `position`, `z-index`, and the hassles that attend their use are particular to this implementation of flexible rounded corners, but most unnecessarily complex styling
  carries comparable baggage. The result of this extraneous *stuff* is always the same:
  the additional markup and styles decrease the flexibility of the site's presentation
  by introducing unintended design constraints.

- More markup and more styles increase the likelihood of input errors and rendering
  bugs.

Something to keep in mind about simplicity—and its absence—is that benefits and
hassles tend to multiply. If you use a single complex implementation in your templates
the consequences will probably be negligible, but complexity beyond the first or second
instance leads ultimately to templates that collapse under their own weight in irresolv-
able conflicts, rendering bugs, and maintenance needs.

If instead one practices simplicity faithfully, the application of CSS Zen in redesigns
and new projects is nearly effortless. Once you strip a template down to its essentials,
there's nothing to get in the way.

The most significant task in enforcing simplicity is to establish firmly what is—or will be—*essential*.

Simplicity and huge sites

The nature of "simple" may change, however, as the scale of the project grows. Development teams responsible for large sites find it extremely difficult to handle all of the special presentation cases and other accents that often achieve approval on smaller sites. Among other things, the demand for improved manageability forces those teams to greatly reduce the number of ids in their product compared to the source examples used in this book, and to rigidly standardize the ids that remain.

In practice, designers are the ones who perform this "trimming" at the encouragement of developers, with the goal of aligning three requirements: business objectives, anticipated visitor objectives, and delivery dates. Such collaboration usually results in the creation of a small number of templates that are themselves often based on a single, very simple template—scaffolding, if you will. The basic layout is divided into smaller, discrete server components, each placed within a container that's assigned an id and often one or more classes, such as:

- #header
- ul#nav
- #content
- #footer

Components inserted into the page can then be populated automatically. The resulting content choices are typically based on the goal to be facilitated by the requested resource, the authentication status of the visitor, and the need for third-party content.

When compared to the source examples found in this book, the source markup of large sites differs especially with respect to its treatment of *navigation*, which is vastly simplified out of necessity. For example, you'll rarely see any kind of image replacement on large sites, because such sites support such a broad variety of use requirements that the resource cost of image replacement techniques is prohibitively high.

Off-the-shelf Content Management Systems and blogging platforms also rely on this design approach. Their use cases cover such a broad spectrum not because of the needs of *visitors* to the sites that run on these platforms, but instead because of the varying objectives of the site operators who install them.

Habit #2: Keeping It Flexible

Maintaining flexibility requires the right balance between near- and long-term definitions of necessity. This habit is far more about people than anything else: every project has (well, *should* have) a unique combination of sponsors, audience, requirements, time line, and expectations of longevity.

Within such a shifting landscape, definitions change. Flexibility in a web application is different from flexibility in a data archive. Event promotion sites are entirely different from both of those; where the first two will focus on flexibility in the face of distant work iterations or outlying use cases, highly time-sensitive sites are most flexible if their assets (including markup) can be used for later, similar projects.

The most significant factors that inform the need for flexibility are process, site objectives, and workplace culture. Successful stylists take all of these into account before starting work. In terms of results:

> A stylist's work product is most flexible when its production values accurately reflect the *real* reasons why it was commissioned in the first place.

The practice of flexibility rests mainly upon two pillars: progressive enhancement, and overbuilding.

Effective implementation of progressive enhancement in web applications often requires that developers write and maintain parallel codebases, one run on the client to reduce server load, and the other run on the server to suit use cases where the user has disabled client-side scripting.

Progressive enhancement was implicitly described in "Separating Content, Structure, Presentation, and Behavior" on page 18. Content rests inside markup, upon which a presentation layer reliant on CSS is laid, and all of those are topped with a final layer of scripting that provides behaviors like error handling and interactivity. When those assets are implemented correctly, the dependencies are unidirectional: implementations of presentation and behavior point back to requirements in content and markup, but if the presentation and behavior "layers" are removed, the site should still be usable.

Some entrenched practices and flaws in the design of the Web increase the difficulty of building flexible work product through progressive enhancement. Those bits of ugliness are described in Chapter 14.

The second pillar of flexibility is *overbuilding*. There are places where markup *might* be inserted into a template to ease the application of things like `class`-based rules and absolute positioning, and whether to add them depends on the long-term needs of the project, or your shop's need to create reusable assets.

In my own deliverables, `class` values such as `section` and `postMetadata` make frequent appearances, even on sites where design requirements are consistent enough to allow their omission. They're applied with an eye on the aesthetic and structural evolution of the site: *initial* requirements might not demand that special styles be added in section or metadata scopes, but such requirements may be added over the medium to long term.

The downside of overbuilding is that it can conflict directly with the goal of simplicity, which illuminates the need to find a good balance. The best test involves three questions:

1. Can a *relevant and descriptive* `class` or `id` value be added to each "extra" element?
2. Is the extra markup meant to support a *range* of possible presentation requirements, or just one?
3. Is there a reasonable expectation that the site will undergo a gradual and extended evolution over an extended period of time?

If the answers to all three of the preceding questions are "yes," then it's not only acceptable but actually desirable to insert the additional markup into your templates. The key to managing the extra structural markup is to practice thoughtful triage, and to normalize the results.

Flexibility, internal libraries, and code reuse

When developers start planning for the long term, they generate the greatest resource savings in *template-based* approaches like those described earlier with respect to flexibility. Teams that operate without significant external support might well attempt to gain that savings by adopting an off-the-shelf publishing system, and develop an internal process for modifying its output.

Longtime freelance developers who prefer to work with web technologies directly often take a different approach: they develop unique libraries of markup, stylesheets, and code over time. Still others, myself included, fall into narrowly defined yet effective production techniques, starting each project from a blank slate (when possible) so that the prototyping process (see "Prototyping and Layout" on page 251) is done manually, but with so little mental effort that the leftover brainpower can instead be devoted to understanding the unique requirements of a given project.

Teams with access to external support and tasked to large sites have the opportunity to get the best of both worlds: for them the best approach is to build new "modules" when new requirements are presented, but otherwise to repurpose existing products. Internal production standards and style guides are critical to such an approach, and those tools affect stylists' work in the following ways:

- Most (if not all) presentation support is stuffed into `class`es, enjoys the benefit of extensive documentation, and can only be altered or extended after an arduous approval process that is deliberately designed to discourage individual team members from cheerleading for edge case support.
- Individual, interchangeable site components are often more "anonymous" than the ideal, and their use cases are documented barely, if at all, within the product itself. This circumstance is owed half to necessity, half to inertia: until CSS gained wide acceptance, `table` nesting (which gained no benefit from inline documentation) was essential to achieving effective site component layout.

- Unavoidable disconnects between graded support requirements (see "Graded Support" on page 273) and browser capabilities are resolved with the brute force provided by JavaScript frameworks and inline stylesheet hacks.

- Overbuilding is comparatively rare, and where present is usually found within smaller content components.

All of these steps lend themselves to the aforementioned need for *balance*. When a team of four to six developers is called upon to accommodate the work of multiple content authors who are far better versed in the editorial and art direction specialties than in web technologies, the latter group's needs *must* be given lower priority for the sake of preserving developers' availability to quality assurance work and other projects.

Habit #3: Keeping to Consistency

Ideally, a stylist can adapt the deliverables from an earlier project to a current project with minimal changes to markup and layout CSS; such an outcome is one example of CSS Zen in action (see "The Functional Principles of CSS Zen" on page 60). To achieve that, a stylist must adopt consistent ways of drawing up and embellishing templates for similar cases. This kind of consistency is harder to achieve in practice than in theory; lack of discipline and manipulative behavior on the part of managers often force line developers (and the stylists among them) to reinvent the proverbial wheel on every project.

Therefore, the habit of consistency demands that a stylist *recognize* familiar circumstances, *prepare* for them, and *act on them with fortitude* whenever possible.

> Consistency is the result of observation, reflection, and preparation.

There are two scopes in which consistency works to your advantage: within a site, and across multiple sites.

Intrasite consistency is one of the central benefits of the cascade. Consider a three-column template; the simplest layout styles for that outline will be contained in comparatively few rules. If you then have a *two*-column presentation that relies on the same template, or have a few pages where the presentation order of two columns is reversed, it becomes necessary to write *additional* styles to handle those cases, like so:

```
                    #main #priorityContent { width: 42em; float: left; }
                #priorityContent #bodyCopy { float: right; width: 24em;
                                             padding: 0 1.5em 0 1.5em; }
                #priorityContent #sidebar { margin-right: 27em; }
                            #main #tertiary { margin-left: 42em; }
       body.mySpecialCase #main #priorityContent { width: auto; }
   body.mySpecialCase #priorityContent #bodyCopy { width: 34.5em; }
   body.mySpecialCase #priorityContent #sidebar { margin-right: 37.5em; }
         body.mySpecialCase #main #tertiary { display: none; }
```

The selectors in this CSS source code example are overloaded, to provide the reader with an idea of elements' parent-child relationships.

The previous styles describe the suggested three-column layout in the first four rules. The rest remove `#tertiary` from the document flow and adjust the layout of the remaining elements to account for the absent column. If there are no special cases, only the first three rules will be necessary.

The extra rules illuminate the benefits of simplicity, which are still enhanced in this example when compared to the prospect of building separate templates for two- and three-column presentation cases. (The compromise, and the most search-friendly practice, is to put the volatile column within a scripted `include` that's invoked only when needed.)

A stylist who writes the preceding styles assumes that the same template will be used for both two- and three-column presentations, which speaks for one kind of consistency. An *additional* template introduces a number of hazards, the foremost being a requirement for more testing. Another notable hazard of implementing separate templates is code forking, where each template is changed as needed, perhaps for wildly variable reasons. Given enough time, the assumptions of the two templates' designs may drift so far apart that the styles used to normalize their presentation multiply far out of proportion to what would be required for a single template.

Another expression of consistency in this scenario is consistency of design. As suggested by the passage of CSS just shown, the styles needed to realize inconsistent design decisions are far greater in number and scope than those used when consistency of design is a priority, thus imposing more unintended interaction between elements, more potential for rendering bugs, and more testing.

The final, highest expression of consistency is expressed through reuse. If you have a library of templates and stylesheets to account for common layout cases, it becomes possible over time to get any styling project off to a quick start: open the template file, alter `class` and `id` values as needed, and adjust the stylesheet's various box and layout properties to account for the designer's idea of the wireframe. After a fraction of an hour's work, you can focus on typesetting, accents, and other finer details, instead of taking hours to gin up new markup and styles from scratch.

When you are certain of your document and template structure from the start, you are freed from the burden of minutiae, having instead the wherewithal to give your undivided attention to the site's user experience design. These benefits will also provide more wherewithal to design good location cues from design accents.

Managing templates to achieve consistency

The explicit discussion of *templates* in this section of the book refers to the idea of *scaffolding*: a simple collection of markup with at most four or five page sections. This outer "frame" accommodates all of the other page or section templates used by a site, so that the context of any layout column or other page component is easily understood by the stylist who is called upon to provide its presentation.

Designers are usually the greatest danger to this "telescoping" approach, because they can be susceptible to the mistaken belief that the resource investment in template management is measured *arithmetically*. In practice, the effort required to manage and document templates is actually *logarithmic*—if two templates require almost twice the effort to manage as one, it's certain that a third will require not *twice* the effort, but somewhat more.

This outsized growth in resource demand occurs because a given template is best created to meet specific business objectives that are *mostly or entirely unique*. This leads to a unique set of component relationships, making it likely that each new template will reveal new bugs and presentation requirements, in addition to the challenges that are expected when a new template is originally signed off on.

Apart from conscientiously reducing the use of `class` and `id` values to intermediate levels, the best way to manage this growth in resource investment is through *process*— to prototype and test each new template only after a preponderance of stakeholders agree upon the need for a new template.

The alternative is to leap to the step of template creation at every opportunity, which inevitably leads to the diffusion and forking described earlier.

Habit #4: Keeping Your Bearings

 The page structure, markup, and nomenclature conventions introduced in this section and used throughout the book are sharply at odds with the production practices encouraged for large sites, a matter discussed later in this section.

The hardest habit to develop is maintaining a sense of place within your deliverables, mostly because it comes only with practice.

The seed of this habit is planted by remembering that *all* web documents exist in multiple contexts and multiple information spaces, and that your project team can only control *some* of them. The point will be made that ease of wayfinding (see "Navigation: Orientation and Wayfinding" on page 63) and clear sense of place are critical to a positive web user experience; if you cannot maintain a similar grasp of your work product, you stand little or no hope of being able to convey them to visitors.

More to the point, the notion of place is the beginning and end of the cascade: elements lie within other elements, which lie within documents, which exist on sites, which are part of a larger system or universe of sites, which itself is in a contestant state of change. The more accurately you can pinpoint where your current task lies within that universe, the easier it will be to write high-quality CSS.

> A skilled web user needs merely to grasp and act upon location cues. A skilled web *developer* needs to know exactly what he's doing and where he's doing it before he can build the location cues that users need.

Consider the following element tree:

- body
  - h1
  - div#main
    - div#priorityContent
      - div#bodyCopy
        - h2
        - div.section
          - ...
      - div#sidebar
        - ...
    - div#tertiary
      - ...
    - ul#primaryNav
    - div#footer
      - ul#secondaryNav
      - p#colophon

This tree presents a minimum of 16 simple contexts in which presentation can be applied. To these are almost certainly added some indication of a document's *scope of content*, by way of `class` and `id` values that can be added to the `body` element (and possibly others).

When a stylist notes and combines these signals of element, document, and site scope, she gains the ability to define the context of any element on the site without respect to its location in source order, its frequency of occurrence, or the significance of its content.

If an arbitrary element can be defined, it can be styled—and if it can be styled, it can serve as a location cue to the visitor. (That's not to say that all elements *should* serve as location cues, just that any element *can*.)

Product documentation as an effective "compass"

The ideal stylesheet documents an entire site by relying on context-dependent selectors and thoughtfully designed document trees, but even the smallest projects benefit from some degree of external product documentation. Much of this documentation addresses design, especially type treatments and grid specifications. There are three other documentation components that prove valuable over time:

Cascade descriptions
> These are typically the easiest to create, but place the greatest demands on a stylist's memory. Any sufficiently complex collection of stylesheet rules falls into rule patterns; the cascade descriptions briefly delineate these rule patterns in one place and point to the site resources that rely on them.

Code/product standards
> These build on the cascade description by describing the markup patterns and types of selectors that are generally applicable to a given type of content. For example, one might call my habit of using `h1` (without an `id`) for the sole purpose of containing the site identity, and using `h2` for the first heading of page content, to be product standards.

Style guides
> These embellish the balance of site documentation by explaining in plain English not only *how* things are done, but also *why* a given approach was taken to the structure and presentation of a given class or item of content.

Effective external documentation holds especially high value for developers who are new to the site that they're working on so that they can quickly form an accurate "mental picture" of a site's information architecture and template structures. The alternative is to throw newcomers head-first into staged product, which forces them to infer and make assumptions about the various objectives that led to a site's design.

Perhaps the greatest value of external documentation is to be found in its raw volume—or more appropriately, its lack thereof. The less need there is for documentation, the more effectively you are applying the four habits introduced in this section.

CSS Zen and the Stylist's Experience

As terms go, "CSS Zen" is something of a misnomer. The practice of Buddhism (of which Zen is one subbranch) emphasizes the interdependence of all things, especially living things, among many points of faith.

As applied to web development, the term is derived from a common English nickname for the Japanese *karesansui* rock gardens, which serve a dedicated aesthetic purpose: demonstrating tangible harmony and precision in spite of evolving surroundings and Nature's unpredictability. The value of *karesansui* to Buddhist meditation (in the course of reflection or upkeep) leads to the moniker "Zen garden," which inspired the name of Dave Shea's immensely popular site, *http://www.csszengarden.com*.

The "CSS Zen Garden" seeks to demonstrate one important idea:

> A single, well-built markup template can support a practically infinite range of design requirements, to a high degree of precision. When done well, such templates create the capacity that enables *design* to be altered while leaving markup untouched in all cases except significant changes to the structure of information published in a document or on a site.

Like *karesansui*, sites that exemplify CSS Zen are molded to their circumstances, particularly project objectives. Moreover, such sites allow their underlying markup templates to remain functionally static, analogous to the rock-stable arrangement of *karesansui* in the midst of seeming chaos.

The Functional Principles of CSS Zen

The habits and ideas discussed in the previous sections are virtuous on account of the efficiency and quality they afford to the stylist's process and work product. On the other hand, the ideal of CSS Zen fits within a framework of principles that encourage a specific perspective on web content and its structure:

1. Information and presentation are distinct from one another, to the point that it *cannot* be declared with any certainty that the nature of one depends upon the nature of the other.

2. It is axiomatic that the flow of information (and therefore of web content) is dictated not by *location*, but instead by *relationships*.

3. Web content is divisible to degrees that are rarely apparent to the casual visitor.

4. Every intersection of environment and information that might apply to a site begs its own ideal *structure*.

Once a stylist integrates these principles into the thought process that he applies at work, his perspective changes. Table 5-1 is a dialectical comparison of common stylist attitudes toward markup and styles, given knowledge or ignorance of the principles of CSS Zen. The order of principles corresponds to the list just given.

Table 5-1. Comparison of stylist attitudes toward markup and styles, given knowledge or ignorance of the principles of CSS Zen

Principle	Ignorance	Knowledge
Separation	Source order and structure are wrangled by presentation requirements.	Source order and structure are dictated by priority and (where needed) taxonomy.
Interconnection	Any given sum of content is indivisible and has an ideal flow.	Content can be subdivided, presented in arbitrary contexts, redesigned, and mashed up; additional context can be provided via hypertext links and metadata.
Divisibility	Markup is informed entirely by presentation and obvious definitions of content; it's often nested, but rarely used to provide additional meaning to the content that it encloses.	Markup and content follow a logical taxonomy and can be arranged within a document tree down to the level of individual syllables and icons, if needed.
Mutability	Document structure is either crammed into a one-size-fits-all structure, or assembled on an entirely *ad hoc* basis.	Content and the arrangement of document trees follow the spirit of the aphorism "a place for everything, and everything in its place"; this can be expressed differently in response to differing project objectives, audiences, and themes.

The faithful application of the principles of CSS Zen results in sites where form follows function on all obvious levels. Since function is what brings in visitors, isn't that a better outcome than the reverse?

Information Architecture and Web Usability

This book has proposed a few key ideas about web development:

- Hypertext links are the beginning, middle, and end of the Web.
- Web resources are fundamentally *n*-dimensional, not linear.
- The infinite number of ways in which content can be linked, cross-linked, subdivided, and combined brightly illuminates the value of effective wayfinding facilities on websites.
- Each website or application is actually a multilayered resource that can be made progressively richer.
- There is no One True Way to build a site, because requirements change according to business objectives and user environments.

The art of *information architecture* (IA) attempts to substantiate these ideas and meet the design challenges posed by them. The principal objective of its practice is to maximize the findability and usability of information; after all, what good is information if it can't be found and used?

This section is intended as an introduction, not an education. Those who desire more information about web information architecture should take advantage of the following resources:

- *Don't Make Me Think: A Common Sense Approach to Web Usability*, 2nd Edition, by Steve Krug (New Riders Press).
- *Information Architecture for the World Wide Web (http://oreilly .com/catalog/9780596527341)*, 3rd Edition, by Peter Morville and Louis Rosenfeld (O'Reilly).
- Boxes and Arrows, a site operated by and for Web User Experience (UX) practitioners at *www.boxesandarrows.com*.
- The American Society for Information Science and Technology, which sponsors Special Interest Groups devoted to Human-Computer Interaction (HCI) and Information Architecture. Their site can be found at *www.asis.org*.

The information architect who specializes in web content and interfaces must treat the previous ideas as facts; the alternative verges on nihilism, since without *any* fundamental facts or assumptions, it becomes impossible to organize a site's content and human interface in an effectively consistent way.

On a practical level, most sites don't need dedicated IA specialists, whether by virtue of limited scope or lack of budget. As a result, conscientious developers should adopt IA as a secondary skill set.

Multidimensionality

As this book has repeatedly pointed out, while traditional sources of information (print, video, audio) are mostly linear, the Web is not. The dimensionality of web content (*not* presentation) can be bounded as follows:

Length
Analogous to the linear nature of traditional information: the obvious beginning and end of a single document's primary content.

Breadth
The position of a web document within the logical domain of all documents that are directly linked to or from it. Related to (but separate from) "situation." *Mind maps* are a newly popular technique for visualizing this dimension of site design.

Depth
Any of the views that can be taken on content, given a particular range of user environments. Evident when progressive enhancement is used.

Entropy
Time-sensitive documents, or those composed to any degree of user-contributed content, can change tremendously during their lifetimes.

Situation

> The position and context of a document, given its position in the history of a visitor's browsing session. "Situation" is separate from "breadth" and "entropy" because it can be perceived and controlled by each visitor.

Use case

> The purpose to which content and structure are put—e.g., RSS feed for posting changes, instead of HTML for normal reading; variant user interfaces in web applications; Search Engine Result Page (SERP) summaries.

Granularity

> The manner in which perception of content changes when parts are subtracted, added, exported, and imported.

Just as changes in our perception of a tangible object's length, breadth, depth, and entropy alter our understanding of that object, so too is our understanding of web content altered by our perception of its characteristics as just described.

People are comfortable thinking in terms of two dimensions, can usually handle thinking in terms of three, and are aware of four. It falls to information architects, site designers, and stylists to decide how many (and which) of the *seven* dimensions described previously to use to define location cues and other navigation guidance.

This is simply a rough description of web content and document structure that references not only the four tangible dimensions, but three others as well. When compared to the bounds of traditional media, it's no wonder that web content can provide people with a good living—even when their principal skill is something so esoteric as helping people find their way through it.

Navigation: Orientation and Wayfinding

Advice about writing effective link text is provided not here, but in "Creating Effective Link Content and title Values" on page 136.

Given the infinitely mutable nature of web content and interfaces, it follows that the most valuable help for the visitor illuminates her location and direction of travel through the site.

Sites typically rely on any of six approaches to giving users their bearings:

Primary and secondary navigation

> Links are set aside in one or two stretches of the page layout, each pointing to a particular document of potential interest to the visitor. These might well be nested in two or more levels according to a hierarchy; in all cases, the displayed document

is ideally identified not only by title, but also by its unlinked nature and contrast against the still-active links in the same design element.

Well-designed breadcrumbs

Like nested navigation, these links are pinned to some hierarchical organization of the site, but are presented in series from highest to lowest level of assigned significance. This approach typically does not provide a clear idea of where a document lies within the information space of an entire site, but it is an excellent addition to printed pages, since breadcrumbs tell the reader of printed content *exactly* how to navigate to the printed page.

Tags

Documents are assigned keywords, and the aggregate list of keyword links is displayed on each page of the site. Following a keyword link delivers a list of links to relevant documents, which can be sorted by one of several criteria (e.g., character set order, date, popularity).

Site maps

The principal difference between nested navigation and a site map is that in the case of a site map, a single page contains links to *all* of the documents and applications on a site.

Inline links

Conscientious content producers will often insert links to relevant material around obvious keywords and phrases, or at least those on the first few "levels" of the site.

Search

Like Google to some degree, only on a much smaller scale. The same content authoring challenges that turn SEO into a chore are no less relevant on a site that provides local search functionality.

The areas of wayfinding implementation that rest on the client side are discussed further in other parts of this book: primary and secondary navigation in the materials about layout and lists.

Like context-specific navigation, site maps are marked up with lists, and sometimes in multiple columns. Tag lists are also marked up within lists with the `display` value of their constituent items set to `inline`, and might be marked up with classes set aside to reflect a site's keyword frequency.

Visit Strategies

The broadest generalizations that can be made about visitors are these:

- The visitor's objective can fall into one (or more) of four categories: information, services, salable products, or entertainment.
- Visitors have two basic methods by which they can reach their goal: browsing or full-text search.

Visitors often prefer third-party search engines because they offer precise information within a range of results among which comparisons can be made. Most visitors also know that some sites—particularly the big social media communities—can satisfy multiple types of session goals.

One of the most significant choices to be made during the design process is to choose *deliberately* how the design and implementation of the site's human interface will accommodate these common goals and strategies.

It's feasible, if not always easy, to implement *all* of the wayfinding strategies discussed here. However, it's important for stylists to know where each one is usually located in page layouts so that they can best apprehend the ideal way to style the cues that will alert site visitors:

Primary navigation
> Horizontally oriented, immediately below the header; sublevel links are often located along the grid row immediately beneath the main "section" links. A site's home page is often linked from the site's identity (i.e., logo), which itself is usually located in the upper-left corner of the layout (in the header).

Footer links
> Laid out across the footer in a list with items set to `display: inline` or `inline-block` and often centered. Type is typically set at a smaller size than that used for body copy.

Breadcrumbs
> Horizontally oriented and placed immediately below the primary navigation, or in lieu of it on print-specific pages.

Tag lists
> To the right of the primary content in a three-column layout; at the bottom of the secondary content in a two-column layout. Immediately below the primary content in those rare instances of single-column layout, but deserving of its own column when used frequently.

Site maps
> Linked from the footer of each page on the site and laid out as primary content on a page of their own, often in columns.

Search
> In the upper-right corner of the header, and sometimes duplicated in the right margin of the footer. Result pages often have single-column layouts, even on sites that rely on a multiple-column layout for regular content. Such output is usually owed to a lack of flexibility in the output of the extension module or appliance deployed to generate search results.

Guideposts for Creating Usable Interfaces

Declaring that "X goes here" is a start: by following established practice, you can take advantage of visitor expectations. However, simply following the crowd is not the only thing you need to do to get it right.

The first and most important goal to follow—again!—is consistency. Given a history of pages that are all scrolled to their respective top margins, the ideal situation for a visitor is one in which everything of wayfinding interest is in exactly the same place on each page: the navigation links, the tag links, the search box, the page title, and so on. Still better is the (far more difficult) case in which you maintain that consistency across a broad section of the page's length, which gives visitors the ability to find their bearings within the page quickly—and just as quickly home in on the nearest wayfinding facility on the page.

When it comes to the various wayfinding techniques, there are design techniques that will make visitors' goals easier to achieve, at least incrementally.

- Navigation and tag link footprints should be made reasonably large, at a minimum by giving each a `display` value of `block` and extra padding as discussed in Chapter 8. The same technique also benefits the usability of submit buttons on search forms.

- "Flying" menus that present sublevel links when moused over, like those in the Applications folder of the Windows Start menu, should be avoided with alacrity since they require enormous amounts of fine motor control. Microsoft can get away with it because they need to conserve display space for the sake of lowest-common-denominator hardware configurations; Windows also provides keyboard support for the Start menu and users with the ability to put links to programs directly on the Desktop, which are far more often used by the typical user. Follow the example set by the Desktop and style your wayfinding links so that they're easily visible.

- Many sites' primary navigation links are set smaller than their body copy, and some sites even reduce the contrast of those links as well. Instead, every effort should be made to increase the size and contrast of wayfinding facilities, short of overwhelming actual page content.

- Label everything clearly. The alternative is what storied web pundit Vincent Flanders calls "Mystery Meat Navigation"—you know that there's *something* in there, but what is it? Do you want to find out and risk going down a blind alley?

- Avoid miniature `input type="text"` fields on search forms, or really any forms. Decreased field size results in less-legible field values, and few things are more frustrating than being unable to read your own input! That's not to say that text inputs should always be huge, just that their contents should always be clearly legible.

- Where the identity of the current document is displayed in a navigation context, distinguish it clearly from its neighbors. If at all possible, remove the a element while preserving its contents.

Disabling links to the current document

Disabling browser behavior related to links is a poor man's way of fooling a user into believing that a document doesn't contain any links to itself, in lieu of running a proper search-and-replace function to remove the anchor tags altogether. You can *apparently* disable a link in two steps.

First, by whatever means, create a class for the purpose of referencing links that should appear inactive. This includes changing a link's cursor property to an appropriate value, which can be found in Chapter 8 and on this book's companion website (*http://www.htmlcssgoodparts.net*). In the example that follows, the class value in question is selfLink.

Next, if you are working within a document served with a MIME type of text/html, add the following JavaScript to a function that is ultimately invoked onload:

```
for (var i = 0; i < document.getElementsByTagName("a").length; i++) {
    if (document.getElementsByTagName("a")[i].href) {
      if (document.getElementsByTagName("a")[i].href == document.location.href) {
        document.getElementsByTagName("a").className = "selfLink";
        document.getElementsByTagName("a")[i].onclick = return false;
      }
    }
}
```

The same class assignment technique suggested earlier is also preferred for notifying users of form input errors.

Finally, note that for security reasons, status bar messages indicating destination URIs *cannot* be cleared in current browsers—which is why disabling link behavior in the browser is considered a poor man's way of altering the user experience.

Predicting Visitor Behavior with Scenarios and User Testing

While broad site navigation speaks for *direction* of travel, where does that leave *location*? Typical practice relies upon fairly basic design choices:

- Prominent page or article titles
- Navigation highlights, hopefully in combination with a deactivated link
- Color-coded backgrounds and page accents
- Unambiguous visited-link styles

As you're probably beginning to realize, current practice is *very poor* when it comes to offering visitors an instant and precise understanding of their location within a site. In practice, the typical user experience gives an indication of the scope of the current page, and otherwise leaves visitors with an impression that they're getting "warmer" or "colder" with respect to any specific objective they might have while browsing the site.

This poverty of precision is an artifact of the Web's absence of boundaries. Beyond a certain point, experienced visitors know better than to form initial expectations of their user experience.

Consider how orienteering works in the real world. Given a map of sufficiently large scale and adequate visibility, someone with sufficient knowledge of his immediate surroundings, map-reading skills, and orienteering skills can ascertain his location, quickly and to within several meters.

Note the way in which that statement is qualified: to get that near a fix on his location, he must know the lay of the land, and must also possess reasonably detailed information in a broader context—conditions that are applicable to anyone's survival in extreme conditions.

On the websites discussed in this book, personal survival is not an issue, and there is absolutely no way that a random visitor can be expected to know the virtual lay of the land. That leaves designers and stylists with the same solution that trained rescuers use to find people: a search pattern of their own.

On the Web, the "search" and "find" tasks are accomplished by testing user behavior. The two main approaches used are *scenarios* and full-smash *user testing*.

Scenarios draw conclusions when project team members role-play the decisions taken by archetypal, fictional users and record the results of the entire process.

User testing amounts to putting real users in front of functional prototypes. This delivers more accurate results, but also requires significant investment in design before it can be attempted.

Both scenarios and user testing improve the opportunity cost of applying *taxonomy* to your site. When done well, taxonomy makes it possible for a visitor to develop a mind map of a site's internal organization after a few page requests.

Taxonomy and Nomenclature

Taxonomy is the practice of creating taxa (rigid and hierarchical forms of classification). The first universally accepted use of taxa was by the Swedish life scientist Carl Linnaeus, who devised a system for categorizing life forms that today functions on seven telescoping levels. Table 5-2 shows these levels as applied to human beings.

Table 5-2. An example of the taxonomy used in biological classification

Level	Nomenclature	Vernacular
Kingdom	Animalia	animals
Phylum	Chordata	possessing a spinal column
Classis	Mammalia	and mammary endocrine tissue
Order	Primates	"of the first order"
Family	Hominidae	"like human beings" (*cf.* "humanoid" as used in science fiction)
Genus	Homo	human
Species	sapiens	"knowing"

Taxa can also be applied to information in general, and to vocabularies that reference any specific context. Many residents of the United States are familiar with the Library of Congress Classification and the North American Industry Classification System, both of which are broadly agreed-upon systems for organizing information in a telescoping, hierarchical manner.

"Nomenclature," meanwhile, is a fancy word for "jargon." Less colloquially, a nomenclature is a specialized vocabulary on which many users agree: a system of naming things. It can be said that taxonomy *organizes* nomenclature, though it also organizes vocabularies that aren't controlled. ("Controlled vocabulary" is a synonym for "nomenclature" often used by professional information scientists.)

Take the following terms:

- Content
- Sidebar
- Hero shot
- Font
- Spacer
- Client

and consider that, in all likelihood, most web developers will understand you perfectly if you use them.

Used effectively, taxonomy and (to a lesser extent) nomenclature can give you the vocabulary you need to create appropriate context for your cascade, particularly with respect to maintaining the habit of flexibility.

Applying Taxonomy Through the Cascade

Taxa can be worked into sites on two different levels: with respect to a site's body of content, and to the structure of its template markup.

Applying taxa to site content points back to the previous discussion of scenarios and user testing: by performing tests, you can learn how a site will be used, and thus how to prioritize the information that it contains.

Consider a small- to medium-size retail business. Its site will likely be used to:

- Find business locations and hours of operation
- Retrieve telephone numbers or other means of contacting store representatives
- Learn about sales and promotions
- Determine the availability and prices of specific goods or classes of goods

As a result, if I'm building a site for a small retailer, I'll recommend the following main categories:

- Store Locations
- Contact Us
- Sales & Events
- Shop Online

On the site's home page, I will attempt to present information from all of these categories by including the following content:

- The street address and operating hours of the company's flagship store
- The main telephone number, customer service email address, and social media points of contact
- Their most significant discount, accompanied by eligibility dates
- Brief product listings and "Add to Cart" facilities for three or four of the most popular products sold in the e-commerce area of the site

If the online store has a particularly large catalog, I'll strongly consider adding links to product category pages in a secondary navigation list as well.

Pages deeper within the site focus on each of the four categories of information, in progressively greater degrees of detail. For example, the destination of the "Shop Online" link will contain a full listing of product categories, and the destination of the "Contact Us" link will contain a reasonably detailed directory of telephone numbers and other points of contact.

Each section of the site—and of all well-designed sites—will provide location cues. Adequately signaling the context of these cues will suggest `class` and `id` values on an element at or near the root of your templates' element trees, such as:

```
<body class="stores" id="KCDetails">
```

Other body elements on the site that reference .stores might be assigned id values like StLouisDetails, SpringfieldDetails, ColumbiaDetails, and so on. These happen to refer to prominent cities on the Interstate highways of Missouri—a larger site designed along similar lines might introduce an intermediate level of detail based upon the states or regions in which the retailer does business.

This method of assigning class and id values to individual pages allows you to target your selectors to an extremely narrow scope, which reduces the work involved in creating specific accents on things like article headings, for example:

```
#KCDetails h2 { background-image: url(/images/heading_kc_store.gif); }
```

Or, consider what can be done for navigation layout, since sublevels are unlikely to have the same number of items from one section to the next:

```
/* #navOnlineStore actually holds two lines of links, #navStores only one */

.stores #nav #navStores { height: 1.5em; padding-bottom: 1.5em; }

/* make the unneeded sublevels GO AWAY */

    .stores #nav #navContact,
      .stores #nav #navPromo,
.stores #nav #navOnlineStore { display: none; }
```

The previous example also deserves notice because it illustrates how elements are nested on the page, like so:

```
<body class="stores" id="StLouisStore">
...
<ul id="nav">
  <li id="navStores">Our Stores
    <ul id="subNavStores">
      <li id="#navKCDetails"><a href="/stores/kc/">Kansas City</a></li>
      <li id="navStLouisDetails">St. Louis</li>
      ...
    </ul>
  </li>
</li>
...
</body>
```

The point is that there is every reason to incorporate your site's content organization into your cascade.

At the page level, taxonomy and nomenclature are more subjective: one man's #sidebar is another man's #highlights, for example.

The good news is that if consistency is practiced with respect to the site's document design, the functions, interrelationships, and typical nesting of a site's various types of content within a single page or template can be assigned documented nomenclature and taxa of their own. My own approach to defining document structure is shown throughout the book, though different projects naturally present differing requirements that may need to be addressed in uncommon ways.

Achieving Granularity on Larger Sites

Especially large sites, or sites operated by large enterprises, are usually unable (for reasons of policy) to make heavy use of `id`s as shown here. In many workplaces, `id`s *might* be replaced with `class`es, but in others even that option will be denied to stylists. Less-complex designs are the trade-off for these constraints. If however you find yourself forced to style a design that makes a poor fit with the constraints imposed by policy, you might perhaps meet your challenge by applying styles via a JavaScript framework such as jQuery.

New Structural Elements (HTML5)

Along with the `nav` element, which will be discussed in Chapter 7, there are several other new proposed structural elements in HTML5:

- `section`
- `article`
- `header`
- `footer`
- `aside`
- `figure`

At the time of writing, there is no native support in current browsers for any of these elements. That said, not much needs to be added to browsers in order to support them, because none of these elements have any special rendering or processing behavior associated with them. Because of that, they are also not features that are likely to have much direct impact on end users; instead, their primary utility is to provide naming convenience to authors.

It's also not clear at this point which of these proposed structural elements will make the cut and actually end up in the HTML5 specification as it makes its way through the standards process. For example, there is general agreement that the `section` element is a useful addition to the language, but much less agreement about the `article` and `aside` elements. There is also some level of agreement in principle about the `header` and `footer` elements being useful for marking up the header and footer parts of pages, but much less agreement about the utility of allowing them within sections. The current HTML5 draft allows `section` elements to have `header` and `footer` children, but page subsections with their own individual headers and footers are not commonly found in existing content.

CHAPTER 6

Solving the Puzzle of CSS Layout

When you create site layouts depending upon CSS, your first and greatest challenge is to put the various pieces of your layout *exactly* where you want them. CSS offers three basic tools for creating layouts: positioning, `float`, and `width/margin`. Unfortunately, the models underlying the use of those techniques are notoriously hard to master.

The CSS Box Model and Element Size Control

When the browser renders block elements, such as `div` or `p`, each element has four telescoping components: content, padding, borders, and margins (from the inside out), as shown in Figure 6-1. In current implementations, the dimensions of such boxes are computed by *adding* three of those four components, so that if a `width` or `height` value is applied to an element, that element's borders and padding (as such) make it yet wider. Margins also affect this process, but only after neighboring margins are taken into consideration.

There are two exceptions to this definition of browsers' layout behavior: mode resets, and the use of `auto` values for content boxes.

Quirks Mode and Strict Mode

Web browsers use two general types of rendering modes: "quirks" mode and "strict" mode. They are invoked by the presence or absence of certain document type declarations, which are described generally in Chapter 2 and listed on this book's companion website (*http://www.htmlcssgoodparts.net*).

Instead of treating box properties *additively*, as strict mode does and the CSS 2.1 box model suggests, quirks mode rendering uses stated `width` and `height` as the primary reference for computing element dimensions, and *subtracts* the other box values from those as appropriate. These behaviors are analogous to the behavior of the CSS3 `box-sizing` property, which has two values: `content-box` and `border-box`.

Figure 6-1. The computed width and height of an element are subdivided into four constituent parts: margins, borders, padding, and content

Quirks mode rendering is the *only* rendering mode available in versions of Internet Explorer prior to IE 6.

auto Values

The default value of both `width` and `height` is `auto`. When the browser applies the computed width of an element with this literal (if implied) value, that means an affected element will expand to fill the `width` of its container. For `height`, the affected element will only expand to fit the length of the content, but only if that element's float value is `none` (the default).

However, when the border and/or padding values of an element with a `width` of `auto` are set, those values are subtracted from the computed `width` value of that element's content, as are any relevant margin values that don't collapse into the margins of other elements.

If you instead assign a discrete `width` value to a block element and change the values of its left and right margins to `auto`, that element will be centered within its container as pictured in Figure 6-2.

This section makes occasional references to "computed" `width` *and* `height`: the dimensions of an element after the user agent has rendered the page. This concept is also mentioned in Chapter 14.

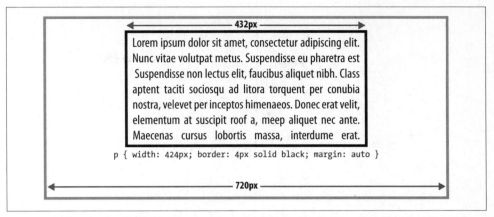

Figure 6-2. *Centering a block of text, as margins are automatically set outside the border*

The overflow Property

An element narrower than its container can be centered horizontally without regard to its specified or computed width, but this doesn't work for element height. The literal height of an element and its container must both be known in advance, before CSS can be used to center one within the other, and then only explicitly.

`height: auto` (whether expressed or implied) tells the browser, "Let this element expand to fully enclose its content, but no further." Because text content will never *certainly* have an intrinsic height, extending the behavior of `margin: auto` to the y-axis by default is more resource-intensive than it's worth.

While vertical centering is a challenge, expanding an element to fill the entire height of its container *can* be accomplished with the `overflow` property.

The `overflow` property describes how content should be rendered when it's larger than its containing element. In fact, `overflow` is the first property mentioned here that enables block elements to overlap one another, allowing the stylist to "break" the rules for block element flow that are spelled out in "Element Flow" on page 83.

The four valid values of the `overflow` property, shown in Figure 6-3, are:

`visible` *(default)*
> All content is visible, regardless of the dimensions of the element. If the dimensions of both the element and any of its content have values other than `auto`, overflowing content will bleed as needed into any elements adjacent to the container, but will not change the dimensions of the container itself or the flow behavior of adjacent elements.

`hidden`
> Overflowing content is removed from the view of the visitor, and the container's dimensions are respected without exception.

Figure 6-3. The overflow property can take on one of four values

scroll

> Vertical and horizontal scroll bars will always be placed on the affected element, and scrolling controls added as needed. The supplied dimensions of the affected element are respected.

auto *(often the user agent value for* html *or* body*)*

> Expressed dimensions are respected, and scrolling controls are placed on the element if necessary. Any scroll bars that are added to the element are placed *within* its expressed dimensions, rather than increasing the element's area.

This last value presents an obscure but potentially useful opportunity. If an element with an `overflow` value of `auto` is also assigned a small percentage `height` value (e.g., 1%), it will expand to encompass the computed height of its content, including any margins that are placed on that content. Note, however, that `width` values do not trigger the same behavior.

`overflow` values are also applied to the x-axes of block elements, but evidence of that is rarely seen since `height: auto` is almost always arbitrary. Cases where evidence of an element's `overflow` value is visible on the x-axis include:

- The presence of uncommonly long lines of text, whether held together by non-breaking spaces, a containing `pre` element, or the `white-space` property.
- The inclusion of replaced elements, particularly images.
- Unexpected insertion of a child element with a computed or intrinsic `width` value greater than the width of the containing element itself. Especially complex web applications or poorly written CSS can trigger this scenario more easily than you might think.

Limiting But Not Fixing Element Dimensions

From time to time, you will encounter situations where you want an element to fill the available space, but only to a point. In other situations, you might want to accommodate a given width or height, while still ensuring that an element will accommodate its intended content. For example:

```
.articleContainer { width: 80%; max-width: 50em; margin: auto; }
    .sidebarItem { float: right; width: 16.667%; min-width: 288px; }
```

The first rule in this example accounts for a scenario in which an element should provide negative space to either side, but still must not grow too wide for the sake of content readability (an issue raised explicitly in Chapter 12). The second rule demands a box that occupies one-sixth of its container's width, but that might also contain an image sized according to house style guidelines, and thus must always occupy a *minimum* amount of horizontal space for the sake of rendering the entire image.

Note that both rules specify the `max-*` property *after* its general counterpart, since the relationship between source order and priority remains operative not only within the document scope, but within the rule scope as well.

Handling the Unpredictable

A stylist is most likely to apply the `overflow` property in a multicolumn layout in situations where a column container (see the section "Implementing Multicolumn Layouts" on page 88) includes background or box properties (see the section "Margins, Borders, and Padding" on page 78) that must be rendered.

However, there are a number of site and application design scenarios where content bounds cannot be predicted, and the `overflow` property will be put to practical use:

Prevention of blowouts in static layouts
> When layout elements are given fixed dimensions (usually specified in pixel units, as described in "Cross-Media Length and Size Units" on page 34) visitor-resized text can cause all kinds of blowouts. Typical users' lack of knowledge of text re-sizing functionality, and the availability of page zoom interfaces, make this a rare contingency, but one that can be predicted and resolved quickly by experienced stylists. The best solution is to use grid-based layouts instead of fixed layouts, but if that's not possible, `overflow: hidden` can serve as an excellent fallback.

Narrowly defined Content Management System (CMS) layouts with overly permissive content bounds
> Consider the possibility that an item with inherent space constraints—say, a text advertisement or sidebar panel—might be populated with more content than accounted for by the approved design. The application of `overflow: hidden` to such elements can discourage disregard of a site's content guidelines. (Such scenarios usually arise as a result of an undisciplined design process.)

Normalizing form layouts
> The juxtaposition of form controls and their associated labels can easily create a situation in which the container of a label/control pair is overrun by one of its child elements. By using the `auto/1%` solution just described, a stylist can ensure that a site's forms will follow the grid suggested by the approved site design.

Bounding the footprint of an Ajax-driven application interface
> When users execute read and update functions in a web application, there may well be occasions when user-generated data (especially images) threaten blowouts. In these cases, `overflow: auto` can account for the outsized content without causing blowouts throughout the application interface.

Current browsers also offer the `overflow-x` and `overflow-y` properties specified by CSS3, which alter behavior with respect to the named axis. Setting differing `overflow-x` and `overflow-y` values might not yield the expected results. A test suite for these properties can be found at this book's companion site.

Finally, stylists should note that when a `scroll` or `auto` value yields a scroll bar, the resulting control is rendered *inside* the specified footprint of the element. Among other possible results, this might cause two scroll bars to appear where only one was expected.

Margins, Borders, and Padding

Composites are often drafted in exhaustive detail, and contract terms can require reproduction of comped layouts at pixel-level accuracy, or at least pixel-level consistency. Element size control is only part of the solution; whitespace and rule (border) control is no less important, and the properties used to effect that control carry a few caveats with their use.

Negative Margins

Apart from values assigned to the properties used to control element positioning, the only *layout* values that can take on negative values are those attached to the various margin properties.

When an affected element is assigned a negative margin value, the element's computed box bleeds into whatever element box might lie adjacent to the negative margin.

As implied by their nature, negative margins *remove* whitespace from a layout instead of adding it. This capacity is more important than it may seem at first glance. For example, consider a heading trailed by interposed whitespace and a custom rule, presumably added with the `background-image` property. If the site design intends this heading to appear in tandem with metadata—as might well be the case with the title of a blog post—the metadata most likely will follow the heading immediately in the markup, and will in turn be followed by the post content itself, as shown in Figure 6-4.

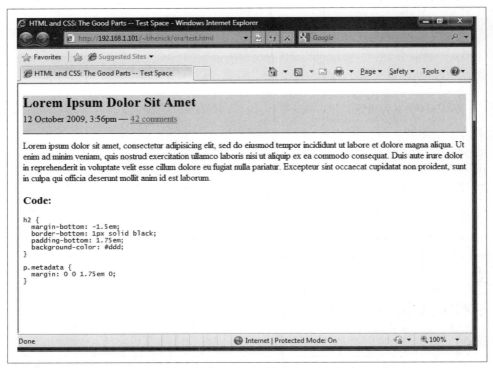

Figure 6-4. Tandem title and metadata using negative margin values

In such a case, the approach that uses the least markup will require a negative `margin-bottom` on the heading or a negative `margin-top` on the metadata, to ensure that the metadata will appear in the intermediate space between the heading copy and the custom rule.

A more likely case for using negative margins is on site footers. If a site footer in a two-column layout is centered within the body copy column rather than the entire document canvas, it will need to exist within the document container, but needs to be placed at the end of it. Therefore, a negative `margin-bottom` will need to be placed on the sidebar element, to ensure that the *apparent* bottom margin of the sidebar is flush with the apparent top margin of the footer.

The usefulness of these techniques might seem limited. However, if you're to obtain the best results from the source order *and* faithfulness to composites, you'll find yourself using negative margins more often than you might think now.

Collapsed Margins

HTML elements start with default display types. Those various elements are further grouped into subtypes. For example, `div` and heading elements are both block elements by default, but the six heading levels also fall into their own discrete heading classification.

When two block elements also lack or share a subtype, their flush margins will always *collapse*. This behavior is most evident in paragraph elements, with user agent styles that look something like the following:

```
         p { margin-top: 1.25em; margin-bottom: 1.25em; }
 p:first-child { margin-top: 0; }
  p:last-child { margin-bottom: 0; }
         p+p { margin-top: 0; }
```

The last of the four rules presented is included solely for the sake of illustration; in practice, the browser's rendering engine identifies two sequential paragraph elements as block elements without a subtype and collapses their margins as a matter of course.

In the sequential paragraph situation described here, the rendered margin between paragraphs is `1.25em` (i.e., the likely default height of one line of copy). If their margins were not collapsed, the rendered margin between them would expand to `2.5em`, an amount that would jar the reader and likely reduce the legibility of the related passage.

The inverse behavior can be tested by alternating a different block element between paragraphs, such as `div`. The top and bottom margins suggested in the preceding rule block will be preserved, and in fact a simple element swap involving the same content will look the same, in spite of the fact that `div` elements have default margins of zero on all four sides.

The display classifications suggested by the HTML 4 specification are provided in the reference tables on this book's companion site.

Borders

The CSS property space offers an extraordinary number of properties that can be used to describe borders (20, in fact). Borders are difficult-to-impossible to avoid and have their own quirks.

The focus on borders in this section of the book pertains not to the presentation effects that require them, but rather to their effect on layout—especially with respect to proportional (i.e., "fluid") layouts.

Borders make a mess when they cross with the greatest limitation of the so-called strict rendering mode: creating fixed-width rules that hew to the visible margins of elements with *proportional* dimensions.

Consider three design elements arranged from left to right in thirds:

```
#attractSection .promo { float: left; width: 32%; height: 11.417em; margin: 3.125%; }
```

In the absence of rendering bugs and rounding problems, the preceding rule will arrange three equally wide elements from left to right across the page, with a margin on both sides of all three equivalent to 1% of the width of `#attractSection`.

Now suppose that the composite insists on a one-pixel border around each of those elements. The addition of those borders will cause the third element to be pushed below its predecessors, since the values applied can't tolerate the addition of six pixels to `#attractSection`'s element box. The solution to the layout problem just got harder.

If the width of `#attractSection` always resolves to a static number of pixels, the easiest solution to the problem is to restate the `width` and `margin` values appropriately in pixel units, then add the borders. If `#attractSection` is instead sized proportionally and its width *isn't* static, the stylist is left with one of two choices:

Relying on the interior elements
> In this scenario, the `.promo` elements are likely to contain a heading and a second element for copy. If the vertical margins and padding of those paired elements are effectively manipulated, their element boxes will both be equal in height (less two pixels) to their containers, and each element can be assigned one-pixel borders on two sides.

Using background images
> Instead of being assigned as CSS properties, the borders can be rendered as background images, then positioned within the `.promo` elements and their child elements as needed. This technique is explained in detail in Chapter 9.

Padding

The greatest design value of padding is that it creates gutters—strips of negative space where the only thing visible is an element's background (if any). Apart from cases of unit-mixing, like those described previously with respect to borders, padding properties rarely cause grief for stylists.

Gutters aside, CSS padding has another useful characteristic: when present in two flush element boxes, it *never* collapses. For this reason, layout objects such as columns often have padding applied to them in situations where margins at first glance seem more intuitive. When dealing with complex layouts, it's easier to visualize the effects of properties that *don't* interact with one another than it is to visualize the effects of properties that *do*.

The Box Behavior of the Document Root Elements

The box properties of the browser canvas and the `body` element behave differently than other elements, especially when documents are served as XML.

By default, all desktop browsers render `text/html` documents with 10 pixels of negative space on each side, a value assigned to the `margin` of the `body` element in nearly all cases.

In current browsers, box properties can be assigned not only to the `body` element, but also to the `html` element—and it's common for stylists to reset them as follows:

```
html, body { margin: 0; padding: 0; }
```

Apart from such resets, the assignment of box values to the `body` and `html` elements should be handled carefully or avoided altogether, for a number of reasons:

- Box values applied to the `html` element will not be applied by Internet Explorer 6.
- Altering the box properties of the `body` element has no effect on the composition of the document's background colors and background images, which are always applied to the document in the context of the entire browser canvas.
- Altering the box properties of the `html` element will alter the edge coordinates of the `body` element, which affects the location of positioned elements in atypical ways.

Box Property Dimensions and the % Value

If you supply any box property except `height` with a percentage value, the result will be proportional to the computed width of the associated element (or of the parent element, if the property in question is `width`).

`height` values set with the % unit are more difficult to apply, because they always resolve to `auto` unless there are one or more elements higher in the cascade (in practice, usually just an immediate parent element) that all resolve to discrete `height` values.

Element Flow

You can lay out elements among their neighbors by specifying one of three types of flow behavior: inline, block, and inline-block, illustrated in Figure 6-5. The HTML specifications are the source for these definitions, and dictate the default flow behavior of all elements.

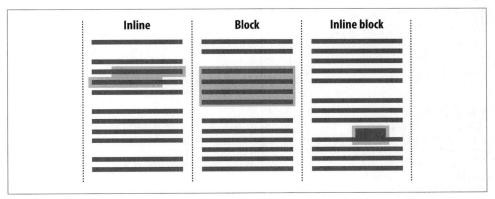

Figure 6-5. The three principal flow types are inline, block, and inline-block

The stylist can further modify these flow behaviors—or in some cases negate them—by applying the `float` or `position` property.

Inline Elements

Inline elements, for example `strong`, are laid out like normal text. The baselines of inline element content are common to those of neighboring text, and linebreaks are arbitrarily applied to their content by default. In current browsers, custom margins, borders, and padding can be applied to inline elements, but those values do not affect the layout of adjacent content.

Most importantly, layout characteristics *other than* margins, borders, padding, and positioning cannot be applied effectively to inline elements.

Text that isn't enclosed by inline markup *behaves* like inline content, but can only be referenced in a stylesheet via their parent element.

Block Elements

Default block element flow follows four simple rules:

1. Block elements expand to fill the available horizontal space within their containing element.

2. They never overlap or are overlapped by other elements, except those that they contain.

3. The content of a given block element must be composed entirely of block elements or entirely by text, inline, and inline-block elements..

4. *All* CSS layout properties can be applied effectively to block elements.

The fourth rule allows you to break the first two rules deliberately.

The third rule introduces the prospect of "anonymous" content boxes, which can cause stretches of content to behave like block elements, yet remain inaccessible to CSS. For this reason, many developers recommend that given a source fragment like this:

```
<div>
  <p>Lorem ipsum dolor sit amet,</p>
  Consectetur adipiscing elit.
</div>
```

the passage outside the paragraph element should be "repaired" by placing it within an *explicit* block element of its own, thus making it fully accessible to CSS.

It's unnecessary to do the same to inline content, unless styling is altered within entirely arbitrary points within an element.

Inline-Block Elements

Many inline-block elements are called "replaced" elements in the W3C's technical literature, because the runtime population of such elements includes images, form controls, and other objects that are usually rendered with the assistance of the operating system underlying the browser.

Inline-block elements acquire the *flow* characteristics of inline elements, which means that they line up on a common baseline. Most notably, source whitespace around and within inline-block elements is rendered on the browser canvas, just as with inline elements. In spite of their flow behavior, inline-block elements can take on the full range of layout properties, just like block elements.

Peculiarities of inline-block flow behavior are raised in the following discussion of the `display` property.

Using the display Property to Change an Element's Flow

The CSS `display` property reliably accepts a range of values corresponding to the flow types explained previously, as well as `none`. The resulting behavior produces a range of desirable effects, all of which are demonstrated on this book's companion site:

- Primary navigation links on "brochure" sites most often assume a horizontal orientation. This is done by changing the `display` value of their constituent list items to `block` (resolving an ambiguity in the HTML Document Type Definitions) and applying a number of other layout properties, particularly `float`. In tandem with assigning `display: block` to hyperlinks, this solution is preferred to applying `#nav li { display: inline; }` in situations where navigation link footprints need to be equally or statically sized.

- Once given a `display` value of `block`, links can be assigned arbitrary `width` and `height` values, which makes them easier to compose within a web application interface. This technique can also be used to increase their footprint, putting into practice the principle of human-computer interaction (HCI) known as Fitts's Law. This asserts that larger interface objects are easier to activate with a pointer device than smaller ones.

- The manner in which ordered and unordered lists are normally arranged with respect to their neighbors can be altered, so that they can be presented serially within other copy.

- By changing the `display` value of form controls to `block`, it becomes possible to lay them out within a predictable grid.

- `display: none;` can be used to enforce template normalization, in the rare but not unheard-of circumstance that an element cannot be removed from a page altogether *and* preserve legible source markup formatting.

- A series of similar text fragments or inline elements that need to run along a common baseline can be assigned a `display` value of `inline-block`. This gives the stylist a double advantage: a common baseline and access to all of the CSS layout properties.

The display Property

The most salient details of the `display` property are associated with its `none` value:

- With respect to layout, elements with a `display` value of `none` are treated by graphical user agents as if they simply do not exist.

- The broad "invisibility" imposed by `display: none` is applied by assistive technology.

The `inline-block` value also creates ample opportunity for unintended consequences. Since inline-block elements have inline flow, source whitespace between inline-block elements and their nonblock neighbors is rendered on the browser canvas, making it impossible to align inline-block elements flush to one another in the absence of adjustments to source formatting. Such adjustments in their turn violate the principle of layer separation, the nature and benefits of which were discussed in Chapters 2 and 3.

In addition to rendering interstitial source whitespace, the inline flow of inline-block elements can force the insertion of soft linebreaks in content when such elements are of an arbitrary width, or when text is resized in a static-width layout.

Finally, the `inline-block` value of the `display` property is supported inconsistently (or not at all) in many older browsing platforms.

The float and clear Properties

The primary effect of the `float` property couldn't be simpler to explain: an element to which it's applied hews to the nearest available margin suggested by that property's value, and following content flows *around* its element box instead of being forced below it. The `clear` property, on the other hand, negates the "flow-around" effects of `float`. These effects are described visually in Figure 6-6.

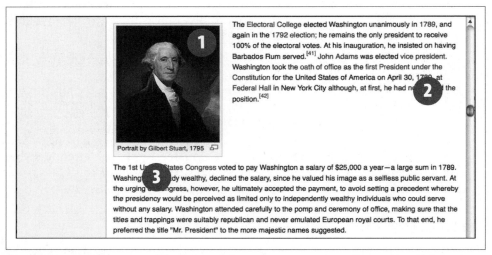

Figure 6-6. A demonstration of the float and clear properties: (1) has a float value of left, (2) has a float value of none, and (3) has a clear value of left

That's the theory, at least. The practice is another story. Because `float` is the only presentation-specific implementation technique that can be used to create variable-height columnar page layouts in CSS 2.1, knowledge of `float` context is actually a vital item in any stylist's toolbox.

The Rules of the float Property

To predict the behavior of an element to which a custom `float` value has been applied, you need to understand the rules that rendering engines follow.

 The following is a brief discussion of rules explained in Sections 9 and 10 of the CSS 2.1 specification.

An element with a `float` value of `left` or `right` *must*:

- Have a discrete width (whether expressed or implied) if the value is to be effective.
- Appear entirely within the content block of its containing element, unless it is *intrinsically* wider or taller than that container (a state that will cause it to affect the layout of other elements in the document).
- Not overlap by more than one line any non-`float`ed element that precedes it in the source order. This is relevant when nearby elements are assigned complementary `float` values.
- Hew first to the highest possible line, then to the one furthest left (or right).
- Be contiguous with the element boxes of affected non-`float`ed elements that it precedes in the source order, but *not* the *contents* of those elements. This behavior is quite relevant when composing multicolumn layouts.

Containing elements are significant in these rules when they have `float` values of their own, as discussed in the following section.

As for `float: none`, one reason why it might be applied explicitly is to supersede a value assigned elsewhere in the stylesheet, thus avoiding the layout chaos that can arise when `float`ed elements are far too large or small to fit easily into the layout specified by a site's designer.

Figure 11-7 in Chapter 11 further illuminates these rules.

This book's companion website describes these rules in still greater detail.

Canceling float Values with Corresponding clear Values

The `clear` property is provided to ensure that an element will not flow around a `float`ed predecessor, but will instead be pushed below it.

The most effective application of the `clear` property is to force the margin of an element to align with, or justify to, a margin of an antecedent element.

Table 6-1. The values of the clear property and their results

Value	Result
none	Affected element flows around `float`ed predecessors per stated rules (default).
left	Affected element is pushed below any predecessor with a `float` value of `left` that would otherwise affect the flow of its contents.
right	Analogous to `left`; applied in relation to any predecessor elements with a `float` value of `right`.
both	Affected element is pushed below *all* `float`ed elements that would otherwise affect the flow of its contents. Default margins change accordingly.

The easiest way to grasp the behavior of `float` and `clear` is to hack at multicolumn layouts, which are explained shortly.

float Context

Like other box and layout properties, the `float` and `clear` properties are applied in a scope determined by the presence of `float` values that are further up the cascade.

The practice of wrapping two columns in a `float`ed element is suggested in the discussions of three-column layout that follow. One effect of this technique is to place those two "wrapped" columns in a float context defined by their parent element, altering the visual scope in which the rules of the `float` and `clear` properties are applied. Working from the same three-column, four-container scenario, this means that any `clear: both` assignment to an element *within* the two-column wrapper element will reset the margins of content to the margins of the two-column wrapper, rather than to the page container.

Implementing Multicolumn Layouts

The two- and three-column layouts we see in such abundance and in Figure 6-7 are a result of inertia, to a degree. Before CSS became reasonably well supported, markup tables were the only available means of exercising any control whatsoever over page layout, short of abusing Flash or images with mapped links.

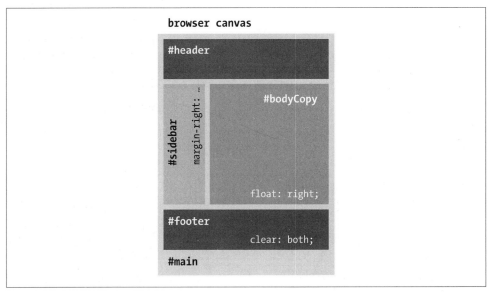

Figure 6-7. The source order of those elements is #main–#header–#bodyCopy–#sidebar–#footer; each ordinal is mated with the float and clear values that apply to that element

Once simplified, typical layout table markup often looked something like this:

```
<div align="center">

<table width="768">
  <tr>
    <td colspan="2">This is the page header.</td>
  </tr>
  <tr>
    <td width="160">This is the sidebar.</td>
    <td>This is the principal content.</td>
  </tr>
  <tr>
    <td colspan="2">This is the footer.</td>
  </tr>
</table>

</div>
```

In practice, the tables that were put into production were vastly more complicated. For one thing, they would include extra rows and cells populated with shim content and inserted to create negative space in page layouts. For example, in early 2002 I drew up a table intended for use in an email campaign that had 40 columns in it, although no section of the layout had more than 4 physical columns. The balance was required to account for rules and changes to the layout grid that were made from one section to the next.

Experienced markup technologists who work on email campaigns are *still* writing that sort of markup, since the extent of CSS support in popular email clients remains egregiously inadequate (with no relief in sight).

Converting the Two-Column Layout from Markup Tables to CSS

If you've experimented at all with multiple-column layouts on your own, it quickly becomes clear that there are lots of ways to fail:

- The presence of `float` and `width` values on all columns appears at first glance to force a relationship between source order and presentation order. This approach also presents a high risk of blowouts, especially in Internet Explorer 6.
- Applying `position: absolute` to your columns reduces the risk of blowouts, but to allow for a proper footer you also need to know the relative lengths of your columns in advance—an unreasonable expectation in the real world.

The solution to the first problem is to place `float` values only on the columns that *must* be floated, and control the remaining columns with judicious use of margin properties. For their part, positioning properties have limited application to multicolumn layouts; there is a good chance that you'll apply them to navigation links, but not to columns of actual content.

Moving to CSS in a simple case like the one illustrated seems at first to involve *extra* work: the element names change, and you use fewer of them—but in the place of the excised elements, you're called upon to write a heap of CSS rules!

Here's the markup (which is also available on this book's companion website):

```
<div id="header">This is the header.</div>

<div id="main">

  <div id="bodycopy">This is the principal content.</div>
  <div id="sidebar">This is the sidebar.</div>

</div>

<div id="footer">This is the footer.</div>
```

and then the styles:

```
                #main { height: 1%; overflow: auto; }
#main, #header, #footer { width: 768px; margin: auto; }
             #bodycopy { float: right; width: 598px; }
              #sidebar { margin-right: 608px; }
               #footer { clear: both; }
```

Figure 6-8 presents this markup in a wireframe context.

How the Two-Column Styles Work

As you can tell from the first rule, the markup and style examples just shown presume a fixed-width layout, just as most table-based layouts take a fixed width. Setting `margin: auto` on the page's three container elements ensures that they will be centered on the browser canvas.

The principal content is assigned an `id` of `bodycopy`. Since it's the first element in `#main` it takes the needed `float` and `width` values. You will also notice that the `overflow: auto` technique described previously is used here; however, it is really only necessary if background properties are applied directly to `#main`.

The secondary (site-meta) content follows next, assigned the token `#sidebar`. Its `width` value remains at `auto` since it lacks a `float` value, and width control is achieved with `margin-right`. This approach to width control is preferred by virtue of the flexibility that margin collapsing affords: if layout values were instead provided with mutable units like `em`, compound `width` values would make the layout more susceptible to rounding variations in computed width, thus increasing the risk of blowouts. Setting the `margin-right` value instead risks slight differences in content width, which are still undesirable but less jarring.

Finally, the assignment of `clear: both` to `#footer` is strictly unnecessary given the application of `overflow: auto` to `#main`—a state of affairs that changes the instant the `overflow` value is removed from the stylesheet. At that turn the footprint of `#main`

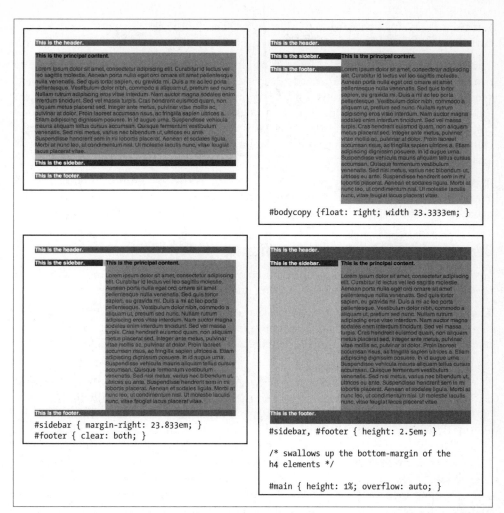

Figure 6-8. The cumulative effect of the style rules applied to the two-column markup example, one rule at a time

terminates on the lower edge of #sidebar; by adding clear: both to #footer, it becomes completely certain that the latter element will always be rendered below both columns of #main, *regardless of which column is taller*. This effect is illustrated in Figure 6-8.

Two issues are left to the imagination in the styles provided earlier. The first of these concerns the navigation that is surely present on the page. In all likelihood, it's contained by either #header or #sidebar, but a more progressive approach is to place it between #main and #footer in the source order, while keeping it close to the top of the layout. However, this requires the application of positioning properties, as well as vertical margins (or a `padding-top` value for `#sidebar`, if the site navigation is to appear at the top of that column).

The second neglected point of interest points to the likelihood of negative margins somewhere nearby `#footer`, particularly if the secondary navigation is *outside* `#footer`. In practice the regions flush to the interior edges of `#header` and `#footer` are lousy with margins, padding, and oftentimes borders. On account of these various combined values, it can become necessary to apply minute adjustments to the margin values associated with those layout regions, a process that as often as not results in at least one negative margin value.

It is also possible to apply opposing `float` values to the two columns, while setting `overflow: auto` and `height: 1%` on `#bodycopy`, an approach given short shrift here because of its annoying tendency to trigger rendering bugs in Internet Explorer 6.

Benefits of Confining Layout Specifications to Stylesheets

Given the umpteen interrelationships and caveats that were just covered, you're wise to question the opportunity cost of relying on advanced CSS for layout.

The answer runs entirely to *simplification*, counterintuitive though that may at first seem. The effort expended on stylesheet authoring gets paid back in the form of lighter markup, which carries a number of benefits. Some of those benefits include:

Content falls in its logical order
> Since there's a direct relationship between the source order of `table` content and its position on a page, the sidebar and the navigation (which usually finds its way into the header or the sidebar on a visual level) are present near the top of the markup. The page's principal content—what is summarized in search results is the likely goal of the visitor—is relegated below these passages of meta-content. The long ubiquity of table-based layout means that to this day, users of assistive platforms *still* expect to find site navigation near what they perceive as the top of the page, since their tools "present" the content in source order.

Elements are added or removed from the body content of templates only when there is content to add or remove
> Less-frequent changes usually mean fewer changes, which in turn mean less work to approve and document. Finally, the increased simplicity that results from these differences makes for easier maintenance in the long run.

The simplified markup carries strong benefits with respect to portability and accessibility
> The most obvious application of this fact has to do with printing: if you feel the need to include a "Print This Page" widget, the document at the far end of that link can use *exactly* the same template as the screen-optimized document. The elements in need of removal will relate to navigation, which can be quickly clobbered with judicious application of `display: none` (or better yet, by wrapping the navigation markup in an appropriate template structure that can be toggled).

For good or ill, presentation outliers can be handled by building a reasonable oversupply of class *and* id *tokens into template markup and code*

> In exchange for the increased use of class and id tokens, developers are called upon to create and maintain fewer templates (or template fragments) on a given site.

Confining presentation in a location separate from the site templates greatly eases development and deployment of enhancements and redesigns

> If your site layout needs a new section of any kind, it can be added to the template quickly, while most of the details are resolved by changes to the stylesheet. Given clean stylesheet rules, it might be possible to remove sections simply by commenting out the relevant template blocks. Compare these abbreviated processes with the sort of extensive changes that need to be made to templates driven by table-based layout: which approach makes more sense, really?

In addition to these benefits, there seems to be considerable faith that reducing the ratio of markup to content—a certain consequence of implementing well-written CSS, as demonstrated in brief by the source examples shown earlier—provides benefits to Search Engine Optimization (SEO) practitioners as well. In the absence of direct comparisons utilizing otherwise equal documents, I'm reluctant to subscribe to that belief without skepticism. However, the willingness of so many experienced people to believe in the SEO benefits of lighter markup must count for something, right?

Moving from Two Columns to Three

Two-column layouts are easy: as long as your backgrounds aren't intricate, you can apply a float value here and a margin value there, and still place your footer at the bottom of the page without risking odd results. There are other ways to a two-column layout; some people like to use float values on both columns.

The techniques that make these layouts work are a combination of Faux Columns and assignment of clear: both to the footer.

When you move to a three-column layout, however, the number of possible basic float/ margin combinations balloons to six. This increase in the number of outcomes is accompanied by the requirement to place two of those columns in a functionally empty container element for the sake of width control. As a rule you'll want to put that container around the first two columns in the source order, though that will be difficult in two of the six possible cases since those columns will not be contiguous in the layout.

There are a total of six ways to arrange and style the columns of a three-column layout. These options are displayed in Figure 6-9 and described in terms of float and margin values in Table 6-2.

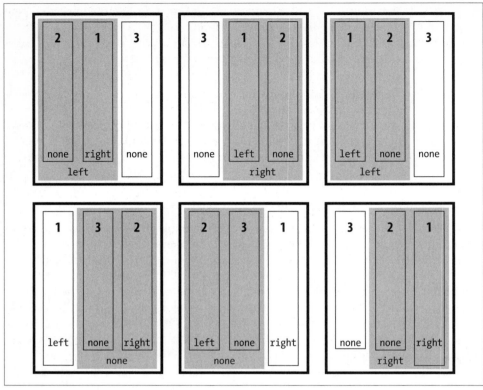

Figure 6-9. Wireframes with source order and float value annotation of the six possible three-column layouts

Table 6-2. Column ordering (from left to right) and float/margin[a] property/value assignment. Columns are numbered by source order; brackets indicate intercolumn container elements

Display order	Container layout	Source column layout		
		Col. 1	Col. 2	Col. 3
[[2, 1], 3]	float: left;	float: right;	margin-right: x;[b]	margin-left: x;
[3, [1, 2]]	float: right;	float: left;	margin-left: x;	margin-right: x;
[[1, 2], 3]	float: left;	float: left;	margin-left: x;	margin-left: x;
[1, [3, 2]]	margin-left: x;	float: left;	float: right;	margin-right: x;
[[2, 3], 1]	margin-right: x;	float: right;	float: left;	margin-left: x;
[3, [2, 1]]	float: right;	float: right;	margin-right: x;	margin-right: x;

[a] Remember that elements assigned a float value need a corresponding width value, while properties assigned a margin-* value should omit a width value in most cases.

[b] x refers here to a variable length, *not* a length that remains constant within a given layout.

If you need to maintain consistent intercolumn container scope between the two "odd" cases and any of the other four that were described in Figure 6-9, the desired results can be achieved in the following steps:

1. Move the intercolumn container to enclose the first two source columns.
2. Unset the `width` property of the intercolumn container.
3. Assign complementary `float` and `width` values to the first two columns.
4. Assign appropriate margin values to the third column, given that the margin values are greater than or equal to the sum of the two `width` values set in step 3.

The two approaches to avoiding collision between main content and footers—`overflow: auto` combined with `height: 1%` on the element containing your columns, and setting `clear: both` on the footer—are viable without regard to the number of columns in your template.

Stylesheets and templates for the six layouts described in Table 6-2 are provided on this book's companion website.

Dealing with More Than Three Columns

As the number of columns in a layout grows, the prospect of using `overflow: auto;` on one or more containers becomes increasingly attractive. Using multiple `float` values in series—and risking blowouts as a result of rounding variations or Internet Explorer bugs—also becomes viable, because once you're past three columns, *any* successful approach to solving layout problems can be considered good enough.

Semantically Empty Containers for Multicolumn Layouts

If you conduct independent investigations into the results that can be obtained with multiple `float` values and positioning, you'll discover that many of the multicolumn layouts discussed here don't require intercolumn containers. (Those who want to skip the investigation can visit this book's companion website instead.)

Creating empty container elements is often assumed to introduce junk markup, which by definition is a poor addition to any page. That's certainly the case if you use one of the three-column templates described earlier, and subsequently need to run a search-and-replace on a series of three-column templates so that the principal content can be moved from an edge to the center of the layout—a step that according to CSS Zen should be entirely unnecessary.

However, the intercolumn container offers the best protection against blowouts and the greatest flexibility with respect to providing distinct, full-height backgrounds for all three columns.

Advanced Layout in CSS3

The current CSS3 module drafts specify support for sequential columns and properties that allow stylists to specify layout behavior like that found in tables.

The multicolumn layout module includes properties that allow a single element to be divided into multiple columns of arbitrary width, height, content length, and gutter width, running from left to right. There is also the `column-span` property, which forces an element into typical block flow, then resumes column rendering from the left edge of the following element's content block.

The template layout module as currently written specifies extensions to the `display` and `position` properties that allow stylists to define a layout grid that mimics the behavior of layout tables like those described in "Implementing Multicolumn Layouts" on page 88.

The `display` extension supports variables encoded within the alphabetic subset of ASCII, as well as two constants. The first constant is `@`, where elements in the "template" context should go, if they aren't explicitly assigned to a position in the defined grid. The second constant is `.` (period; `%2E`), which defines gutters within a layout.

The jQuery JavaScript framework includes a module that allows stylists to emulate this template module behavior by defining a prefix token for custom `display` and `position` properties (e.g., `-mygrid-display`) and the name of the CSS file containing the template layout rules.

CSS Positioning Properties

The `position` property takes one of four values (of which `static` is the default) and allows the stylist to place any element anywhere in the layout.

More importantly, the assignment of any `position` value other than `static` alters the positioning context of elements, which is briefly described in Chapter 3.

How Positioning Works

Consider the following values:

```
#someDiv { ... left: 160px; top: 96px; }
```

Suppose that those styles are applied to the following markup:

```
... <body><div id="main"> ... <div id="someDiv">The quick
red fox jumps over the lazy brown dog.</div> ... </div></body>
```

The four `position` values that can be applied to `#someDiv` will yield the following results:

static
> `left` and `top` values are not applied; the element *retains* its expected position in the layout flow of the document.

absolute

> The upper-left corner of `#someDiv` appears 96 pixels below and 160 pixels to the right of the upper-left corner of the browser canvas. The margin applied to `body` is disregarded. The element is *removed* from the layout flow of the document.

fixed

> Yields the same result as `position: absolute`, except that the element will retain its position on the browser canvas regardless of any content scrolling. The element is *removed* from the layout flow of the document.

relative

> Instead of being offset from the upper-left corner of the browser canvas, `#someDiv` is offset from where it would normally appear in the document layout. The element *retains* its expected position in the layout flow of the document, apart from the changes imposed by the left and top values supplied in the stylesheet.

Let's add the following stylesheet rule:

```
#main { position: relative; margin: 20px; }
```

The `top`, `right`, `bottom`, and `left` properties of `#main` default to zero, but the assignment of `position: relative` changes the positioning context of `#someDiv` so that instead of being offset from the upper-left corner of the browser canvas, `#someDiv` is instead offset from the upper-left corner of `#main`, yielding a displacement of 20 pixels rightward and downward when compared to the first set of examples, as suggested by the upper-right panel in Figure 6-10. The storyboard in the figure is based on the markup and styles used for the two-column layout demonstration (see "Converting the Two-Column Layout from Markup Tables to CSS" on page 89).

A bit more about the effects of element positioning on the flow of surrounding elements. An element that is *removed* has the same effect as an element with a `display` value of none, except that the element remains visible at the coordinates specified by the stylist. *Retained* flow behavior means that while the position of the element might be altered (in the case of `position: relative`), it still affects the layout of nearby elements according to the behavior suggested by its `display` value.

Finally, note that Internet Explorer 6 and 7 render margins differently than other browsers when `position: relative` is used to reset positioning context, as in the navigation layout techniques discussed later. In practice, these deviations should be repaired by providing appropriate reset values in a conditionally requested stylesheet.

```
#sidebar p { position: static; }
```

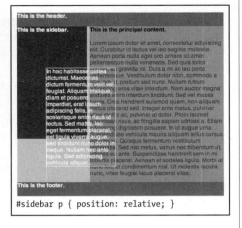

```
#sidebar p { position: relative; }
```

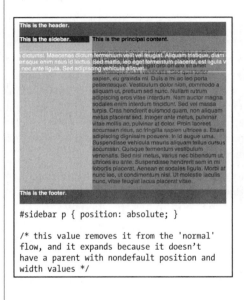

```
#sidebar p { position: absolute; }

/* this value removes it from the 'normal'
flow, and it expands because it doesn't
have a parent with nondefault position and
width values */
```

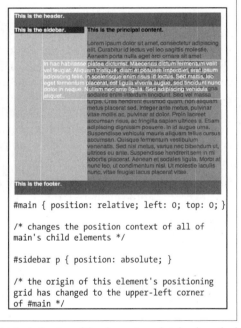

```
#main { position: relative; left: 0; top: 0; }

/* changes the position context of all of
main's child elements */

#sidebar p { position: absolute; }

/* the origin of this element's positioning
grid has changed to the upper-left corner
of #main */
```

Figure 6-10. A storyboard displaying from left to right the behavior of the elements and styles described in this section

Bounding Positioned Elements

The `top` and `left` properties—which can be set with the same units as the box properties—are accompanied by the `right` and `bottom` properties, which tend to be less frequently used due to the unpredictability of browser canvas size.

However, in all current browsers, complementary values can be assigned together in lieu of assigning `width` (or less often `height`) values. Consider the following:

```
#someDiv { position: absolute; left: 25%; right: 25%; }
```

which yields the same result as:

```
#someDiv { position: absolute; left: 25%; width: 50%; }
```

This bounding technique can prove helpful in the execution of variable-width layouts that require margin offsets in units other than percentages.

As with `top` and `left`, negative `right` and `bottom` values move corresponding margins outside the margins of the element that sets the positioning context, as described in Figure 6-11.

---

width: auto and Nondefault position/float Values

In the absence of an assigned `width` value, elements with a `position` value of `absolute` or `static` will expand to fill the horizontal space available, just as normal elements will. This means that given a set `left` or `right` value, the unset complement has a functional value of zero.

Things become more interesting if an absolutely positioned or floated element contains nothing but content of an intrinsic width (e.g., images and form controls). In these cases, the containing element with a `width` value of `auto` will "shrink to fit" the contents at their widest point.

Section 10.3 of the CSS 2.1 specification goes into seemingly interminable detail about the rules applied to the calculation of element widths.

The visibility and z-index Properties

The various box and positioning properties speak for manipulating page layout in two dimensions, and there are two additional properties that stylists need to manipulate layout in three dimensions.

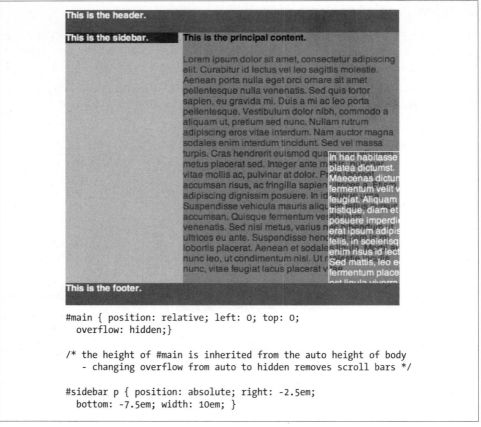

```
#main { position: relative; left: 0; top: 0;
   overflow: hidden;}

/* the height of #main is inherited from the auto height of body
   - changing overflow from auto to hidden removes scroll bars */

#sidebar p { position: absolute; right: -2.5em;
   bottom: -7.5em; width: 10em; }
```

Figure 6-11. Negative right and bottom values move affected elements outside (rather than inside) their default position

Altering Visibility Without Affecting Document Flow

display: none is tremendously useful, but it affects the overall flow of documents in which it's used. The visibility property and its single well-supported custom value—namely, hidden—make it possible to remove content from view without affecting the overall flow of the document's layout. Where the assignment of display: none to an element causes its neighbors to be rendered as if it didn't exist, visibility: hidden merely removes that element's contents from view and renders its (apparently empty) element box.

visibility: hidden and opacity: 0 deliver the same result. The primary difference between them is with respect to support. visibility was part of an addendum to the original CSS specification drafted in 1996, while opacity is unevenly supported, although part of the CSS3 feature set.

Stacking

Where two elements overlap—in the simplest case, because one is contained by another—the latter element in the source order will be displayed *over* its predecessor. That's all well and good, but matters are complicated by the nature of positioning and by the fact that any element contains at least two layers of its own.

For a *normal* block element, matter is stacked in the following order, from bottom to top:

1. Background color
2. Background image
3. Borders
4. Inline content
5. Floated content

Inline and floated elements can have their own backgrounds, borders, and contents, which gives them their own stacking order.

Trailing and distinct from that list are elements with any `position` value other than `static`. Each of these takes on its own stacking *context*, which is shared in the same manner as positioning context. Where two positioned elements share a stacking context, their stacking order will be determined by their source order as suggested earlier.

The `z-index` property serves the purpose of manipulating the stacking order of positioned elements. Suppose that you have a series of deliberately positioned elements with the same positioning context; if they overlap at all, the element visible in the intersecting region will be the last in the document source order by default.

If those elements need to be stacked "out of order," `z-index` values (which default to `auto`) can be assigned, yielding the following changes to the stacking order:

• Elements are stacked according to negative `z-index` value, below...
• Elements with `z-index` values of zero and `auto`, which are stacked in source order but below...
• Elements with `z-index` values greater than zero, which are stacked likewise according to their `z-index` value.

In general, elements with identical positioning context and identical `z-index` values will be stacked in source order, again with the earliest on the bottom of the stack.

The most significant limitation of the `z-index` property is that elements *must* share a positioning context before they can be arranged arbitrarily with respect to one another along a document's notional z-axis.

Finally, note that if you ever need to stack "normal" content over a floated neighbor, you can move it to a higher position in the stacking order by assigning to it a `position` value of `relative`.

Obtaining Precise Navigation Source Order and Layout

"Styling Navigation Elements" on page 121 describes list markup and styling and includes a list of steps that explains how to lay out a site's primary navigation elements. Step 5 avoids details, however—it simply suggests that navigation item layout involves a heap of box and layout properties.

 All selectors used in this section are deliberately written in the most generic manner possible.

The following material assumes that the first four steps of the process have been followed, resulting in a reset list with all of its items set to `display: block`.

 Chapter 13 also discusses complex page layouts in fine detail.

Orienting the List

Regardless of where the primary navigation has been placed in a template's source order, it's easiest to explain the layout process by first orienting the navigation as a whole, as shown in Figure 6-12.

Three issues affect navigation list item orientation:

- Overall horizontal or vertical orientation
- Presence or absence of sublevels
- Overall orientation of sublevel items

Establishing a horizontal orientation—the most prevalent orientation for primary site navigation on commercial English-language sites—is best accomplished by writing stylesheet rules similar to the following, with length values altered as needed:

```
#nav { display: block; height: 1.5em; overflow: hidden; }
#nav li { width: 8.333em; float: left; overflow: hidden; }
```

The result is displayed in Figure 6-12. Note that `#nav` actually takes its positioning context from `#main`, thus allowing it to lie *below* the principal content in the source order. The space in which `#nav` lies is provided by padding that has been added to `#main`, as indicated by the gray negative space present on each side—space that is needed to account for rounding differences between browsing platforms.

If the use of `float` fails to yield acceptable results due to cross-browser rounding differences or Internet Explorer rendering bugs, another approach is to assign

---

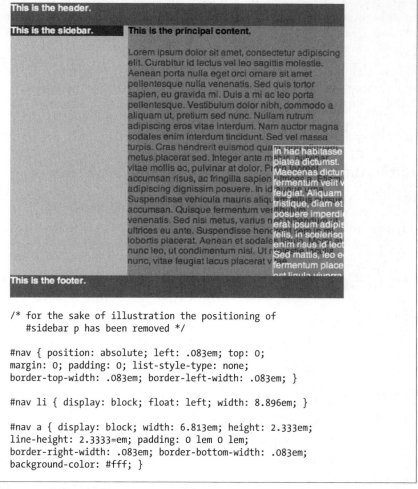

```
/* for the sake of illustration the positioning of
   #sidebar p has been removed */

#nav { position: absolute; left: .083em; top: 0;
margin: 0; padding: 0; list-style-type: none;
border-top-width: .083em; border-left-width: .083em; }

#nav li { display: block; float: left; width: 8.896em; }

#nav a { display: block; width: 6.813em; height: 2.333em;
line-height: 2.3333=em; padding: 0 lem 0 lem;
border-right-width: .083em; border-bottom-width: .083em;
background-color: #fff; }
```

Figure 6-12. Horizontally oriented navigation

position: relative to the containing list (unless position: absolute has already been applied to work around source order), then assign position: absolute to each of the individual list items, along with the desired layout coordinates.

The reason for preferring float: left to position: absolute when laying out navigation list items goes back to the "stacking context" issues described earlier. Elements that have odd stacking characteristics tend to encourage the proliferation of position and z-index values in arbitrary parts of a document—an outcome that usually brings trouble during the testing phase of a project. That trouble grows even worse when encountered in the context of brokered advertising or content contributed to a CMS by untrained users.

Vertically oriented navigation is categorically easier to style. The biggest challenge lies in accounting for items that run onto two lines of link text rather than one; however, the practice of assigning an `id` to each list item contained in the primary navigation (if possible) simplifies the requirement to account for that case.

Where the horizontally oriented navigation is bounded in terms of `height`, the vertically oriented navigation is bounded in terms of `width` and sheds all need for `float` values, yielding simpler rules; for example:

```
#nav { display: block; width: 10em; overflow: hidden; }
#nav li { height: 1.5em; overflow: hidden; }
```

Forcing the Navigation List into the Desired Coordinates

In typical cases, the list containing your primary navigation links will fall at one of two locations in the template source, and at one of two locations in the template layout. In addition, the depth of the primary navigation list in the document tree is significant. The first two scenarios presented here assume the following page structure:

1. Document root
   A. Content container
      I. Header
      II. Primary navigation
         i. Individual links
            a. Sublevels
      III. Content columns
      IV. Footer
         i. Secondary navigation
            a. Individual links
         ii. Rights statements, etc.

The latter two scenarios assume that 1.A.II. and 1.A.III. (the primary navigation and content columns) are transposed with respect to the source order just outlined.

The apparent (layout) location of primary navigation links always lies within or adjacent to the header except in the rarest of cases; the principal question is whether they're oriented in a column flush to the left margin of the entire layout (and probably above secondary content), or oriented horizontally along a line contiguous to the bottom of the header (and likely spanning all columns in the layout).

The particulars of laying out navigation *links* within their parent list are discussed in the previous section and in Chapter 7; the question answered here is how to put them in the desired place on the visible page.

In keeping with the examples used in the rest of this chapter, Figure 6-13 assumes that the navigation list will be placed at the end of #main. This approach is not without its disadvantages, but it leads to the most logical ordering of content according to priority.

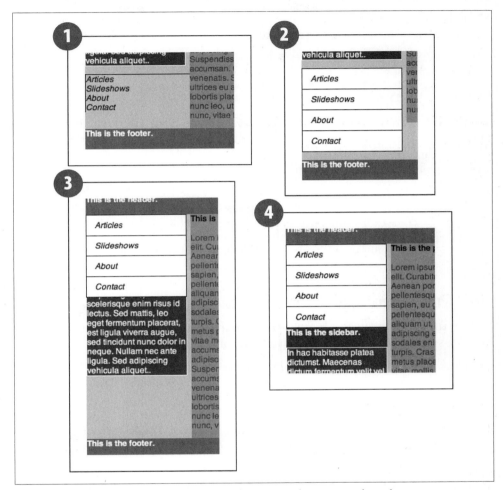

Figure 6-13. The layout of a vertically oriented navigation list, presented step by step

Things get a little more complicated if the links are vertically oriented, as shown in Figure 6-13, and contiguous with the left column of the layout. Using Figure 6-13 as a guide, consider the default disposition of a vertically oriented navigation list at that position in the source order, and think through the following steps:

1. Reset the list by applying `list-style-type: none` to the list and setting `padding-left: 0` on the list items.

2. Set the desired box properties on the list items, and on the list itself. In this case, padding and two borders have been applied to all four sides of each list item, and two borders to the list, in a manner similar to that suggested by Figure 10-3 (shown in Chapter 10).

3. Relying on the positioning context established by `@main`, the navigation list is moved over the top of the left column.

4. An appropriate `padding-top` value is applied to the left column.

Layout Types and Canvas Grids

You must address two concerns when you create a page layout: the width of the layout in relation to the browser canvas, and the grid that will be applied within the layout. There are three popular approaches to linking layout width and canvas width, and two levels at which layout grids are applied.

 You'll find warnings about the dangers of mixing fixed units with percentages. The most frequently encountered involve borders and rounded corners, both of which tend to work far better when resolved to static units, notwithstanding the desirability of applying them to elements of proportional width.

Fixed, Proportional, and Flexible Layouts

Even in the ever-changing web browser environment, a site's designer must ask three questions before starting work on a wireframe or (perhaps) a composite:

- How much space do I need to communicate the site's message?
- How much space can fit within the browser canvas of the site's typical visitors?
- Will it serve visitors' needs to use the entire canvas?

To some extent, these questions should also be answered with respect to separate *components* of a site's design: "How much space do I need in x, and for what reasons?"

Because the answers to these questions vary from one project to the next and from one designer to the next, there are no universally correct answers. However, there are a number of design concepts that affect the horizontal composition of a layout:

Type sizes
> Since there is an ideal number of words per line, and since the most frequently used words in a given language are well known, it follows that narrower layouts best accommodate small type sizes, while wider layouts are needed for larger type sizes.

Image sizes
> If photographs or other illustrations are to comprise a significant portion of the site's content, their aspect ratios and sizes will have a strong impact on the design

of the site as a whole—particularly since they cannot be sized proportionally within proportional layouts on account of their fixed size.

Negative space and contrast

Apart from the negative space created in a wide browser window that contains a proportionally narrow layout, there remains the need to place negative space (e.g., gutters and paragraph margins) in various parts of the layout. Regions of high contrast also benefit from being padded with generous amounts of negative space around content.

Browser constraints

Inexperienced stylists will encounter significant rendering bugs when implementing proportional and flexible layouts.

The Rule of Thirds, the Golden Ratio, and the Fibonacci Sequence

When composing the "over-the-fold" space of a landing page or the area of a page section, you can rely on these ubiquitous series of numbers to establish column widths and other metrics.

The characteristics, advantages, and disadvantages of the three basic layout types are summarized in Table 6-3.

Table 6-3. Layout types: their characteristics, advantages, and disadvantages

Layout Type	Characteristics	Advantages	Disadvantages
Fixed	All layouts are assigned in px units; columns probably will be as well	• Most accommodating to gutters, rules, and detailed accents • Least vulnerable to rendering bugs • Well suited to image-heavy sites	• Least accessible to visually impaired users • Most vulnerable to blowouts at all levels
Proportional	Most or all layout values are assigned in % units	• Layouts remain consistent regardless of the size of a visitor's browser canvas • Most accessible to visually impaired users	• floated elements are difficult to manage when fixed units are provided for gutters and borders • Especially long lines are rendered within wide browser windows, leading to a loss of content readability
Flexible	Most or all layout values are assigned in em units	• Offers the best compromise between accessibility and readability; handles Text Zoom well • Essential to successful grid management • Little or no need for unit-mixing; all length/size values can be assigned in em units without fear of blowouts	• Extensive fraction-to-decimal conversion and multiplicative calculation of type sizes required on the part of the stylist • Fares poorly on small canvases when combined with type sizes greater than 12px (or its equivalent)

In practice, the most significant contributor to your decisions about layout width and type will be driven by the expectation that most of your visitors will be browsing at a particular canvas size and display resolution. As I write this, the lowest common denominator is usually 1024×768 fully maximized, which yields a smallest likely canvas of roughly 1000×600 (in Internet Explorer 7 with multiple tabs and toolbars enabled). Most page layouts are then centered to account for larger browser windows in larger displays, like the 1280×800 window I run within a 1680×1050 display.

If your site has especially broad or ambitious objectives (and a desired audience to match), it might also pay to account for 800×600 display resolution. This can be handled in one of two ways:

- Shrink the width of your layout to fit within an 800×600 display, while taking into account the requirements of accommodating ideal line length.
- Maintain 1024×768 as your lowest common denominator for browser window dimensions, but set the column widths of your site to fit primary page content within the space made available at 800×600.

The Web Developer Toolbar extension for Firefox offers the best "poor man's solution" for testing layouts at various window sizes; it supports a dialog that allows you to specify an arbitrary number of window sizes, and then creates menu items that you can select to switch between the sizes that you've provided. For their part, accessibility and user experience experts will advocate that you test display resolutions natively, in no small part because of the variations in display pitch that are described in Table 3-3.

Defining Grids

Consistency is often considered the highest virtue of effective graphic design, and the Web offers few excuses to ignore the value of consistency to the user experience. In fact, the nature of the cascade (see "Applying Taxonomy Through the Cascade" on page 70) greatly promotes consistency in design.

In its turn, consistency is greatly aided by the creation of *grids*. Grids are applied at all levels of a site's design, most notably at the atomic level and the page/template level.

An atomic grid is exactly what its name suggests: the division of a layout into a pattern of small, identical rectangles, which are often (but not always) squares. Many design platforms, including and especially Adobe Photoshop, include support for square grids as a matter of course. Grids can be activated in Photoshop by navigating to View → Show Grid or pressing Ctrl/Cmd-[apostrophe]. Those grid lines can and should inform the distance between lines of text and the possible locations of column stops.

Page grids are more arbitrary, but in their way no less consistent. A page's grid specifies the widths of the columns in the layout, offers a preferred height for blocks of content, and specifies the circumstances under which the `clear` property should be used.

The alternative to a page grid—dumping content into one or more columns without regard for the vertical space it occupies, building page sections with different column widths, and eschewing consistency with respect to assets such as images or heading composition—results in a patchwork effect, as demonstrated by Figure 6-14, which shows the Weather Channel and Weather Underground home pages as they appeared at the same time. (Note the amount of clutter between gridlines in the capture of Weather Underground, displayed at the top.) Neither layout is superlative in its adherence to a page grid, but in the case of the Weather Channel's site, it's apparent even to the casual visitor that at least somebody *tried* to follow a page grid.

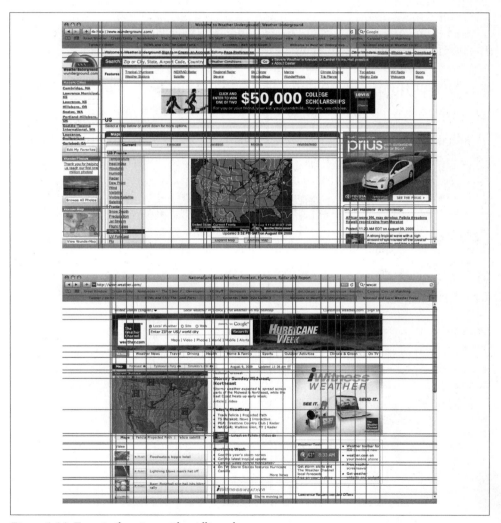

Figure 6-14. Two similar sites, with gridlines drawn

Not so with Weather Underground. Content on that site is also poured into three columns, but with far less attention to the y-axis of the page layout. On both sites, advertising is piled up between the page content and the footer, and again the difference is apparent: the Weather Channel site divides the main column to position its text ads, while Weather Underground divides its *entire* content area for the same purpose.

Note that most of the visible problems at Weather Underground point to ads that are dumped into outsized footprints. Thus:

> If you intend to sell advertising on a site, design for its presence from the beginning.

Because it can be difficult to predict the height of a block of content, vertical composition challenges need to be met with editorial discipline and planning. In situations where height control is critical to the execution of a page layout, you should consider the prospect of using `overflow: hidden`.

The Rule of Thirds, the Golden Ratio, and the Fibonacci Sequence

The similar concepts of the Rule of Thirds, the Golden Ratio, and the Fibonacci sequence are particularly relevant to page layout. The Rule of Thirds is the easiest to comprehend and calculate; it proposes that given an arbitrary composition, viewer focus is most easily maintained at the four points that rest at one-third of the distance between its edges.

The Golden Ratio or ϕ is a constant approximately equal to 1.618034, such that if it is divided into 1 and that quotient subsequently added to 1, the resulting sum will equal ϕ.

The Fibonacci sequence is the series of numbers such that $x_n + x_{(n+1)} = x_{(n+2)}$, given that the lowest possible value of $x_{(n+2)}$ is 1 (i.e., 0 + 1). Starting with the second instance of 1, the first 10 numbers in the Fibonacci sequence are 1, 2, 3, 5, 8, 13, 21, 34, 55, and 89.

The Rule of Thirds yields a ratio of 3:2, which is an extremely rough approximation of the Golden Ratio, and that in turn is the number toward which the ratios of successive Fibonacci numbers trend.

Figure 6-15 describes the Rule of Thirds and the Fibonacci sequence. Those grids make excellent starting points for determining your own layout grids, specifically with respect to column widths and the proportion of the target canvas height that will be occupied by the site header and footer.

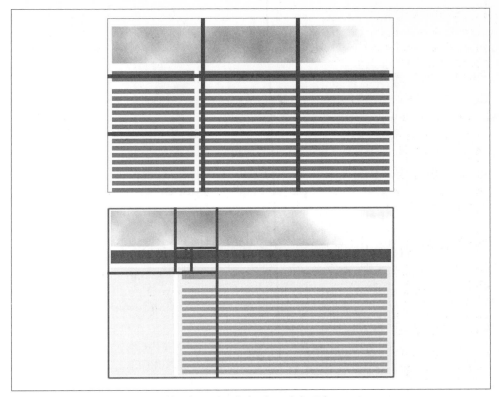

Figure 6-15. The grids suggested by the Rule of Thirds and the Fibonacci sequence

Implementing a Flexible Page Grid

 One part of the standards track work on CSS3 is a method for defining atomic grid units of an arbitrary size. The relevant draft specification is linked from this book's companion website.

Most atomic grids that are applied to page layouts follow one basic rule: the height of the grid's rows are equivalent to one line of text with leading. If I put the following into a stylesheet:

```
body { ... font-size: 14px; line-height: 1.714em; ... }
```

I'm suggesting a grid that will have rows 24 pixels in height unless some sort of zoom is applied—and even if Text Zoom *is* applied, the leading of my copy will remain proportionally constant.

Text Zoom is mentioned here because it's a valuable accessibility aid, and because it tends to wreak havoc on the composition of layouts that aren't tightly em- and grid-based. A summary of zoom support in current browsers is provided in Table 6-4.

Table 6-4. Summary of zoom support in web browsers

Zoom type	IE 8	IE 7	IE 6[a]	Firefox 3	Firefox 2	Safari 4	Safari 3
Text Zoom	✓	✓	✓	✓	✓	✓	✓
Page Zoom	✓	✓	n/a	✓	n/a	✓	n/a

[a] Unsupported for text that inherits its font-size from a value stated in px units.

Atomic column width can take any value. Column width that yields squares seems logical, but doesn't always yield pleasant gutter widths. Other candidates include:

- Row height divided (or multiplied) by ϕ
- 1em or multiples of ems
- The width of a common word in your default typeface

When implementing an atomic grid, again the main thing to remember is *consistency*. Your column widths and any other lines on your page layout grid should correspond to lines on your atomic grid, and if you're trying for a flexible layout, all values should be expressed in em units.

For example, suppose that I use the Fibonacci sequence as the basis for a two-column layout on a square grid. This will yield the following proportions before gutters and margins are inserted:

Header and footer height	8x
Sidebar width	13x
Primary content width	21x
Likely width of inline photos	8x
Likely heading sizes (with leading)	3x and/or 5x

The task before me is to solve for *x*. Given the proportion of the body copy width to the sidebar width, I'll want a line length at the shorter end of the optimal range: 12 words, which resolves to something like 36em in many typefaces. That yields a value for x of .618em.

Since I can't very well have lines that are .618em high, I can double that coefficient, leading to a line-height value of 1.235em (which turns out to be pretty close to the default for many typefaces). If I move onto the next item in the Fibonacci series I obtain a line-height value of 1.853em, which is probably too large.

Alternatively I can look at my layout in terms of proportions (13:21 sidebar:body ratio, yielding a total width of 34 units) and divide that into my canvas width. The result of that arithmetic will fall somewhere in the range of 28–30 pixels per grid unit, which in its turn suggests larger type on shorter lines of copy.

Regardless of which value I choose, I can codify the results into my stylesheet by simply deciding on grid dimensions, assigning dimensions to each significant class of content on the site, and getting the most from stylesheet selectors in the course of assigning my layout and composition values.

CHAPTER 7

Working with Lists

Lists are everywhere: checklists, shopping lists, to-do lists, "Best of" and "Worst of" lists, procedure lists, and simple rankings turn up every day. Lists are pretty easy to find in web markup, too, used for all of those purposes and often for navigation. HTML supports three types of lists: ordered, unordered, and definition lists.

Ordered and Unordered Lists

The principal difference between ordered and unordered lists is semantics: sometimes there's a need to rank items by some criterion (e.g., importance, order of execution, time, order of addition, alphabetic order), and sometimes a list contains nothing more than a group of data with something in common.

User Agent Default Styles for Ordered and Unordered Lists

At first glance, unstyled lists look like block elements (which they are) containing a series of still more block elements, each of which is offset from the apparent left margin of the list. However, current browsers apply different user agent styles to lists than their legacy counterparts, as shown in Table 7-1.

Table 7-1. User agent styles for unordered, ordered, and definition lists (ul, ol, dl)

User agents	User agent style
• Firefox 2+ • Internet Explorer 7+ • Safari 3+	`margin: 1em auto 1em 0; padding-left: 40px;`
• Firefox 1.0.x–1.4.x • Internet Explorer 6 • Quirks rendering modes	`margin: 1em auto 1em 40px;`

Note the `40px` values. Their consequence is that if type is especially large and an ordered list runs long, list item markers are likely to be obscured in part at the left margin. Such an outcome can be avoided when necessary, by increasing the appropriate `margin-left` and `padding-left` values and supplying them in em rather than px units.

A list layout behavior test suite can be found at this book's companion site (*www .htmlcssgoodparts.net*).

Creating Valid Ordered and Unordered Lists

Building valid lists isn't difficult, but there are a few key rules to follow:

- A list must contain at least one item.
- A list cannot contain anything other than items.
- The direct parent of a list item must be a list.
- All elements that are valid children of `div`s are also valid children of list items, including bare text and other lists.
- HTML 4.01 permits list items without closing tags.
- The `start` attribute of `ol`, the `value` attribute of `li` within `ol`, and the `type` attribute of both are valid within Transitional document types, but not Strict document types.
- Ordered list item counters do not increment on items that have a `display` value of `none`.

The list-style-type Property and the type Attribute

Ordered list items can be annotated with a full range of cardinal markers. The default is decimal numbers, while both Latin letters and Roman numerals are available in lower- and uppercase forms.

Unordered lists nominally have three types of item markers: discs (i.e., bullets), circles, and squares.

Well-supported values for the `list-style-type` property are shown below, followed by their analogous HTML `type` values in parentheses:

- `circle` (`type="circle"`)
- `disc` (`type="disc"`) [default for unnested unordered lists]
- `decimal` (`type="1"`) [default for ordered lists]
- `lower-alpha` (`type="a"`)
- `lower-roman` (`type="i"`)
- `none`
- `square` (`type="square"`)

- upper-alpha (`type="A"`)
- upper-roman (`type="I"`)

The `none` value turns up frequently, because site navigation rarely appears with list bullets intact—especially when image replacement (see "Bitmapped Copy and Fahrner Image Replacement" on page 157) techniques are used.

There is also limited support for a `list-style-image` attribute, which replaces the generated marker with a custom image. However, the results of using this property are almost universally disappointing, so it's usually better to include such custom markers via the `background-image` and `background-repeat` properties, discussed in Chapter 9.

CSS 2.1 also provides for `lower-latin`, `upper-latin`, `lower-greek`, and `upper-greek` markers, but these are unevenly supported.

The nav Element (HTML5)

Among the new elements in HTML5 intended for adding richer structure to HTML documents, the `nav` element is arguably the most important. While the other proposed structural elements, such as the `section` element, are great features for authors, they don't have much direct impact on end users. The `nav` element, on the other hand, is a different case. It is important in that it gives you a standard way to mark up navigational content so that user agents can identify it and handle it differently if they choose to— which means that user agents can use `nav` to significantly improve the user experience.

Navigational content—that is, the lists of hyperlinks that each page of a website or web application provides for the purpose of navigating to other parts of a site, other features of an application, or specific parts of a page—can appear in a variety of places in a page or application. For example, in a page that uses a multicolumn layout, you might put primary navigation in the leftmost column of the page and secondary navigation in the rightmost column. Or, in another page design or a web application, you might put primary navigation in menus at the top of the page that expand to show their contents when the user selects them, and secondary navigation in the footer of the page.

Lacking the `nav` element, you would most likely mark up navigational content using a `div` with a particular `class` attribute. The `class` value "nav" is in fact one of the twenty or so most commonly used `class` values on the Web. Sites also use values like `primary Nav` and `secondaryNav` to further distinguish between separate classes of navigational content.

The problem with using `class` values exclusively to mark up navigational content is the lack of agreed-upon standard values that are used consistently across different sites. The `nav` element solves that problem by providing a common standard element that all web authors can use for the same purpose. In turn, having a standard `nav` element helps with a common dilemma that faces many authors: the need to decide where to place navigational content in the source order of a document to try to ensure it does not negatively affect document accessibility, or limit usability on small-screen mobile devices.

Accessibility and usability concerns

A number of accessibility issues affect the decision about where to place navigational content in the source order of the document. For example:

1. There is a common concern that if you don't place primary navigation near the top of a document, the document will be less accessible to users of AT (accessibility technology) products such as screen readers. The worry is that such users are accustomed to finding the primary navigation at the top of any given document and won't be able to locate it elsewhere.

2. Paradoxically, there is a conflicting concern that if you place primary navigation at the top of a document in source order, it will make your content *less* accessible. That's because in a typical site design, most every page of the site will have the same long set of navigational links that users of AT tools need to wade through to get to the main content. This can be frustrating and time-consuming.

3. Closely related to the second concern is the question of usability of content in browsers on small-screen mobile devices. A number of mobile browsers have a built-in means for intelligently reformatting content into a single column to make it more usable on a small screen. Mobile browsers typically do that reformatting based on the source order of the content, so if the primary navigation appears at the top of each page in source order, users of such browsers end up facing the same problem that users of AT tools face. On each and every page they are confronted with a long list of primary navigation that they then need to scroll through to get to the main content.

In practice, a common way that authors address the second and third concerns is to provide something like a "Skip to main content" or "Skip past navigation" hyperlink on each page prior to the primary navigation. This helps, but it is essentially a hack to work around the fact that prior to HTML5 there was no standard way (without using heuristics) that a screen reader or a browser on a mobile device could determine what part of document is navigation and what part is actual content.

Enabling user agents to present navigation through alternate means

With the addition of the nav element to HTML5, user agents now have a standard element to look for that they know contains navigational content. They can then provide alternative means for presenting that navigational content to users, as a note in the current draft of the HTML5 specification explains:

> User agents (such as screen readers) that are targeted at users who can benefit from navigation information being omitted in the initial rendering, or who can benefit from navigation information being immediately available, can use this element as a way to determine what content on the page to initially skip and/or provide on request.

Screen readers are not the only type of user agent for which nav is especially useful; it is extremely useful for browsers on small-screen mobile devices as well. Such browsers might, for example, make nav content accessible through a soft-key menu rather than rendering it within the main text flow of a page.

Of course, all the wonderful utility of the nav element is just a pipe dream unless AT tools, browsers on mobile devices, and other user agents actually add some features to their user interfaces to take advantage it.

Changing the Range of an Ordered List

Consider an ordered list like the following:

Greater Wavelengths

1. Red
2. Orange
3. Yellow
4. Green

Shorter Wavelengths

5. Blue
6. Indigo
7. Violet

The literal source of these lists is written as follows:

```
<h5>Greater Wavelengths</h5>
<ol>
  <li>Red</li>
  <li>Orange</li>
  <li>Yellow</li>
  <li>Green</li>
</ol>
<h5>Shorter Wavelengths</h5>
<ol start="5">
  <li>Blue</li>
  <li>Indigo</li>
  <li>Violet</li>
</ol>
```

The relationship between these two lists should be obvious, as should their layout. However, note the use of the start attribute; only Transitional types of HTML will validate the implementation shown here, because the only *reliable* way to interrupt and then resume an ordered list is with HTML 4's deprecated start and value attributes. The value attribute arbitrarily increments or decrements a list's item counter on a one-time basis.

CSS 2.1 specifies a counter implementation, but it's difficult to understand and can only be activated via the `:before` pseudoclass. In the case of a list, this prevents content and item markers from being justified to a common margin. In addition, the counter implementation is currently unsupported by Internet Explorer.

To start an ordered list at an arbitrary point, apply the `start` attribute to the list, or the `value` attribute to its first item. The values provided for both must be Arabic integers, regardless of the list's associated `type` or `list-style-type` value (which will be preserved).

Other Uses for Lists

Lists have two other fairly straightforward uses: outlines and inline serial lists.

Outlines

At its simplest, an HTML outline is nothing more than a series of appropriately nested ordered lists, accompanied by the following styles:

```
            ol { list-style-type: upper-roman; }
         ol ol { list-style-type: upper-alpha; }
      ol ol ol { list-style-type: decimal; }
   ol ol ol ol { list-style-type: lower-alpha; }
ol ol ol ol ol { list-style-type: lower-roman; }
```

Outline levels 6–10 repeat the same sequence as needed, though the second pass should probably involve deemphasized type (whether smaller or lighter) in tandem with the default indentation.

Inline Serial Lists

An uncommon but not unheard-of scenario involves the extensive use of the serial comma to separate several items in a list. There are a number of reasons why this approach might be taken in a web document, the most likely being to save space. Almost as likely is an editor's insistence on seeing that list presented in serial format.

To implement an inline list, place your source paragraph within a `div` that's been assigned a `class` of your choosing and split it on the list, which should leave you with two separate paragraphs separated by a list. Then add the following styles:

```
.foo p, .foo ul, .foo li { display: inline; }
            .foo ul { list-style-type: none; }
```

If the content of each list item ends properly with a comma and a space (or the penultimate "and", as needed), the result will satisfy both severe editorial *and* severe semantic requirements. The apparently extra `div` isn't superfluous, as the content in question started life as a single paragraph anyway.

Altering the Layout of Footer Links

The behavior of `inline-block` layout was discussed in Chapter 6, and that behavior is especially valuable when working with footer links. Instead of mucking about with `float` solutions, you can settle for the following, simpler approach, given appropriate reset styles:

```
#footer ul { list-style-type: none; text-align: center; }
#footer li { display: inline-block; }
```

If custom bullets on footer links are desired, you can change the `padding-left` value of the list items and use a background image as needed.

Bullets in Backgrounds?

Yes, you read that right. The CSS `list-style-image` property is set aside *specifically* for inserting custom bullets, but it suffers from three serious drawbacks.

The first drawback of `list-style-image` is that the image it calls is always rendered on the baseline, forcing the stylist to execute the composition of the intended bullet in their graphics editor on a pixel-by-pixel basis—a requirement that roundly defeats the goal of separating content from presentation.

The second drawback follows from the first: if the visitor zooms in on the page, bullets are composed in odd proportion to their accompanying text.

The third drawback is the fact that without composition values like those that a stylist can supply for background properties, there is no hope of applying sprites—fraught with danger though their implementation might be in this case—to custom bullets specified by the `list-style-image` property.

Styling Navigation Elements

In this section, the shorthand term "nav" will be used to refer both to the list containing the separate primary site navigation items ("nav items"), and to the analogous design element as it will appear on the production site. The links within the nav will be referred to explicitly.

 There are two basic orientations for primary site navigation: vertical and horizontal. The latter has its constituent items `float`ed left-to-right, while the former is stacked into a column. The other steps to creating navigation are fairly similar for both orientations.

Placing the Primary Site Navigation Within the Source Order

The first question to ask is: "Where does my nav go in the source order of the template markup?" There are a number of issues to consider when answering this question:

Users of assistive software usually expect to see (or hear) the nav early in the source order
    This expectation is an artifact of 1990s design trends and tools, when the primary nav was almost certain to comprise the second chunk of a page's source order (after the site header).

However, it's marginally more respectful of an assistive technology user's time to place a page's unique content as close as possible to the beginning of that page's source order
    The need to act on this criterion is mitigated by list-skipping functionality and user expectations, but should not be ignored. Pushing down the primary nav might also provide incidental Search Engine Optimization (SEO) benefits.

Placing the nav just below the header section will permit you to apply styles that are simpler (to a point)
    Placing the primary nav at the end of a page's source order offers a near-absolute guarantee that you'll be forced to rely on positioning context to put it where you want it on the page—a requirement that will add complexity to your stylesheet.

Navigation is more easily maintained when it's amalgamated into a single include file
    Also, your template setup might reduce the number of included files by one—not a big deal on most sites, but on a high-volume site, even one include file means less performance drag.

The Primary Navigation Layout Recipe

Once you've composed your primary nav and decided upon its location in the source order, you can finish plugging it into your site layout:

1. *Append ids to the nav and its constituent items.* The question of how to name the ids is addressed in "Applying Taxonomy Through the Cascade" on page 70.

2. *Strip the user agent styles from your nav and its constituent items.* This is as simple as inserting something like...{ `margin: 0; padding: 0; list-style-type: none; }` into your stylesheet.

3. *Place the nav list where it will appear in the layout.* The styles used to accomplish this step will vary according to the orientation, source order position, and layout position of the nav, as well as the overall page layout scheme. The method most likely to be bug-proof requires that the nav be inside the page's content container, which is then relatively positioned so that the nav itself can be positioned absolutely within the page container's margins.

4. *Assign new display and box values to the nav items, as needed.* On most sites, the links will have equal footprints and a horizontal orientation, so many of your item styles will be contained within `#nav li`.

5. *Arrange the nav items as needed.* For horizontally oriented nav items, this can be done with `float: left` or `position: relative`. The latter approach results in a stylesheet that is more difficult to adapt to design changes, while the former is more prone to bugs in Internet Explorer 6. Vertically oriented nav items will likely only require `display: block` during this step, but are more likely to be nested. If a vertically oriented nav contains more than one level, the lists that contain sublevels should be assigned their own `ids`, (e.g., `#navSubAbout`). More details about this step are explained in "Obtaining Precise Navigation Source Order and Layout" on page 102.

6. *Expand the nav links to the full width and height of their containing items.* This is done by first setting the links to `display: block`, a step with benefits that are fully explained in Chapter 8. Finding the right `width, height,` and `padding` values will probably take some number crunching, and it might be wise to add `overflow: hidden` to the containing items as well.

7. *Implement Fahrner Image Replacement on your items and links, if desired.* Fahrner Image Replacement is described in Chapter 9. If this step is taken, background images might well be assigned to both the nav items and the nav links, so that a link in hover state displays a different background image than its containing (and underlying) list item.

The Footer Navigation Recipe

Secondary navigation is typically easier to style than primary navigation; for one thing, there's usually little doubt as to its position in the source order (nearly at the bottom, just above the rights-and-terms statement). For another, its constituent links are rarely set to constant dimensions.

It's most likely that your site's secondary navigation will be laid out in one of three ways:

Centered within the overall page layout, given generous negative space on all sides, and allowed to flow as deeply as needed
> One example of this layout can be found on PayPal's public pages. In this approach, list items are set to `display: inline` and given borders to one side (either right or left).

More or less flush to one bottom corner of the page layout
> This approach can be seen on Facebook user pages. The main differences between this approach and the centering approach lie with justification (`text-align: right` instead of `text-align: center`) and vertical footprint (confined to one line, rather than sometimes breaking onto two or more lines).

As a minimally styled list at the end of the site's tertiary content
> This approach has been growing in popularity on weblogs. Such secondary nav elements might well be inside the tertiary column's markup as well as its footprint.

The last layout described is no challenge at all; the other two offer minor obstacles with respect to dividers and whitespace. Here's how they're assembled and styled:

1. Set `list-style-type: none` on the list or its items.

2. If the list is to be centered, assign it appropriate `width` and x-axis margins.

3. Set the desired `text-align` value on the nav list, and `display: inline` on its separate items.

4. Set appropriate `padding` and `line-height` values on both the list and the list items—unless `display: inline-block` has been assigned to your links, in which case the links should take the box and text properties in question. Setting equal `padding` values for both left and right sides of each item will be easier in the long run, even if it doesn't seem that way at first.

5. Add your item separators. If these are bullets of any kind, they should probably be reset as background images.

6. Add whatever `class`es or `id`s that are required to remove separators on apparent initial and terminal items, and to break the list into the desired number of lines. In many cases, the `white-space` property might be a good fit for the latter task, though if items on common lines also share some discernible semantic quality, there's nothing wrong with breaking them into multiple lists.

7. Adjust as needed to meet the balance of the composite's requirements.

Definition Lists

Where ordered and unordered lists are simple heaps of data with members that share a *vague* classification, definition lists imply definite relationships between their terms (indicated by `dt` elements) and their definitions (indicated by `dd` elements). Each term is followed by one or more definitions, which are understood to relate strictly to the term.

To be valid, a definition list must contain at least one `dt` or `dd` element; to be semantically useful, it must contain at least one of each. `dt` elements may only contain text and inline elements, while `dd` elements can contain the same broad range of content as `li` elements. There is no restriction on the number or arrangement of `dd` and `dt` elements within a given definition list; it's left to content authors to ensure that definition list elements are arranged sensibly.

Styling Definition Lists

The user agent styles applied to definition lists are minimal, and can be described as follows:

- `dt` elements are not unlike paragraphs without margins.
- `dd` elements are offset with `margin-left`, but never take a marker.

- `dd` elements have the same (lack of) constraints on valid contents as `li` elements.
- Definition list text content is set in unstyled type by default.

The most common uses for a definition list are lexica (e.g., glossaries, dictionaries) and transcribed dialogue. The first of these is fairly straightforward, and the user agent styles will usually be adequate to that purpose, with the caveat that a particularly typography-conscious designer might prefer to see `dt` elements set in bold type.

Dialogue styling requires different values. The changes to make are as follows:

- The `width` of `dt` elements should be set to a discrete and constant value, and `clear: left` applied as well.
- `dd` elements should take a `margin-left` value slightly greater than the width of the `dt` elements.
- Some kind of variant typesetting (e.g., `font-weight: bold` or `text-transform: uppercase`) should be applied to the `dt` elements.

Since the forms just described are directly inspired by print, there's every good reason to duplicate them in the following sections.

Dictionary Example

Adapted from the *American Heritage® Dictionary of the English Language*, Fourth Edition:

e·con·o·my *n*. Inflected forms: *pl*. e·con·o·mies **1. a.** Careful, thrifty management of resources, such as money, materials, or labor: *learned to practice economy in making out the household budget*. **b.** An example or result of such management; a saving. **2. a.** The system or range of economic activity in a country, region, or community: *Effects of inflation were felt at every level of the economy*. **b.** A specific type of economic system: *an industrial economy; a planned economy*. **3.** An orderly, functional arrangement of parts; an organized system: *"the sense that there is a moral economy in the world, that good is rewarded and evil is punished"* (George F. Will). **4.** Efficient, sparing, or conservative use: *wrote with an economy of language*. **5.** The least expensive class of accommodations, especially on an airplane. **6.** *Theology* The method of God's government of and activity within the world. *adj*. Economical or inexpensive to buy or use: *an economy car; an economy motel*.

Here's the source markup for the dictionary passage:

```
<dl>
  <dt>e&middot;con&middot;o&middot;my</dt>
  <dd>
  <span class="partOfSpeech"><abbr title="noun">n.</abbr></span>
  <span class="variants">Inflected forms: <span class="partOfSpeech"><abbr
    title="plural">pl.</abbr></span> e&middot;con&middot;o&middot;mies</span>
  <ol>
    <li>
      <ol>
        <li>Careful, thrifty management of resources, such as money, materials,
```

```
        or labor:
        <span class="usageEx">learned to practice economy in making out the
        household budget.</span></li>
      <li>An example or result of such management; a saving.</li>
    </ol>
  </li>
  <li>
    <ol>
      <li>The system or range of economic activity in a country, region, or
        community: <span class="usageEx">Effects of inflation were felt at
        every level of the economy.</span></li>
      <li>A specific type of economic system: <span class="usageEx">an
        industrial economy; a planned economy.</span></li>
    </ol>
  </li>
  <li>An orderly, functional arrangement of parts; an organized system: <span
    class="usageEx"><q>the sense that there is a moral economy in the world,
    that good is rewarded and evil is punished</q> <cite>(George F. Will).
    </cite></span></li>
  <li>Efficient, sparing, or conservative use: <span class="usageEx">wrote with an
    economy of language.</span></li>
  <li>The least expensive class of accommodations, especially on an airplane.</li>
  <li><span class="subjectFocus">Theology</span> The method of God&rsquo;s
    government of and activity within the world.</li>
  </ol>
  <span class="partOfSpeech"><abbr title="adjective">adj.</abbr></span> Economical
    or inexpensive to buy or use: <span class="usageEx">an economy car; an economy
    motel.</span>
  </dd>
</dl>
```

The styles that accompany this example are available on this book's companion website.

This markup reveals some interesting quirks:

The various definitions are enclosed within ordered lists rather than sequential dd *elements*
This was done because the stylist—that is to say, I—decided that it was better to preserve the numbering than to get stuck on an incredibly fine semantic point. If Internet Explorer supported generated numbering like its competitors, I would not have been forced to make that choice, but support shortcomings in various browsers force skilled stylists to make these kinds of choices every working day.

Users of browsers other than Internet Explorer will see the various definitions presented inline
However, assigning a value of display: inline to list items causes their item markers to disappear, so those items must be assigned markers all over again via the counter() function that can be supplied as a value for the content property. If a stylist adds an appropriate reset rule in a conditional stylesheet, Internet Explorer users see ordinary ordered lists.

The source is littered with instances of spans *and* classes.

The abundance of inline markup illuminates the case made by microformats advocates, who propose that if something *can* be given a semantic label, in many cases it *should* be. From a stylist's perspective, the extra markup allows differing labels (in the case) to be styled in different ways.

If the numbering and finer details are omitted, a more typical dt/dd structure can be used:

```
<dt>economy</dt>
  <dd>Careful, thrifty management of resources, such as money, materials, or labor:
    <span class="usageEx">learned to practice economy in making out the household
    budget.</span></dd>
  <dd>An example or result of such management; a saving. The system or range of
    economic activity in a country, region, or community: <span class="usageEx">
    Effects of inflation were felt at every level of the economy.</span></dd>
  <dd>A specific type of economic system: an industrial economy; a planned economy.
      An orderly, functional arrangement of parts; an organized system:
    <span class="usageEx">&ldquo;the sense that there is a moral economy in
      the world,
    that good is rewarded and evil is punished&rdquo; (George F. Will).</span></dd>
  <dd>Efficient, sparing, or conservative use: <span class="usageEx">wrote with an
    economy of language.</span></dd>
  <dd>The least expensive class of accommodations, especially on an airplane.</dd>
  <dd>The method of God&rsquo;s government of and activity within the world.</dd>
  <dd>Economical or inexpensive to buy or use: an economy car; an economy motel.</dd>
...
```

Dialogue Example

A dialogue isn't quite the same as a definition list, but the parts fit easily together. Here's a passage from *Pygmalion*, Act IV, by George Bernard Shaw.

HIGGINS: *[In despairing wrath outside]* What the devil have I done with my slippers? *[He appears at the door]*

LIZA: *[Snatching up the slippers, and hurling them at him one after the other with all her force]* There are your slippers. And there. Take your slippers; and may you never have a day's luck with them!

HIGGINS: *[Astounded]* What on earth—! *[He comes to her]* What's the matter? Get up. *[He pulls her up]* Anything wrong?

LIZA: *[Breathless]* Nothing wrong—with *you*. I've won your bet for you, haven't I? That's enough for you. I don't matter, I suppose.

HIGGINS: *You* won my bet! You! Presumptuous insect! I won it. What did you throw those slippers at me for?

LIZA: Because I wanted to smash your face. I'd like to kill you, you selfish brute. Why didn't you leave me where you picked me out of—in the gutter? You thank God it's all over, and that now you can throw me back again there, do you? *[She crisps her fingers frantically]*

The source markup is shown below:

```
<dl>
  <dt>Higgins</dt>
  <dd><span class="stageDir">In despairing wrath outside</span> What the devil have
    I done with my slippers? <span class="stageDir">He appears at the door</span></dd>
  <dt>Liza</dt>
  <dd><span class="stageDir">Snatching up the slippers, and hurling them at him one
    after the other with all her force</span> There are your slippers. And there.
    Take your slippers; and may you never have a day&rsquo;s luck with them!</dd>
  <dt>Higgins</dt>
  <dd><span class="stageDir">Astounded</span> What on earth&mdash;!
  <span class="stageDir">
    He comes to her</span> What&rsquo;s the matter? Get up. <span class="stageDir">
    He pulls her up</span> Anything wrong?</dd>
  <dt>Liza</dt>
  <dd><span class="stageDir">Breathless</span> Nothing wrong &mdash; with
    <em>you</em>.
    I&rsquo;ve won your bet for you, hav&rsquo;n&rsquo;t I? That&rsquo;s enough
    for you. Idon&rsquo;t matter, I suppose.</dd>
  <dt>Higgins</dt>
  <dd><em>You</em> won my bet! You! Presumptuous insect! I won it. What did you throw
    those slippers at me for?</dd>
  <dt>Liza</dt>
  <dd>Because I wanted to smash your face. I&rsquo;d like to kill you, you selfish
    brute. Why didn&rsquo;t you leave me where you picked me out of &mdash; in the
    gutter? You thank God it&rsquo;s all over, and that now you can throw me back
    again there, do you? <span class="stageDir">She crisps her fingers
    frantically</span>
</dl>
```

Like the dictionary example, this one relies on spans and classes to convey an additional layer of information, in this case stage direction.

With respect to styling, the general approach is indistinguishable from the one described earlier, except for the addition of clear: left to the dt elements. The last significant difference between the rendered play and the source markup is the appearance of the characters' names in uppercase. This accent is handled by the text-transform property, which is described in Chapter 12.

The exact stylesheet rules for the dialogue example are available on this book's companion website.

At one point, HTML5 had proposed a dialog element for these cases, but it was removed from the specification.

It's only when web developers pay attention to the use of lists in their work product that they gain an understanding of their ubiquity. As it turns out, the only thing greater than the utility and ubiquity of lists is the challenge that sometimes must be met when styling them.

CHAPTER 8

Headings, Hyperlinks, Inline Elements, and Quotations

The need for powerful site styling definitely *begins* with layout, but it *ends* with accents. HTML and CSS offer no shortage of accents, particularly with respect to headings and hyperlinks.

HTML also defines a number of inline elements that can lend useful shades of meaning to their content.

Headings and Good Writing

HTML provides six levels of headings: h1 (most significant) through h6 (least significant), as displayed in Figure 8-1. (The sizes and margins shown are rendered in Internet Explorer 8's user agent styles.) To the uninitiated, headings are painful to use: user agent styles for the three most significant heading levels result in type so large that it jars the casual reader, and managing headings' top and bottom margins can turn into a major chore.

HTML and CSS are well equipped *by design* to mitigate all of the problems a developer might face when working with headings. When headings are properly associated with the elements used to delineate sections of content, they illuminate potentially important details of document structure and allow the stylist more opportunities to "zero in" on specific groups of headings as needed.

Headings in Print

Putting aside for the moment the matter of *how* to style headings, questions remain. How should they be used to identify content, and why would anyone *want* to use them? The use of headings in print provides a good explanation.

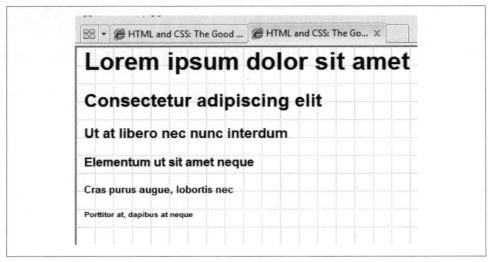

Figure 8-1. Headings can be assigned to one of six levels, as rendered by Internet Explorer 7

All but the briefest print content can be broken up into smaller parts, which are labeled singly and in aggregate by headings. In the case of a nonfiction book—such as this one—each larger section of the book (which contains one or more chapters) takes a first-order heading or "A-head" (i.e., h1), since the book title itself has a unique context in publication design. B-heads (h2) are reserved for chapter titles, C-heads (h3) for main sections within a chapter, and so on. In other books, sections are treated like books of their own, which means that each section gets a title page while individual chapters take the A-heads. In any case, in addition to giving the reader an idea of a passage's relationship to the document as a whole and signaling changes in focus, this approach also breaks copy into easily digested parts.

All of these section and heading assignments are handled in the context of the book as a whole; things like data tables and illustrations are captioned, but those captions don't qualify as headings, since they're considered labels for tertiary (albeit valuable) material.

In HTML, the h1–h6 hierarchy corresponds to headings as they're used in print books and articles, with two additional considerations:

The only place where the content of the **title** *element is persistently rendered is on the browser's title bar*

> This forces conscientious developers to *repeat* that information within an h1 (or perhaps an h2) near the beginning of a given document's source order, even if the document title introduces a broad scope like that suggested in the following section.

If the site operator's online identity is especially valuable, as in cases where visitors frequently run web searches against the operator's name, a site will benefit slightly by inserting that identity within h1

This point of interest relies on the assumption that each page contains only a single instance of h1, positioned at or near the top of the page's source order.

Optimal Heading Insertion

Traditionally, the higher the level of a heading, the broader the scope of the content it introduces to the reader.

Heading use is a counterpart to the "wrapper elements" suggested by the source fragments in "Working with Document Trees" on page 19 and "Habit #4: Keeping Your Bearings" on page 57. Each properly assigned wrapper points to the context of a passage, and enhances the modularity of content. On the Web, the highest purpose of headings is to identify those modular bits at a human-readable level.

If a stylist or developer uses heading elements assiduously, it follows that each "scoping" div will lead with a heading of the appropriate level.

Since all of this markup is meant to signal scope from broad to narrow, it's usually assumed that the first heading should be an h1 element, followed by h2, h3, and so on with each narrowing of scope. Up-level headings should be used at appropriate locations and levels; meanwhile, skipping levels when inserting down-level headings is strongly discouraged. Cross-media and assistive tools can organize documents according to their heading arrangement, and that functionality suffers when heading levels are skipped.

My own approach to headings is to enclose the site title and home page link in an h1 element (print practice notwithstanding), the page headline or title in an h2 element, and the various section headings in the other four heading elements, as needed.

Even if you don't use div elements to indicate scope, software can use heading arrangement to infer the scope of intervening content, at least well enough to generate a table of contents on the fly.

Finally, the content of heading elements—particularly h1 and h2—has an outsized influence on search result ranking, the degree of which varies from one search provider to the next.

Styling Heading Elements

Headings present different margin behavior than most block elements, which makes their composition one of the more annoying tasks stylists face.

Heading Sizes and Type Treatments

Almost every high-value design is going to specify heading sizes that differ from the user agent defaults, in no small part because—let's face it—the user agent styles for headings make them universally big and ugly.

The first step to attractive headings involves a *type treatment*. This will specify the size, leading (`line-height`), font, color, and box behavior of all the type used on the site.

In the case of headings, at minimum the type treatment will specify a different graduation of sizes that will be based on the number of scope levels in the content and the intent of the site's designers.

Type treatments are explored at length in Chapter 12.

Normalizing Heading Dimensions

The *very first* thing stylists should do before working with headings is to *reset* their user agent default styles, making sure to set all box and `font-size` values. For box values, I recommend something like:

```
h2 { margin: 0 0 1.5em 0; padding: 0; border: 0; ... }
```

However, that work won't resolve potential composition issues by itself. `line-height` will likely also need to be taken into account, and still more important will be the position of headings within the page's overall structure. If each heading is mated to a section container with custom box values of its own, the work that goes into heading resets is reduced; otherwise, the relationship between headings and adjacent block predecessors will also require resets. Given stringent composition demands, the stylist can even address these resets on a case-by-case basis with the + (next sibling) selector, for the sake of browsers that parse it correctly.

An even greater challenge is posed when attempting to control heading height in environments where strict grid obedience or space constraints are critical. The cheapest solution is to set a discrete height on headings and enforce a length limitation with `overflow: hidden`, but the inflexibility of this approach makes it impractical for the sites that make the best use of headings.

Yet another approach to controlling heading height values in a grid is to set large body copy `line-height` values, so that all type sizes can be accommodated in one line with varying `line-height` values. However, this approach is ill-suited to sites that pose minimal scrolling as a requirement.

Another possible solution is to rely on a combination of size and contrast adjustments, with the intent of reducing variability in type size (and thus leading).

The best approach to heading height control varies from project to project, and from designer to designer. However, this goal of controlling heading height also serves as an excellent example of the need for effective collaboration between stylists, designers, and content producers.

Heading Accents

A site's headings may also contain *rules*: lines of arbitrary length, color, and style that are placed in tandem with a block of copy, usually along one of its margins or, in the case of headings, sometimes on its baseline. In the case of simple, solid lines placed on a heading's margin, rules can be created easily enough by setting a heading's `border-bottom` (or perhaps `border-top`) property, for example, `h3 { border-bottom: 1px solid rgb(85,170,255); }`.

Most of the other accents likely to find their way into headings are controlled through the use of background images, which are discussed in Chapter 9.

Link Markup

 All instances of "link" as used in this section refer to arbitrary hyperlinks that are created with the `a` element. Readers who are interested in the `link` attribute should consult Chapter 3 and this book's companion website (*www.htmlcssgoodparts.net*).

HTML's inline elements as a group provide nuances of meaning to words, phrases, or short passages within longer blocks of content. Apart from hyperlinks—which are the point to the whole endeavor, of course—and form elements, the best known of these are used to provide emphasis.

Form elements are explained in Chapter 13, and the semantically oriented inline elements will be explained at the end of this chapter.

There are a number of reasons to give close attention to the implementation of links:

- Links are categorically interactive; by activating a link, the user causes something new to happen. For this reason alone, links should always be easy to distinguish from surrounding content.
- The design cues styled into links can imply relationships to particular visitor objectives.
- The user agent styles provided for links are based on antiquated environmental assumptions that rarely apply on contemporary sites.

Link Attributes

Link elements support the following notable attributes:

href
: The beating heart of the Web's application layer. This specifies the destination of the link, saving the user the trouble of typing or pasting URIs into the browser's Location bar.

target
: This attribute takes as its value the name of the window, tab, or frame in which the destination of the link should load. It is unsupported in Strict DTDs, which relegate the associated functionality to the site's behavior layer. This attribute is also a vital component of links that exist in the context of a `frame`, which is discussed in Chapter 14.

rel
: As with `link` elements, this attribute briefly describes the relationship between the current document and the destination of the link. Its most common use in hyperlinks appends the custom value `"nofollow"`, which signals to search engine crawler agents that the destination URI link should not be indexed. The `"nofollow"` facility was created by Google as a means for site operators to ensure that spam links in their user-generated content are assigned null weight in result ranking algorithms. It should be noted that with the possible exception of `"nofollow"`, the `rel` attribute as used in hyperlinks does not have any universally agreed-upon values.

There are also universal attributes, among which `title` is especially relevant to links.

Virtuous Use of the href Attribute

Since they're so ubiquitous, `href` attributes are easy to overlook—you supply their values, then move on. However, there are four principles that should be followed when creating links:

Accuracy
: Input errors and links have a long, sick, and twisted relationship, so it's critical to proofread and activate links in staged copy *before* a site is put into production.

Validity
: URIs are structured according to a detailed specification (IETF RFC 2396, *http://www.ietf.org/rfc/rfc2396.txt*) that guides how their contents should be arranged. Certain characters within URIs need to be escaped if valid documents are a priority; this escaping process is called *URL encoding* and is discussed in "The Fine Print of URL Encoding: ASCII Entities" on page 248.

Currency
: Over time, web documents have a tendency to disappear or move, which results in a phenomenon known as "link rot." Good web citizenship insists that site

operators set up redirects or other fallbacks for documents that they move, clobber, or put out of reach—but sadly, good web citizenship is actually uncommon. In any case, *someone* needs to take responsibility for checking the currency of links; I recommend that *deliberate* currency checks be performed once per quarter, if at all possible. Problems and solutions related to link currency—for example, the feasibility of automated link checks—are discussed on this book's companion website.

Brevity

Unless Search Engine Optimization (SEO) is a concern, `href` values should be kept as short as possible without obscuring all hints about the nature of the destination content. Shorter `href` values result in increased markup legibility and a reduction in the likelihood of input errors.

Linking to Specific Passages Within Documents

Readers whose knowledge of HTML is based principally on dated sources will be familiar with the `name` attribute, which is discussed at length in Chapter 14. Current practice lends greater simplicity and meaning to inline link destinations by relying on `id` values, so that:

```
<a href="http://www.example.com/docs/swallow_airspeed.html#european" ... > ...
```

will cause the browser to automatically scroll to the element with the `id` value of `european` if the link is activated and if `swallow_airspeed.html` finishes loading.

If visitors need to know that such a link destination exists (e.g., "permalinks"), one popular approach that works in most current browsers is to add a "self-link" at the end of its immediate block-level parent, populate that link with a consistently used symbol, and add styles and markup like the following:

```
        p.containsInlineLink a { color: #fff; } /* same as background color, actually */
    p.containsInlineLink:hover a { color: #999; } /* some contrast, but not as much given
                                                    to the body copy */
    ...
    <p class="containsInlineLink" id="european">The airspeed of an unladen European
    swallow is the subject of extensive speculation, much of it ironic. <a href=
    "#european" title="Permalink to the discussion of the airspeed of an unladen
    European swallow.">&rarr;</a></p>
```

Given this facility, visitors who are familiar with the site can then copy the `href` value of the inline link for insertion into their own web content.

Creating Effective Link Content and title Values

Ideal link content can be difficult to publish for a number of reasons:

- Many links are framed as part of a site's interface rather than its content, which encourages designers to fill links with ideographic content or the briefest of keywords.

- On pages created specifically to facilitate purchases or user account creation, many links will be—for good reason—populated with calls to action (e.g., "click here"), rather than properly descriptive language.

- Sometimes, a site (or part of a site) will be designed around the assumption that the user is able to examine its content in a particular context.

- A designer may choose to use a logo or some other image for link content.

When such circumstances can be avoided, the best link content attains three of the four virtues described for `href` values: brevity, accuracy, and currency, in that order.

The frequent circumstances that make fully descriptive links impossible will lead you to the `title` attribute, which is particularly helpful to users of assistive technology.

Working from the scenarios just given, effective link `title` values might appear respectively, as follows:

Interface keywords

```
<a href="/contact/"
title="Telephone numbers, e-mail addresses, and driving directions.">Contact</a>
```

Calls to action

```
...To add your name to our mailing list, <a href="/promo/signup.php"
title="Mailing list signup form.">click here</a>.
```

Single context

```
<a href="/gallery.php?user=persist1&imgfile=DSC2112.JPG"
title="See 'Playing Frisbee' in Ben's 'Day at the Dog Park' photoset."><img
src="/persist1/images/DSC2111.JPG" alt="A Shih Tzu makes scary faces at
the camera." class="lggallerypic" /></a>
```

Logo image as link content

```
<h4>This item is available at:</h4>
<ul>
...
  <li><a href="http://www.powells.com/" title="Buy this item at powells.com.">
  <img src="/images/powells_logotype.png" alt="Powells.com" /></a></li>
```

Take special notice of the "calls to action" example, which actually *relies* upon the link's `title` value for context. The copywriting technique used here is frequently held up as an example of something to *avoid*, but even so, effective landing pages *need* to

---

contain succinct calls to action. If possible, copywriters should try to find concise alternatives to "click here."

An additional benefit of the `title` attribute is that conscientious use allows a document's content and outgoing links to be summarized programmatically. Just as headings speak for the broader structure of a document, the values of `title` attributes can speak for content at even finer levels of detail.

Along with the benefits discussed here, the `title` attribute also carries some limitations. The most significant is its inaccessibility to users who rely on the keyboard for page navigation, which can only be repaired (after a fashion) with custom JavaScript. For this reason and others, content critical to reader comprehension should always be presented in plain view.

Styling Links

As the elements that most readily respond to user interactivity—even without the benefit of scripting—links deserve a proportionally large amount of a stylist's attention.

When rendered with user agent styles, links suffer from two serious flaws:

- The colors assigned to links by default are at worst unattractive, and at best ill-suited to most color palettes.
- As inline-level elements, links only occupy as much canvas area as needed. If there's no graceful way to fill important links with ideal amounts of content, they can be difficult for users to find and activate, or disruptively large and ragged.

Because of their interactivity, links require greater effort to style than most elements. Much of this effort relies on rules written around pseudoclasses.

Link Pseudoclasses

Because links can express several states, it's logical but not really feasible to assign styles to links with the element selector alone.

To account for the various link states, CSS offers the `:link`, `:visited`, `:hover`, and `:active` pseudoclasses. The first two describe usable links and those that point to already-visited destinations, respectively; the latter two describe the link under the mouse pointer, and that same link while the primary mouse button is depressed.

In a stylesheet, selectors with common scope that include these pseudoclasses should apply them in the order `:link`–`:visited`–`:hover`–`:active`, all preceded by the analogous rule that lacks pseudoclasses. I suggest the following mnemonic: Life's Very Hurried Always.

The reason for this ordering follows the rules of selector weight—specifically the rule that selectors with equal weight are given priority in reverse source order. Links are unvisited at first, but that changes—and in any case neither state involves a hovering mouse pointer. Chances are that you want hover states to stand out from the others, and of course a link can't be activated by a pointer unless it's already in a hover state.

If you were to consider the *negative* case and place the pseudoclass-oriented rules in the *reverse* of the suggested order, the hover and active states would always be ignored by the rendering engine, because in that order the "usable" state takes priority over the "hover" and "active" states, even when one of the latter states is true.

There are no special constraints on the validity of property/value pairs that are assigned to rules defined with selectors that contain pseudoclasses.

There is one important exception to the normal expectations of selector priority. If a property is set in a rule that references a *without* any pseudoclasses, conflicting references to that property in rules *with* pseudoclasses in their selectors will not be applied in Firefox and Internet Explorer. In other words, if you apply a `{ color: #00f; }`, then `a:visited { color: #808; }` will be ignored. If `a:link { color: #00f; }` is supplied instead, then the `a:visited` rule is *not* ignored.

Finally, CSS specifies the `:focus` pseudoclass, to be applied when an element is in active focus but is not actually being activated. This is also unsupported in all versions of Internet Explorer before IE 8. The `:focus` use case arises when the visitor relies on a keyboard, or drags the mouse pointer off a link mid-click. When used, it should fall between the `:hover` and `:active` selectors.

Using display: block to Increase the Footprint of a Link

When a link is part of a site's interface (i.e., navigation) or is intended to convey a call to action, implementing a button-like behavior can be a useful interface enhancement.

The relationship between link interactivity and the cursor is also discussed briefly in "Disabling links to the current document" on page 67.

The first step in achieving this effect is to assign `display: block` to the link. With the link's `display` value changed, the balance of formatting is handled with the `width` and `height` elements for basic dimensions, and perhaps the `padding` property or the various background properties (via Fahrner Image Replacement) for formatting (see "Bitmapped Copy and Fahrner Image Replacement" on page 157).

Before composing such interface-style links, the stylist needs to take the following conditions into account:

Container `display` *value*
> To produce the desired behavior, these links need to be placed within elements with a `display` value of `block` or `inline-block`.

Static versus flexible layouts

Background images (whether for backgrounds alone, or as part of Fahrner Image Replacement need little attention to positioning in static layouts. In proportional or grid layouts, however, they are best centered within their containing link.

Calculating link dimensions

In the simplest case, links can be assigned a `height` of `100%`. If finer attention to detail is called for, a link's dimensions, borders (if present), and padding can be calculated and assigned separately.

Link formatting techniques are also discussed in the context of navigation in Chapters 5 and 7, and the behavior of the cursor property is demonstrated on this book's companion website.

Styling :hover and :active Links

When you're starting to work with CSS, it can be tempting to change the weight, text size, or dimensions of links that are in the midst of user-initiated events.

In a word: *don't*. Styles that change the footprint of an element without warning turn the entire page layout into a moving target, which can frustrate user attempts to interact with (or even merely follow) the page.

This rule can be relaxed if both links and their surrounding content are reliably anchored to static points in the layout, but excellent results in this regard require high levels of training and experience from both designers and developers.

The text-decoration Property

On certain occasions, it can be useful to place lines under, over, or through brief passages.

The `text-decoration` property supports the following values:

`underline`
The default value for the `a` and `ins` elements

`line-through`
The default value for the `del` attribute

`overline`
The counterpart to `underline`; rarely used

The `blink` value is also referenced in CSS 2.1 but is only supported by Firefox, and only if it's deliberately enabled via the `about:config` pane.

The cursor Property

CSS provides an interface to its host operating system's library of mouse pointer objects via the cursor property, the default value of which is auto. Custom values include:

- default (the arrow pointer)
- pointer (the default for links)
- crosshair
- text (the default for plain-text content)
- help
- progress
- wait

Of these, the help pointer is most often used to cue the visitor to wait for an element's associated tool tip to appear. It can also be used to indicate links that point to Frequently Asked Questions and other visitor support resources.

Custom uses for the other values are best confined to web applications, and the efficacy of those custom uses should be verified through user testing.

Adding Semantic Value with Inline Elements

In addition to links, there are a number of other inline elements that can lend nuances of meaning to content. These elements are summarized in Table 8-1.

Table 8-1. A survey of HTML 4 inline elements

Element	Long name	"Presentation" equivalent	Notes
em	emphasis	i, u	
strong	strong emphasis	b	
cite	source citation	i	Applied to titles of books, periodicals, broadcast program series, and long form audio/visual media, but not to other proper names
code	code passage	tt	*cf.* kbd, samp
kbd	user-supplied keyboard input	tt	
samp	program output sample	tt	According to the HTML 4.01 specification, distinguished from code by the fact that code content implies executability, while samp refers to program output
abbr	abbreviation	[none]	
acronym	acronym	[none]	Acronyms and abbreviations expand in mutually exclusive ways; acronyms are formatted differently from one country to the next

Element	Long name	"Presentation" equivalent	Notes
sup	superscript	[none]	Best assigned an infinitesimal `line-height` value
sub	subscript	[none]	
ins	insertion	[none]	Styled with an underline, by default
del	deletion	strike	Best followed by content within `ins`, in cases where "backspace and overstrike" is implied
q	inline quote	[none]	Behavior varies by user agent; prefer `blockquote` for long quoted passages
var	variable; irrational number	i	E.g., $2\pi r$, $(\sin^2\theta + \cos^2\theta) = 1$
dfn	definition	i and em (in context)	Marks up terms that are presented *inline* to their definition, as a complement to definition lists ("Definition Lists" on page 124); especially effective when assigned an `id` value for the purpose of being a link destination unto itself

Most of the elements in Table 8-1 are fairly straightfoward, once their user agent styles are taken into account. Two in particular take no user agent styles at all, and deserve special attention: `abbr` and `acronym`.

As mentioned previously (see "Creating Effective Link Content and title Values" on page 136), users will sometimes find themselves viewing web content out of context. This becomes an issue when using abbreviations and acronyms, which often run to the technical (or colloquial) and pose a mystery to site visitors who aren't familiar with their contexts, to the point of making site copy incomprehensible.

On the other hand, if you include clues to the expansions of acronyms and abbreviations by using effective `title` values, copy becomes more accessible to all comers. In recent versions of Firefox, the following rules are included in the user agent stylesheet:

```
acronym, abbr { border-bottom: 1px dotted; }
```

It's accepted, if somewhat rare, to add `cursor: help` to rules like this one. The benefits of this practice are explained in "The cursor Property" on page 140.

The support state of the `abbr` and `acronym` elements is described in Table 8-2.

Table 8-2. Support state of the abbr and acronym elements as of Q2 2009

Element	Features	IE 6	IE 7	IE 8	FF 2	FF 3	Safari 3	Safari 4
abbr	DOM		✓	✓	✓	✓	✓	✓
	Styles	✓	✓	✓	✓	✓		✓
acronym	DOM	✓	✓	✓	✓	✓	✓	✓
	Styles		✓	✓	✓	✓		✓

Quotations

HTML provides the inline-level q and block-level blockquote elements for quotations. The HTML 4.01 specification declares that these elements are supposed to support the cite attribute, which is meant to store a URI that qualifies as a primary source. In practice, this requirement is ignored by all browsers except Internet Explorer 8, and thus forces user-facing citations to be crammed into the cite and a elements. However, for the sake of preserving metadata, the URI values that are valid for the cite attribute should still be provided.

The blockquote element has three salient characteristics: user agent styles apply a discernible margin-left value to it, quotation marks must be added deliberately to its content, and Strict DTDs require that it contain at least one block element (usually a paragraph).

Quotation markup provides only limited support for the :before and :after pseudoelements, which are unsupported by all versions of Internet Explorer except 8. In browsers that *do* support :before and :after pseudoelements, opening and closing quotes are specified by the user agent stylesheet for the content of the q element; in no current environment is the blockquote element likewise endowed. To *add* typographically appropriate quotation marks to blockquote elements in those browsers, you should add the following lines to a style block:

```
blockquote:before { content: open-quote; }
blockquote:after { content: close-quote; }
```

The :before and :after pseudoelements are used as a matter of course in the same fashion as they're used for the q element; without the content property, they're useless. As much to the point, the content property can only be applied with these selectors.

content values can also be used to nullify user agent defaults like those set for the q element, which leaves content producers free to reintroduce literal characters into content. This production method is more labor-intensive, but improves compatibility with the requirements of assistive technology.

The content property itself consistently takes as its value open-quote, close-quote, or an arbitrary quoted string of ASCII characters. Higher-bit characters, literal generic quotes, and encoded newlines need to be escaped, a requirement explained in detail in Chapter 14.

CHAPTER 9

Colors and Backgrounds

Most of us take color for granted. For web professionals, it's a big heap of details. Experienced developers need to know how to relate color data to their literal counterparts, and the body of related knowledge gets trickier and more subjective from there. Web color is about the numbers *and* the art, and it never hurts to understand the two together.

Backgrounds offer challenges of their own. Assigning a flat background color to an element is a straightforward task, but once images enter the picture the implementation questions start to multiply.

 This book doesn't cover web color and graphics in depth, but there are plenty of good resources out there. A number of sites are linked from this book's companion site (*http://www.htmlcssgoodparts.net*). I also recommend the following books:

- *Web Style Guide*, Third Edition, by Sarah Horton and Patrick Lynch (Yale University Press)
- *Painting the Web* (*http://oreilly.com/catalog/9780596515096/*) by Shelley Powers (O'Reilly)

Color Theory and Web Color Practice

The CSS 2.1 properties that can take color values are the various background and border properties. There's also the `color` property, which sets the text and underline colors of the elements to which it is applied.

Usability, Accessibility, and Color

When assigning colors and background colors to two elements, adhere to the following:

- Where `background` or `background-color` is used in a stylesheet rule, `color` should follow—and a background color reference should always precede a `color` value. This prevents odd user agent or user stylesheet defaults from making copy illegible.

- Where background images are used, a compatible background color should be assigned deliberately, also for reasons of legibility.

- Accessibility is maximized when there's significant contrast between the foreground and background colors of an element, particularly with respect to brightness.

You should also consider the visual acuity of older site visitors. As people age, the structures of the eye become less adaptable, making it more difficult to discern detail and color. This loss is especially noticeable at close ranges, and is the result of a condition called *presbyopia*.

Color blindness is another vision condition that can be accommodated by the creation of high-contrast designs. Consider the following:

- The most prevalent form of color blindness by far is red-green color blindness, which is experienced by at least 7% of American men (HHMI, 2002).

- The functional effect of color blindness is to render certain wavelengths of light completely dark. Much as infrared and ultraviolet wavelengths of light cannot be detected directly by the human eye, color-blind visitors are likewise deficient with respect to bands of the ordinarily visible spectrum.

- Red-deficient visitors see ordinarily red hues with a strong blue or green tint, while green-deficient visitors will see ordinarily green hues with a strong red or blue tint. In cases where the deficiency is total, all evidence of the color at issue is absent from the sufferer's vision, which can also affect the brightness of the remaining colors.

- The remaining wavelengths that are visible to the color-blind can still combine into something they will perceive as white light; however, the range of light so perceived will be broader than for visitors with normal color vision. The inverse is true with respect to black.

Links to color-blindness simulators and other contrast evaluation resources are available on this book's companion site.

The Additive Color Model

Additive color is named for the process of steady addition of materials. It's the model taught in art instruction, since it applies to paints and other pigments. When applied to a white or off-white medium, approximately blue, red, and yellow pigments are mixed to create other hues, so that:

- blue + red = purple
- blue + yellow = green
- red + yellow = orange

To these a black or white pigment (classically, charcoal and treated lead, respectively) can be added to create the desired color on a moment's notice. In color printing, the lightness of a color is controlled by pigment (e.g., ink, toner) coverage and saturation.

The HSB Color Model

For the task of rapidly identifying colors in the absence of experience with paints, the HSB (hue, saturation, and brightness) model is the most accessible. It arranges all of the visible *hues* (from red to violet and everything in between) in descending order of wavelength, usually on a 360-degree scale since there are three primary colors. In HSB notation 0° refers to red, 120° to green, and 240° to blue.

When identifying colors according to their HSB values, the important rules to remember are:

- Hue values progress *through the rainbow*, with red at the lowest end and violet (in application, hot pink) at the highest.
- Saturation values progress from neutral to the most intense hue possible at a given position on the color wheel; to yield white or any shade of gray, the saturation value *must* be zero.
- Brightness values progress from zero to 100%. A brightness value of zero always yields black, but a brightness value of 100% can yield white or any variety of colors.

The Subtractive Color Model

In the United States the additive color model is taught in grade school, and the subtractive color model is taught in high school physics. That fact by itself should give you some idea of the subtractive color model's underlying complexity.

In the physical world, all visible light is reflected. Where a pigment is present (whether deliberately laid on a substrate, naturally present on a surface, or created by a natural process), it *absorbs* all wavelengths of light that *don't* correspond to its color. The darker or more saturated the color, the less light it reflects—thus the term "subtractive."

Modern display hardware works through emission rather than reflection, however. A cathode ray tube (CRT) or liquid crystal diode (LCD) projects a given pixel in narrow red, green, or blue wavelength bands, at varying levels of intensity. White is the result when all three channels are at maximum intensity, while black is displayed when all three channels are at minimum intensity. If two channels are active at full intensity, the secondary colors are displayed:

- red + green = yellow
- green + blue = cyan
- blue + red = magenta

Colors that are neither primary nor secondary are yielded when all three color channels are at different levels of intensity.

The 24-bit color space currently supported by web browsers' CSS implementations gives the stylist access to more than 16 million colors, based on 256 intensity graduations of each channel. The closer the aggregate color value is to zero—i.e., rgb(0,0,0)— the darker the color. The values of the 256 grays are easy to distinguish because their channel values are always equal.

More detailed demonstrations of subtractive color are provided on this book's companion website.

Design, Contrast, and Complements

A well-designed site is typically founded on the basis of design briefs and requirements documents, which are drafted to summarize many of the known facts and opinions about likely visitor and business objectives. The *functional* nature of design is a significant driver of the process: unlike fine art, effective graphic design endeavors to communicate concise ideas and help its beholder achieve (or decide upon) concrete goals. Aesthetics do play a vital role in design, but that role is entirely in the service of communicating the ideas behind a design.

Ideally, once briefs are in hand and there's some agreement on how a site will be built, motifs and other design guidelines are determined, keeping in mind the expectations of customers and vendors in addition to visitor and business goals.

A significant visual component of any site design (and its underlying motifs) is its *palette*: the colors used by the design to communicate ideas. Palettes almost always have at least three colors or grays: foreground, background, and accent colors. Palettes of six colors or more are not unheard of.

In the discussion of vision dysfunction, it was mentioned that contrast is desirable. This fact also holds true for users with full visual acuity. To obtain high contrast, oftentimes designers will choose *complements* for foreground and background colors. Complements can be defined broadly in terms of hues, or precisely in terms of colors; given a hue, its complement is found at the opposite end of the color wheel defined by the HSB model—yellow is the complement of blue, for example. Complementary colors account for saturation and brightness as well, and can be found in the subtractive model by inverting a color's channel values as demonstrated in Table 9-1.

Table 9-1. Examples of complementary colors, as defined by the subtractive/RGB model

Base color			Complement		
Red	Green	Blue	Red	Green	Blue
255	255	255	0	0	0
255	255	0	0	0	255
51	102	153	204	153	102
43	61	21	212	194	234
143	34	69	112	221	186
192	114	12	63	141	243

"Inverse" refers to the value obtained when the first value is subtracted from 255 (the maximum decimal value for a single channel in 24-bit color). If you look at the two values for each channel in a given row, you'll notice that they create a sum of 255.

Identifying Colors, in Brief

It's possible to get the hang of identifying colors on sight, both from display and from stylesheet rule fragments. Unfortunately, plain old practice is the only way to do it; all you can gain here is general guidance:

- An experienced eye can look at a six-digit hexadecimal color value and break it into three channels without effort.
- The ability to convert hexadecimal numbers into decimal numbers in one's head is nice, but hardly necessary. If you can get used to the idea of A, B, C, D, E, and F as numbers, you'll do fine. To paraphrase Tom Lehrer, "Don't panic—base 16 is just like base 10, really...if you've got six extra fingers."
- The higher a color value across all three channels, the brighter it is.
- The greater the aggregate proportional differences between channel values, the greater the saturation of the color.
- Mentally separating the color wheel into subspectra between primary and secondary colors often makes color identification easier; the rest is just arithmetic.
- When all else fails, use an eyedropper tool, copy, and paste.

A Firefox extension called ColorZilla (*https://addons.mozilla.org/en-US/firefox/addon/271*), shown in Figure 9-1, can help. Once installed, ColorZilla places a hotspot at the left edge of the Firefox status bar that turns the mouse pointer into an eyedropper tool when clicked. Macintosh users can also run a comparable (albeit less usable) application called DigitalColor Meter, found in the Utilities folder.

Figure 9-1. ColorZilla activates an eyedropper tool, allowing you to sample and copy colors

Display Environments and the Web-Safe Palette

The passage about CSS Units (see "CSS Units" on page 33) covers the variability of display pitches in the wild and explains how to include color values in a stylesheet, but says nothing about the likely results.

Every display technology in existence reproduces color according to assumptions about the environment in which it will be used. The faithfulness of a display's color reproduction is influenced by its era of manufacture, quality of components, and quality of assembly.

Because of these display variances, most people will see mostly inaccurate colors, most of the time. This raises the profile of three-digit hexadecimal color values, of which a tiny fraction comprise the range of the *web-safe palette*. To create so-called web-safe colors, use the channel intensities described in Table 9-2.

Table 9-2. "Web-safe" channel values

Hexadecimal	8-bit decimal	Percentage[a]
00	0	0%
33	51	20%
66	102	40%
99	153	60%
cc	204	80%
ff	255	100%

[a] Provided here for reference; though originally slated for implementation as part of CSS1, percentage values never caught on.

The web-safe palette first got its name because its space of 216 colors was the domain most likely to be reproduced faithfully by the weak graphics hardware of the 1990s. Today, the web-safe palette is still relevant, but for an entirely different reason: older consumer-grade LCD displays are incapable of reproducing the full depth of 24-bit gradients (see Figure 9-2).

HD-capable monitors and CRT displays connected to capable graphics hardware usually do not suffer from the same color reproduction deficits as cheaper LCD displays, but are used by only half of the developed world's web user base, *at best*.

The challenges of faithful color reproduction also affect images and their embedded color profiles (see "Working with Color Profiles" on page 185).

Creating Your Own Palettes

If you're doing commissioned work or working full-time for an established company, there's an excellent chance that at least two of your palette colors have already been chosen for you. There are two popular-yet-systematic methods for making the balance of your choices: relying on math, and using found colors.

The "math" approach creates what are called dyads, triads, and tetrads: sets of hues with obvious relationships to an original color. In the case of triads, one can suppose that two palette colors have already been chosen. For this example, let's assume hues close to the ever-popular blue and green—205° and 105°, which are more or less teal and chartreuse.

The angle that bisects those two is 155°, where the hue is described as an aquamarine or sea green. Either this hue or its complement (335°, violet) can be used for the third hue in the triad. The challenges that remain are to choose a color in that hue that has compatible saturation and brightness, and to integrate that color into your design.

Figure 9-2. Older consumer-grade LCD displays do a poor job of representing gradients

The most popular alternative to playing with angles is to use found colors. In this approach, you take an attractive photo, use an eyedropper tool to take colors from it, and decide for yourself which of those colors will make the most desirable palette.

The subject of palette creation is discussed in much greater detail on this book's companion website.

CSS Backgrounds

You can use CSS background images in many places. If it has an element box, you can almost always apply a background to it.

The best place to start is with a survey of the CSS properties that affect background appearance, shown in Table 9-3.

Table 9-3. CSS background properties (default values shown in boldface)

Property	Purpose	Values
`background`	Shorthand property, aggregates property/value pairs	
`background-attachment`	Prevents backgrounds of elements with scroll bars from scrolling along with content	• `fixed` • **`scroll`**
`background-color`	Defines the background color	• [color] • **`transparent`**
`background-image`	Specifies the background image to be applied to the element, which will be stacked *over* any background color	• **`none`** • [url]
`background-position`	Contains horizontal and vertical values separated by a space; defines the relationship between the edges of the element and the edges of a background image	• [length] • [percentage] • `bottom` • `center` • `left` • `right` • `top`
`background-repeat`	Specifies the axes along which the background image should repeat, if at all	• `no-repeat` • **`repeat`** • `repeat-x` • `repeat-y`

Setting background-position Values

When a `background-position` value is provided, it should contain two components: the left offset and the top offset. When length units such as `px` or `em` are used, the results are straightforward: the background image is offset to the element coordinates specified. If any of the values are negative, the top-left corner of the "first" instance of the background image will be laid out of view.

If percentage or keyword values are used instead, the behavior of the `background-position` property changes. Instead of placing the image a specific distance from the upper-left corner of its element, the rendering engine lines up the stated coordinate of the image with the stated coordinate of the element. A value of `33% 33%` will align the image coordinates one-third from its upper left corner with the same coordinates of the element. This "mutual alignment" is diagrammed in Figure 9-3.

The keyword values of the `background-position` property correspond exactly to values of zero, `50%`, and `100%`, each as called for.

For designers who want to utilize the Rule of Thirds or the Golden Ratio in their designs, this approach can pose real challenges. For example, what if the image in Figure 9-3 ought to be *centered* at the `33%` coordinates?

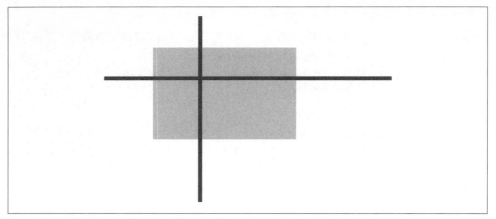

Figure 9-3. A background image with its background-position value set to 33% 33%; lines were added for illustration purposes

The only effective way to meet this challenge is to fix the dimensions of your layout, which carries challenges of its own and probably isn't worth it, if your only goal is to put background images exactly where you want them.

CSS3 calls for a `background-size` property, but this is currently unsupported by the mass-market web browsers.

The CSS background Shorthand Property

Just as `margin`, `border`, `padding`, and `font` are all shorthand properties, so is `background`. Its values are space-separated, in the following order:

```
background-color background-image background-repeat background-position
background-attachment
```

Like the other shorthand properties, `background` is a wonderful space-saver, but has one severe drawback: when individual values are omitted from a reference to the `background` property, the results can be inconsistent.

Composing Background Images

As it turns out, *composing* background images can be even more challenging than putting them into production on a website. For starters, there are a number of different *types* of background images, as shown in Figure 9-4, which poses its own technical challenges.

"Faux Columns"

Faux Columns are wide and narrow bands of color, one of which might actually be transparent. In the discussion of multicolumn layouts (see "Implementing Multicolumn Layouts" on page 88), it was pointed out that *forcing* an element to

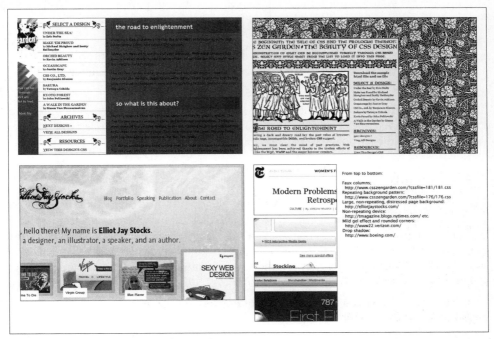

Figure 9-4. Popular styles for background images

expand to the height of its contents is not strictly impossible, but often more trouble than it's worth. If a column container is assigned a background image that mimics those columns, the result is a convenient illusion.

In cases where the heights of the columns in a layout can't be predicted with any certainty, this technique might also be used to place vertical rules between columns, as an alternative to using the `border-left` or `border-right` properties.

Background textures and patterns

Textured and distressed backgrounds are brilliantly popular—more so in some years than others—because they lend a flavor of wear to a design, as if to say that the associated content claims great longevity or justifies heavy use. These might consist of tiled (repeating elements), or be composed as single large images.

Nonrepeating motifs and devices

Devices are usually far less detailed than patterns, and are typically anchored to a corner of the browser canvas.

Drop shadows and gel effects

Drop shadows give an element the appearance of being closer to the visitor than the surrounding canvas, and have enjoyed the same kind of popularity as textured backgrounds. Gel effects are often used on links and buttons—especially on sites operated by companies that self-identify as being part of the "Web 2.0" movement—and require similar image composition techniques.

Rounded corners

While the composition techniques used to create rounded corners are entirely different from those used for drop shadows, the implementation challenges they impose on stylists are not.

To these background implementations we can add bitmapped copy, which is often "typeset" with a technique called Fahrner Image Replacement, discussed in "Bitmapped Copy and Fahrner Image Replacement" on page 157.

"Faux Columns"

Consider a two-column design with variable-height columns. Regardless of the CSS rules that you use to implement the layout, one challenge remains constant: one column will almost certainly have less content than the other. Using `... { overflow: auto; height: 1%; }` on the element containing the columns gives you another element to which you can usefully apply backgrounds, but the original challenge remains: making it appear to the visitor as if there are two (or more) full-height columns in your layout.

When you are presented with a requirement for two columns that have a banded background behind them, follow these steps:

1. Assign `... { overflow: auto; height: 1%; }` to your column container. This step isn't strictly *necessary*, but increases the flexibility with which you can approach the layout markup.

2. The background image should always be wider than your layout, to account for rounding errors, user-initiated changes to the browsing environment, and future layout tweaks. The actual width will vary according to the characteristics of your layout, and the means by which you're applying the background image to the layout. If you're using one of the flexible layout approaches, you'll probably want to make your background image *considerably* larger than the intended width of your layout.

3. To conserve bandwidth, background images that effect patterns should be no taller than needed to produce the desired tiling effect.

4. In most cases you'll want to calculate the *proportional* width of your columns, unless you intend for one column to assume a static width at all times without regard to user manipulation of the browsing environment.

5. Paint/fill your bands proportionally for flexible layouts. For layouts with at least one fixed column, calculate the width of the band corresponding to the fixed column by adding the column width (in pixels) and the bleed width. In cases where you're applying a custom full-height rule rather than column bands, simply place that rule at the X-coordinate where color bands would normally meet.

6. Your supplemental property/value pairs should work out as follows:

`background-color`
> In most cases, the background color should be the same as the color intended for the most prominent column.

`background-repeat`
> If you want to be cautious, `repeat-y` is recommended.

`background-position`
> Apply a similar X value (the first of the two provided here) to the one you used to decide on the width of the color bands in the image, whether static or proportional. In the case of fixed layouts, that value will be the inverse of the bleed, so that a bleed of five pixels would yield `background-position: -5px 0`.

Normally, your column background won't contain any transparent pixels, and the `background-color` of your column container will be assigned to suit the colors used in the primary column. The only likely exception to this practice arises when column colors are used as a location cue; in many of those cases, resources can be conserved by using a single background image that utilizes transparent pixels in the "adaptive" column, and relegating that column's `background-color` to the stylesheet rules that address the column container (on a location-by-location basis).

This advice works well for two-column layouts, but three-column variable-width layouts provide additional challenges. (Fixed-width backgrounds can usually be confined to the `body` element.) In instances where a three-column layout needs three distinct background bands, you'll be applying *two* background images: one to the `body` or the broadest container element, and another to the intercolumn container (explained in Chapter 6). The steps just suggested can then be executed twice in succession.

Tiled Background Textures and Patterns

The default behavior of background images is to tile themselves across and down the browser canvas, with top and left edges flush to the top and left edges of the affected element box.

Tiled backgrounds are more difficult to create from asymmetrical source images, but offer the advantage of reduced bandwidth. To create and apply them, Adobe Photoshop users can use the following (zoom- and squint-heavy) process:

1. Apply Filters → Other → Offset to *center* the "seams" that result from the source image's lack of symmetry. These seams should form the illusion of a cross.
2. Abut your source image with two duplicates (one on each axis). Use of a custom grid (View → Grid → Snap To → Grid) will take much of the tedium out of this task.
3. Merge the three copies of the source image into a single layer.
4. Use a combination of clone, healing, smudge, and move tools to obscure the seams. Avoid Blur filters, which create as many problems as they solve unless they're only

applied to a tiny area of the image. Your tool choice will come about as a result of experimentation and experience.

This step should first be performed on the regions where the seams intersect with the edges of your source image. Some of those repairs will apply only to the duplicates; paste and merge those repairs into the corresponding regions of the original.

5. Crop your working image back to its original size.

6. Repeat step 2–4 on the seams in the central region of the image. Plan on frequent use of the Undo command and History palette.

7. Save the image, upload it, and apply it to the element. The remaining user agent default styles for backgrounds should be adequate to the task.

Images that *are* symmetrical should still be offset, either at creation, or with the `background-position` property. Otherwise, "rivers" of negative space will appear along the top and left edges of the element.

Large Background Textures and Nonrepeating Devices

Larger background images can be adapted from existing stock with a minimum of effort, but usually consume logarithmically larger amounts of bandwidth. The trick to working with large backgrounds is to find the best compromise between image file size, image dimensions, and useful detail; the first of these is always reduced at the expense of the other two.

When the background in question is applied to the `body` element, the challenge of compromise grows still more difficult, since the dimensions of your background image need to be *at least* 1680×1050 pixels. Dimensions of 1920×1200 pixels will cover all but a tiny fraction of use cases.

Except in those rare cases where your large background image is either several times taller than the element to which it is applied, or carefully mated to an element with certainly fixed dimensions, the related stylesheet rule fragment should resemble the following:

```
#foo {
  background-image: url(/my/path/bar.ext);
  background-attachment: fixed;
  background-position: 50% 50%; }
```

If you create a background image that incorporates a device (e.g., an ideogram, geometric shape, famous public domain illustration, or some part of the site sponsor's visual identity), it will almost certainly be smaller than a texture. The composition of this background image and the CSS associated with it should follow the guidelines below:

• Apply more contrast than you would to a texture, but not so much that the legibility of overlying content is compromised.

- If the size of the background image is far smaller than the footprint of its element, anchor it to one edge or corner of that element; the results will be more predictable.

- In most cases, `background-attachment: fixed` will be most appropriate.

- Safeguard the content legibility of an element with a bottom-fixed background image by setting that element's `padding-bottom` value roughly equal to the native height of your background image.

Drop Shadows, Gel Effects, and Rounded Corners

To create drop shadows, gel effects, and rounded corners, Photoshop users can use the Effects dialog of the Layers palette, or a tedious combination of tools and filters.

These three background effects are discussed separately from others because the designer who employs them relies on a fixed-width layout, pushes corners of drop shadows across the visible margin of the layout (usually the top and bottom of the browser canvas), or likely forces the stylist to write junk markup.

The reality behind these choices points back to one of the fundamental characteristics of element flow: it's *impossible* to predict the height of any element other than a plug-in instance or an image with any certainty. Since background images can't be arbitrarily scaled by current browsers, effects that *need* to appear at predictable layout coordinates (i.e., corners, as is the case with rounded corners and the corner regions of drop shadows) within an element of unpredictable dimensions must be placed *one at a time*. The markup and styles used for rounded corners are described at the beginning of "Habit #1: Keeping It Simple" on page 50, as part of a negative demonstration of the value of simplicity.

Firefox and Safari support their own CSS extensions to specify rounded corners (`-moz-border-radius` and `-webkit-border-radius`, respectively), but Internet Explorer offers nothing similar. The unextended `border-radius` property is specified by CSS3.

Bitmapped Copy and Fahrner Image Replacement

Chapter 12 discusses the wilderness of letterforms at a minute level of detail. Two hazards of this wilderness are relevant to any discussion of background images: the narrow range of universally available typefaces for use on the Web, and the benefits gained by heavily anti-aliasing instances of large type.

Inline and background images guarantee designers' access to attractive web typography, a state of affairs that has held true since web browsers began supporting inline images in 1993. In the first half of 2002, several CSS experts (myself included) independently worked out techniques that made it possible to move bitmapped type out of markup and into stylesheets. The application of the simplest of these techniques is summarized in Figure 9-5. Collectively these techniques are called Fahrner Image

Replacement (FIR), in honor of Todd Fahrner, an early pioneer of applied CSS who was among the first to work out and publicize the underlying ideas.

Lorem ipsum dolor sit amet

Consectetur adipiscing elit. Curabitur id lectus vel leo sagittis molesti mi ac leo porta pellentesque. Vestibulum dolor nibh, commodo a alic tincidunt. Sed vel massa turpis. Cras hendrerit euismod quam, non ali

Lorem ipsum dolor sit amet

Consectetur adipiscing elit. Curabitur id lectus vel leo sagittis molesti mi ac leo porta pellentesque. Vestibulum dolor nibh, commodo a alic tincidunt. Sed vel massa turpis. Cras hendrerit euismod quam, non ali

Lorem ipsum dolor sit amet

Consectetur adipiscing elit. Curabitur id lectus vel leo sagittis molesti mi ac leo porta pellentesque. Vestibulum dolor nibh, commodo a alic tincidunt. Sed vel massa turpis. Cras hendrerit euismod quam, non ali fringilla sapien ultrices a. Etiam adipiscing dignissim posuere. In id aug

Figure 9-5. The three steps from a plain heading to a FIR-enhanced heading, (1) shows the plain heading, (2) shows the heading with its new background image, and (3) shows the final result after a text-indent value has been applied

The basic point to FIR is that an image shouldn't exist in the content layer of a site unless it's *actually* content. How, then, does one retain the benefits of images, while moving the images themselves into the presentation layer where they belong?

The obvious part of the solution is to use the background properties. However, that step alone does nothing for the text that still lives in an element to which FIR is applied. To solve that problem, a stylist must use one of the modalities for moving content out of view, without affecting the composition of the principal element.

The first of these approaches to gain notice was to place a junk `span` within the principal element, then apply `display: none` to it. However, this approach creates a problem of its own: assistive technology platforms parse the `display: none` pair (media type conflicts notwithstanding) and ignore it, just like a browser rendering content for screen display.

Several other junk-markup-dependent approaches to the FIR concept were tested by various developers, each depending on a different means of using CSS (such as visibility and positioning) to move text content out of view. After a while, one developer by the name of Mike Rundle hit on the idea of using the `text-indent` property to move text off-canvas, while another named Russ Weakley suggested hiding tiny (and I mean *tiny*) text against a background of the same color and simultaneously providing enough of a gutter on the edge of the element to render that text completely invisible.

The FIR Stylesheet Rules

The CSS source for the Rundle and Weakley methods, which assumes `<h2>Lorem ipsum dolor sit amet, consectetur adipiscing elit</h2>` and a background image of 30 pixels in height, is displayed below:

```
/* *** Rundle (Phark) Method *** */
h2 {
  height: 30px;
  margin: 0;
  text-indent: -10000px;
  background-image: url(/my/path/foo.ext);
  background-repeat: no-repeat;
}

/* ***     Weakley Method     *** */

h2 {
  height: 1px;
  margin-bottom: -1px;
  padding-top: 30px;
  color: #fff;
  background-color: #fff;
  background-image: url(/my/path/foo.ext);
  background-repeat: no-repeat;
  font-size: 1px;
  line-height: 1;
}
```

The Weakley method is far more verbose, but sidesteps a brutal rendering problem in Internet Explorer 6 that's exposed when `text-indent` is applied to a link with a `float` value: the text itself responds to the `text-indent` value, but the underline doesn't.

It should also be noted that small, obscured text like that employed by the Weakley method, can gain a website a spot on search providers' blacklists when used solely for the sake of Search Engine Optimization (SEO).

Drawbacks of FIR

Fahrner Image Replacement has two major drawbacks: stylists have no control over the appearance of the background images on the printed page (where they probably won't render at all), and the small population of users who run their browsers with images disabled will be at a loss to read copy that you enhance by using FIR.

A lesser concern relating to bitmapped type in general is that most users are unaware that underlying content or `alt` values of bitmapped text can still be copied to the system clipboard. For this reason, content that is at all likely to be copied—such as contact information—should always be presented in normal text, or at least *repeated* in normal text.

Reducing Server Load with Sprites

A year after FIR started to gain notice, the webzine *A List Apart* published an article by Dave Shea that invoked an artifact of 8-bit gaming history: sprites. In retro gaming, these are the groups of images that together form the "landscape" of an older side-scrolling, platform-type, or overhead-view video game, and that are arranged as needed by the console hardware that runs the game.

A similar design approach can be used by stylists to combine several similar background images into a single file, with the goal of reducing server traffic and maintenance requirements.

Sprites have obvious application to navigation links. In many circumstances, site navigation can be exported to combined link and hover state bitmaps exactly as comped.

Consider a navigation setup like the one in Figure 9-6: its various items are set in bitmaps and rendered with the assistance of FIR, because the desired typeface is well outside the families of "web fonts" supported by various operating system vendors.

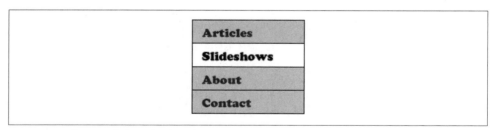

Figure 9-6. The intended result of applying sprites to a navigation list, as described here

The layout of bitmap exports like these can be arbitrary; in a case like this I would probably place the hover state bitmap under the default state bitmap, but you might arrange things differently. The important thing is to record the origin coordinates of each bitmap fragment, which are needed for later use as `background-position` values.

To apply normal state and hover state FIR bitmaps from a single image to a site navigation, proceed through the following steps:

1. Apply the layout to your navigation described in "The Primary Navigation Layout Recipe" on page 122.

2. Set the same `background-image` value for both the list items that contain your navigation links and the hover states of the links themselves. At this point your navigation should display the same bitmapped type in each item (see Figure 9-7).

3. Provide unique `background-position` values for the various normal and hover state rules (e.g., `#nav li { ... }` and `#nav li a:hover { ... }`). The relevant styles used for the demonstration available at this book's companion website are reproduced in this section.

```
             #nav li { background-image: url(/images/bg_nav.gif); }
           #nav li a { display: block; width: 100%; height: 100%; }
             #nav li,
           #nav li a { text-indent: -10000px; }
      #nav li a:link,
   #nav li a:visited { background-image: none; }

   #navAbout { background-position: 0 0; }
 #navContact { background-position: -144px 0; }
   #navForum { background-position: -288px 0; }
 #navGallery { background-position: -432px 0; }

   #navAbout a:hover { background-position: 0 -24px; }
 #navContact a:hover { background-position: -144px -24px; }
   #navForum a:hover { background-position: -288px -24px; }
 #navGallery a:hover { background-position: -432px -24px; }
```

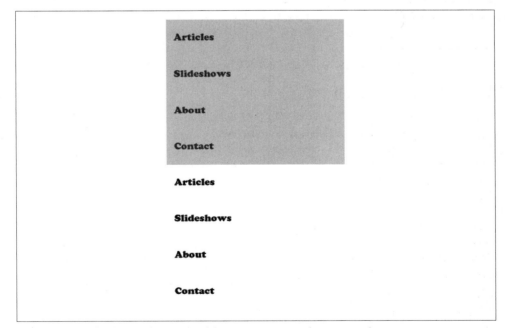

Figure 9-7. The background image used for a sprite-equipped navigation list

CHAPTER 10
(Data) Tables

If you've been doing web design for a few years, chances are good that you own a book that recommends the use of `table` elements for layout. Once upon a time, this was the only reliable page layout mechanism that web browsers offered—and as the discussion of multicolumn layouts suggested (see the section "Implementing Multicolumn Layouts" on page 88), layout tables are comparatively easy to implement.

But in a word, *don't*.

The Disadvantages of Layout Tables

Layout tables offer few unpleasant surprises on launch day, but using them means surrendering opportunities to make your sites more usable and maintainable. Table-based layout might be easier to develop when you first build a new site, but maintenance and extension quickly become major headaches.

Source Order: Square Peg, Round Hole

When you use tables for page layout, you're forced to implement your entire site around the table-rendering algorithm. This algorithm was always intended to display data, and as a result calls for content structure that's better suited to spreadsheets than to documents containing text passages. (Would you write a school paper or an interoffice memo in Microsoft Excel? Didn't think so.)

The first class of users disadvantaged by such an outcome are users of assistive technology, who rely on their tools to make sense of the Web. Since the creators of assistive software cannot read web designers' minds in aggregate, much less singly, table content is displayed in source order. One consequence of this approach is that 15 years after table support was first unleashed on unwary web users, assistive technology users *still* expect to encounter site navigation at the top of the page, regardless of its *real* importance.

On sites where sidebar content is contained in a leftward column, content priority is inverted further. Imagine being *forced* to wade through three hundred disjointed words of tertiary *crap* before you even encounter the title, to say nothing of the body copy, of the article that led you to the site...and you have a small idea of what impaired users deal with every time they use the Web.

CSS Zen Becomes a Myth

When faithfully applied, the paradigm of CSS Zen (see "The Functional Principles of CSS Zen" on page 60) creates unlimited opportunities for quick redesigns. Structurally driven markup and `class`/`id` values make that flexibility possible. In turn, that flexibility drastically reduces implementation time—for example, three of my last four redesigns of henick.net were each executed in a significant fraction of one day.

Even on a *huge* site, careful attention to site structure, page structure, and the virtues of thoughtful overbuilding makes it possible for a team to implement an entirely new look and feel in the space of days.

But when tables are used for layout, *you can't do that*—the design is supposed to embellish the markup, while layout tables *dictate* the markup. The practical consequence is that *any* redesign undertaken with existing markup winds up being confined to colors and accents; new content, deletions of old content, and broad layout changes would force the creation of brand-new site templates.

Template Slavery Is Unavoidable

Unless you use *heaps* of templates on a site, the layout flexibility of table-driven markup trends toward zero. If you work in a larger shop that insists on detailed approval processes, the result is a site design that might as well be etched into stone on launch day. This is categorically frustrating—and what happens if there's some broad problem with the site? Users affected by these problems are the *second* group of disadvantaged users, and failure to respond quickly to their problems with your site can be costly.

Chances are that within weeks of launch, the team that produced a table-based site will take a look at the problems revealed by visitor feedback and start thinking about the *next* design, which will hold the promise of no less travail. In fact, when the time comes for a team to make the leap to CSS, the work will actually be *more* difficult as team members acclimate themselves to the terseness and reference points of CSS.

What better time is there than the present to get *that* over with?

Positioning Is Rendered Useless

If `float` carries most of the hassles in CSS-driven layout, `position` lends many of its virtues.

When you use tables for layout, positioning properties lose practically all of their power. Layout tension, content stacking, and a host of useful layout tweaks are put out of reach. Table layout leaves designers *absolutely* no choice but to think *inside* the box, because the display characteristics of table cells leave no alternative.

And that's *enough* doom and gloom!

The Parts of a Data Table

The best understanding of data table markup begins with an examination of the smaller parts of a table, as illustrated in Figure 10-1.

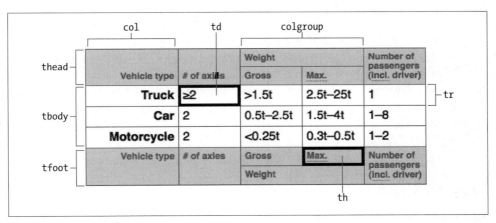

Figure 10-1. Data table anatomy

Rows and cells: tr *and* td
> These will typically contain all of the data points that relate to a single item. Rows are themselves divided into cells (td), and analogous cells in separate rows are always rendered into consistent columns. Apart from tbody, rows and cells are the two elements that *must* be present in a table.
>
> Readers who are familiar with relational databases will recognize that tr elements signal the bounds of a single record.

Columns and column groups: col *and* colgroup
> Just as a row relates to a single item, a column relates to a common class of data. Each column in a table corresponds to the table cells found at an interval of n, given that n equals the number of cells in each row.

Row and column headings: th
> th functions as an alternative to td, and defines the character of data found in a particular row or column.

th elements are distinct from td elements not only in terms of presentation, but also because they are set aside *specifically* to create table cells that do *not* contain actual data.

Captions: `caption`

Headings are assigned to normal copy; in spite of their name, `caption`s serve an analogous role for data tables. They are always rendered at the top of tables, as a heading would be in relation to the copy that it describes.

Table headers and footers: `thead` *and* `tfoot`

These serve as convenient "baskets" for describing the types of data to be found in a table's various columns and (less often) rows. They are distinct from plain rows for two reasons:

- An arbitrary number of rows might be needed to label types of data; for example, the first row of a table header might group broad data *classes*, while the second row defines each type on a column-by-column basis.

- According to the specifications for HTML and CSS, in paged media the `thead` and `tfoot` elements should be present on every page of a multipage table. Systems of generic rows and columns are ill-suited to this usability enhancement.

Note the `thead` and `tfoot` elements are *optional* with respect to validity, where `tbody` is not.

The table body: `tbody`

The table body contains all of the table cells that have actual *data* in them, as opposed to metadata.

Example: The Full Smash of Table Markup

A table that uses all of the elements just described would contain markup not unlike the following:

```
<table summary="Trucks, cars, and motorcycles, described according to their number of
axles, vehicle weight, and passenger capacity.">
<caption>Types of gasoline- and diesel-fueled road vehicles.</caption>
<colgroup id="type"></colgroup>
<colgroup id="axlect"></colgroup>
<colgroup id="wt">
  <col id="gvw" />
  <col id="mvw" />
</colgroup>
<colgroup id="pax"></colgroup>
<thead>
  <tr>
    <th rowspan="2" scope="colgroup" abbr="Type">Vehicle type</th>
    <th rowspan="2" scope="colgroup">#  of axles</th>
    <th colspan="2" scope="colgroup">Weight</th>
    <th rowspan="2" scope="colgroup" abbr="Passengers">Number of passengers (incl.
    driver)</th>
  </tr>
  <tr>
```

```
          <th scope="col">Gross</th>
          <th scope="col"><abbr title="maximum">Max.</abbr></th>
        </tr>
      </thead>
      <tfoot>
        <tr>
          <th rowspan="2" scope="col" abbr="Type">Vehicle type</th>
          <th rowspan="2" scope="col"># of axles</th>
          <th scope="col">Gross</th>
          <th scope="col"><abbr title="maximum">Max.</abbr></th>
          <th rowspan="2" scope="col" abbr="Passengers">Number of passengers (incl.
          driver)</th>
        </tr>
        <tr>
          <th colspan="2" scope="colgroup">Weight</th>
        </tr>
      </tfoot>
      <tbody>
        <tr>
          <th scope="row">Truck</th>
          <td>&ge;2</td>
          <td>&gt;1.5t</td>
          <td>2.5t&ndash;25t</td>
          <td>1</td>
        </tr>
        <tr>
          <th scope="row">Car</th>
          <td>2</td>
          <td>0.5t&ndash;2.5t</td>
          <td>1.5t&ndash;4t</td>
          <td>1&ndash;8</td>
        </tr>
        <tr>
          <th scope="row">Motorcycle</th>
          <td>2</td>
          <td>&lt;0.25t</td>
          <td>0.3t&ndash;0.5t</td>
          <td>1&ndash;2</td>
        </tr>
      </tbody>
    </table>
```

A close look at the previous markup illuminates some interesting details:

- caption is a direct child of table, and appears at the top of the table. caption elements are optional, but when used must be the first immediate child of table when used, if the table is to validate.

- summary takes the *functional* place of title, when it's used at all.

- colgroup can be used to identify column "groups" with only one member apiece, while col is reserved for individual columns that share scope.

- `colgroup` elements without contents still include a closing tag, due to the requirements of valid XHTML. In HTML documents, closing tags are *optional* on `colgroup` elements.

- The `rowspan` and `colspan` elements make it easier (in the case of a data table) to indicate that a datum is repeated across several records or fields, and in `thead` organization to better reflect field grouping.

- Each of the column and column group elements has been assigned an `id` so that CSS `width` values can be assigned to columns, rather than to the cells of the first row of the table.

- The row and cell presentation of the footer is inverted, compared to that of the header.

- The use of the `scope` attribute of each `th` element in the header and body of the table make it easier to generate metadata. The `td` element in turn supports the `headers` attribute, which takes a space-separated list of `id`s attached to that cell's associated `th` elements.

- The markup further embellishes `th` elements with the `abbr` element. User agents can apply its value as an alternative to verbose normal content, in situations where space and time are at a premium.

- The `tfoot` element follows `thead` rather than `tbody`. This is an obscure requirement of valid markup that's also referenced in Chapter 14 .

An attribute *not* used in the example table is `headers`. This attribute is attached to `td` elements, and takes as its value a space-separated list of the `id`s assigned to the `th` elements corresponding to a given table cell. Browsers with full attribute selector support thus allow individual cells to be styled according to *context*, in lieu of forcing stylists to apply the `:nth-child()` pseudoelement selector (explained in "Attribute and Child Selectors" on page 173) to cells without regard for the data that they actually contain.

 The various attributes apart from `colspan` and `rowspan` that can be used to control the layout of tables and table parts are still amply supported, but setting values on those attributes instead of controlling layout from a stylesheet reduces the flexibility of a proper data table—particularly one that holds user-generated content.

Composing Cells

Before you nail down details like custom column widths and backgrounds, it's best to ensure that individual cells have the desired appearance. The focus here is on cells because among all the various table elements, cells apply the broadest range of properties.

The best place to start is with borders. A close look at random passages of legacy markup reveals many `table` tags that look like this:

```
<table border="0" cellspacing="0" cellpadding="0">
```

Those attribute/value pairs ensure that the various cells of a table will align flush with their neighbors, an effect that's achieved with the following CSS fragment:

```
table { border-collapse: collapse; }
td, th { padding: 0; }
```

The result is shown in Figure 10-2.

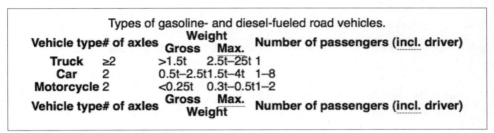

Types of gasoline- and diesel-fueled road vehicles.				
Vehicle type	# of axles	Weight Gross	Max.	Number of passengers (incl. driver)
Truck	≥2	>1.5t	2.5t–25t	1
Car	2	0.5t–2.5t	1.5t–4t	1–8
Motorcycle	2	<0.25t	0.3t–0.5t	1–2
Vehicle type	# of axles	Gross Max. Weight		Number of passengers (incl. driver)

Figure 10-2. Data table without borders and intracell padding

With that task out of the way, the next step is to differentiate cells by adding borders to them. Since each cell is flush to its neighbors, only two borders are needed, as shown in Figure 10-3. Note that all three cells have top and left borders; the border effect on cell 1 is completed by the borders rendered in cells 2 and 3 by way of the following styles:

```
td, th { border-top: 1px solid #000; border-left: 1px solid #000; }
```

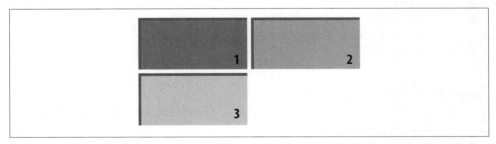

Figure 10-3. When borders are only applied to two sides of a table cell (1), the other two borders are resolved by the flush placement of neighboring cells (2) and (3)

The borders might be removed later; unless a width value is assigned to both the table and its individual columns (a step that's discouraged), the presence or absence of cell borders won't expose any bugs or layout conflicts. With the borders present in the meantime, the table now appears as shown in Figure 10-4.

None of the styles used thus far account for bottom or right borders, and the border-collapse value hides the left borders at the edge of the table. Finally, let's face it: as it stands, without negative space the table trends to illegibility (which defeats the whole

Types of gasoline- and diesel-fueled road vehicles.				
Vehicle type	**# of axles**	**Weight**		**Number of passengers (incl. driver)**
		Gross	**Max.**	
Truck	≥2	>1.5t	2.5t–25t	1
Car	2	0.5t–2.5t	1.5t–4t	1–8
Motorcycle	2	<0.25t	0.3t–0.5t	1–2
Vehicle type	**# of axles**	**Gross**	**Max.**	**Number of passengers (incl. driver)**
		Weight		

Figure 10-4. Previous table render, plus cell borders

purpose of data tables). Thus, the following styles should be added, with results pictured in Figure 10-5.

```
table { margin-left: 1px; border-right: 1px solid #000; border-bottom:
1px solid #000; } td, th { padding: 5px; }
```

Types of gasoline- and diesel-fueled road vehicles.				
Vehicle type	**# of axles**	**Weight**		**Number of passengers (incl. driver)**
		Gross	**Max.**	
Truck	≥2	>1.5t	2.5t–25t	1
Car	2	0.5t–2.5t	1.5t–4t	1–8
Motorcycle	2	<0.25t	0.3t–0.5t	1–2
Vehicle type	**# of axles**	**Gross**	**Max.**	**Number of passengers (incl. driver)**
		Weight		

Figure 10-5. Previous table render, plus remaining borders and whitespace

Table and Data Composition

The finer points of table rendering are complex to the point of frustration, though experience does give developers the ability to predict intuitively how an unstyled table will be laid out. However, stylists can be certain that the ideal layout of a table will be far different from what the browser provides as a starting point.

The first step of composing table data is to set the alignment of cell contents with respect to cell margins. The default alignment values for cells and headers are provided in Table 10-1.

Table 10-1. Default alignment styles for LTR (left-to-right) table data

Element	text-align	vertical-align
td	left	middle
th	center	middle

In general, data composition should obey the following rules:

- Literal data should be left-justified and top-aligned.
- `th` content within `thead` should be justified like the data that it describes, and bottom-aligned.

However, consider that these rules are especially subject to exceptions. There are two prominent examples:

- Designers often like to justify the first two columns of a table to a common margin, in order to emphasize the leftmost column of data.
- When several adjacent cells contain duplicate data, it's not uncommon to apply the appropriate `rowspan` or `colspan` value to the first such instance of data, and center it within the resulting large cell (at the cost of reducing accessibility).

The challenge inherent to applying table composition standards lies not in *values*, but rather in *selectors*. Internet Explorer lags behind its alternatives (see "Absent or Poor Selector Support" on page 267) when it comes to supporting the selectors that makes it possible to provide *precise* table layout without abusing `class` values.

In addition to *aligning* table *data*, it's also often necessary to apply custom column widths. These are best specified via `id` values attached to `colgroup` and `col` elements, which lead to rules like the following:

```
 #type { width: 8em; }
#axlect { width: 8em; }
   #gvw { width: 4em; }
   #mvw { width: 4em; }
   #pax { width: 8em; }
```

Figure 10-6 shows the results. If the policies under which you work make it impossible to tune tables on a case-by-case basis, you might get approval of a plan to standardize the column widths of the tables you build. The result would be comparable to the class-based form field sizes discussed in "Grouping Controls by Appearance" on page 254.

Before you examine Figure 10-6 to consider the results, you'll probably notice that each column has been referenced by its own rule. While there's nothing strictly *wrong* with styling multiple columns in a single rule, doing so might create priority conflicts in the future—thus the separate rules.

Even though `width` and background properties are the only properties that can be assigned to `col` and `colgroup` elements with any expectation of positive results, there is another reason to rely on these elements when applying presentation. If the layout or contents of a table need to be changed, reliance upon HTML attributes to control column presentation might fail in the face of `overflow` conditions or other unexpected results, forcing extensive revisions to table markup. When instead you confine data table presentation to a series of styles, markup changes will usually be confined to data and source order alone.

Types of gasoline- and diesel-fueled road vehicles.				
Vehicle type	**# of axles**	**Weight**		**Number of passengers (incl. driver)**
		Gross	**Max.**	
Truck	≥2	>1.5t	2.5t–25t	1
Car	2	0.5t–2.5t	1.5t–4t	1–8
Motorcycle	2	<0.25t	0.3t–0.5t	1–2
Vehicle type	**# of axles**	**Gross**	**Max.**	**Number of passengers (incl. driver)**
		Weight		

Figure 10-6. Previous table render, with normalized columns

Table Headers, Footers, and Heading Cells

When data is aligned to predictable margins, the results tend to be more legible. Figure 10-7 shows the table when the following `text-align` and `vertical-align` styles are applied to the various heading cells:

```
tbody th { text-align: right; }
thead th { vertical-align: bottom; }
tfoot th { vertical-align: top; }
thead th, tfoot th { text-align: left; }

thead th[rowspan]:first-child,
tfoot th[rowspan]:first-child {
  text-align: right;
}
```

Types of gasoline- and diesel-fueled road vehicles.				
Vehicle type	**# of axles**	**Weight**		**Number of passengers (incl. driver)**
		Gross	**Max.**	
Truck	≥2	>1.5t	2.5t–25t	1
Car	2	0.5t–2.5t	1.5t–4t	1–8
Motorcycle	2	<0.25t	0.3t–0.5t	1–2
Vehicle type	**# of axles**	**Gross**	**Max.**	**Number of passengers (incl. driver)**
		Weight		

Figure 10-7. Previous table render, with well-aligned heading cells

Attribute and Child Selectors

If you look at the stylesheet rules earlier, the last of them is notable for its use of odd selectors. In English, the selector refers to any th elements that are the initial, direct child elements of any element within thead or tfoot, and that also have a rowspan value.

It's entirely possible that you're looking at those selectors and thinking that they were pulled from thin air—but they weren't. When attribute and :nth-child() selectors are considered, the cascade can account for almost any element you can dream up, without forcing you to add ids or classes to arbitrary elements.

Of course, Internet Explorer fails to support any of the advanced selectors that are under discussion, so it becomes necessary to add classes to the markup you want to style just-so, or let the absent support wear its proverbial boxer shorts in public. In the case of IE 8 this support gap verges on frustrating, because IE 8 *does* support the attribute selector *by itself*—just not in combination with element selectors.

It should also be noted that support for :last-child is absent from all versions of Internet Explorer, while support for :nth-child is a newcomer to Firefox. As a result, you'll find yourself adding arbitrary classes to table elements if you want to use striped background colors (among other effects).

```
tbody tr:nth-child(2n+1) td { background-color: #ccc; }
```

The following two steps bring you to the argument of your :nth-child() selector:

1. Define the interval between elements, which falls before n.
2. Determine the ordinal location of the first element to be styled. This value becomes the addend.

Using the previous selector as the example, the argument provided yields the set of all odd members counting from an index of one (just as 2n by itself would yield the set of all even members).

Reducing Header and Footer Contrast

The existing typesetting of the table still has one flaw: the header and footer content competes with the actual data for the reader's focus. There are two easy ways to solve this problem: with reduced contrast and reduced type size—and there's no reason why both can't be applied. To make this happen for the table styled here, the following styles are applied:

```
thead th, tfoot th { font-size: .75em; background-color: #ddd; color: #777; }
```

Another way to increase the contrast of data relative to the rest of the table is to increase the brightness of the table's borders. The results of the heading cell and border changes are displayed in Figure 10-8.

Types of gasoline- and diesel-fueled road vehicles.				
		Weight		Number of passengers (incl. driver)
Vehicle type	# of axles	Gross	Max.	
Truck	≥2	>1.5t	2.5t–25t	1
Car	2	0.5t–2.5t	1.5t–4t	1–8
Motorcycle	2	<0.25t	0.3t–0.5t	1–2
Vehicle type	# of axles	Gross	Max.	Number of passengers (incl. driver)
		Weight		

Figure 10-8. Previous table render, reduced size and contrast on heading cells; reduced contrast on borders

The final steps are to alter the caption and adjust the column widths again, since the second column is too wide and the third and fourth expand slightly to account for their content:

```
caption {
    padding-bottom: .413em;
    color: #777;
    font-size: 75%;
    font-weight: bold;
    text-align: left;
}

  #type { width: 7.5em; }
#axlect { width: 5em; }
  #gvw { width: 5em; }
  #mvw { width: 5em; }
  #pax { width: 5em; }
```

The applied results of those styles are displayed in Figure 10-9, and a before-and-after view is shown in Figure 10-10.

Types of gasoline- and diesel-fueled road vehicles.				
		Weight		Number of passengers (incl. driver)
Vehicle type	# of axles	Gross	Max.	
Truck	≥2	>1.5t	2.5t–25t	1
Car	2	0.5t–2.5t	1.5t–4t	1–8
Motorcycle	2	<0.25t	0.3t–0.5t	1–2
Vehicle type	# of axles	Gross	Max.	Number of passengers (incl. driver)
		Weight		

Figure 10-9. Previous table render, adjustments to caption and column widths

Types of gasoline- and diesel-fueled road vehicles.

Vehicle type	# of axles	Weight		Number of passengers (incl. driver)
		Gross	Max.	
Truck	≥2	>1.5t	2.5t–25t	1
Car	2	0.5t–2.5t	1.5t–4t	1–8
Motorcycle	2	<0.25t	0.3t–0.5t	1–2
Vehicle type	# of axles	Gross	Max.	Number of passengers (incl. driver)
		Weight		

Figure 10-10. Before-and-after view of the table styling demo

The point to all of the apparent accent styling should now be clear: of the two table designs in Figure 10-10, which would you rather see in your web document?

Adding Rollover Accents to a Table

Tables that are especially wide or reliant on `rowspan`/`colspan` elements to accurately display data can benefit from the use of rollover effects. The simplest such effect is a table row highlight, which can be added in a rule like the following. It will be applied in every major browser except Internet Explorer 6:

```
tr:hover { background-color: #fcc; }
```

However, to apply column highlights it's necessary to use scripting. Given that a cell is being moused over, its analogs in other rows of the table body can be sussed out with the DOM API and altered via their `style` properties or ad hoc `class` assignments.

Finally, there are cell `titles`, which aren't used in the applied example but can define the intersection at which a cell lies, e.g., [Range of truck gross vehicle weights]. Such a detailed approach is verbose, and might decrease the screen-medium usability of small tables. For larger tables, it will likely reduce the amount of scanning required to make sense of data.

Whether they interact with user-initiated events or not, there's a lot more to do with data tables than stripping their internal negative space—and the stylist tasked with implementing effective information design will find that CSS has plenty of tools that are up to the task.

Images and Multimedia

It's hard to imagine today, but the first web pages were just text. You could link to images and view them in separate windows, but the rest of the page and images were presented separately. The NCSA Mosaic browser felt revolutionary in large part because it supported images presented inline with the text, and other inline media followed suit shortly thereafter, especially after the authoring platform known today as Flash was launched in 1996.

Many of the production principles worked out during the Web's infancy remain relevant after 15 years, in no small part because support for the two basic multimedia elements—`img` and `object`—has evolved *slowly* since their introduction. Those principles are applied alongside more recently developed practices intended to minimize the demands placed upon server and browser software.

Replaced Elements

If you look through the HTML 4.01 and CSS 2.1 specifications, you'll discover that some elements are described as "replaced." However, the specifications are predictably obtuse about what replaced elements are, and how they behave. Section 3.1 of the CSS 2.1 specification has this to say:

> [A replaced element is] an element whose content is *outside the scope* [emphasis mine] of the CSS formatting model, such as an image, embedded document, or applet. For example, the content of the HTML IMG element is often replaced by the image that its "src" attribute designates. Replaced elements often have intrinsic dimensions: an intrinsic width, an intrinsic height, and an intrinsic ratio.

To simplify:

> The layout characteristics of a replaced element can only be altered by the *direct intervention* of a stylist, if at all, regardless of context.

The one thing that's typical of replaced elements is that their content is rendered by some component of the local host *other than* the browser's rendering engine, which merely receives the content as input and inserts it in the page layout.

As replaced elements, images have discrete width and height; among other things, that means that if you apply a layout property to an image, the value will work. However, in the absence of layout values, an image will be laid out as if it were a word in a passage of text: its bottom margin will be aligned with the baseline of adjoining inline text.

Assigning `display: inline-block` to any inline nonreplaced element will cause it to emulate the behavior of replaced elements. This is unreliable in Internet Explorer 6, however, which only applies `display: inline-block` to elements that are defined as inline elements in the HTML 4 specification.

In practice, you'll discover that most image layout begins with assigning `display: block` to the various images you use in your layouts, or to container elements that hold both images and captions. This puts a halt to the odd baseline-to-margin alignment of images under default conditions, and enhances source markup readability by making it possible to leave space characters between images in the source markup, while preserving zero margins between consecutive images.

In this last case, consider three images in a row, i.e., `<img /> <img /> <img />`. When the user agent default styles are applied, those interstitial spaces will be rendered. When instead those images are assigned a `display` value of `block`, they can be lined up in source order with additional use of a `float` value, and their margins will lie flush to one another unless the width of the containing element forces an image to drop below its predecessor in the document flow. In fact, when both source formatting and pixel-perfect rendering take high priority, it becomes nearly impossible to achieve both without applying `display: block` to images.

However, if for any reason image slices are called for—as might be the case with sites to which legacy technical requirements apply—it's universally better to ditch the goal of squeaky-clean source markup formatting and remove the whitespace (including linebreaks) between image elements. These blocks can still be formatted by starting each line of source on the first attribute/value pair, rather than at the beginning of each `img` tag.

Preparing Images for Production

If your work process begins with a Photoshop document full of assets and layout instructions, the most important decision to make is one of purpose: can a given graphic be defined as a design accent, or is it actual content?

Design accents should generally be relegated to background images, with the possible (and sometimes likely) exception of bitmapped heading type. For more information about the composition and styling of such images, consult Chapter 9.

If instead an image is identified as content, such as a photo or an illustration of statements made in the document, it should be referenced in an `img` element, which will declare at least the image's URI and alternative text content.

The alt Attribute Explained

The `alt` attribute is critical to the experience of impaired visitors; it diminishes in importance only when images are loaded into the page *and* viewed *exactly* as intended. In all other cases its value is displayed, which is vital to any effort at making sense of images as content—so an `alt` value should convey meaningful information, or none at all. An excellent approach is to treat the `alt` attribute like a caption, or as an opportunity to label the image's subject if a caption already exists.

When inline images are used for design accents that do not have a meaningful text equivalent (i.e., all such accents except for bitmapped heading type), their `alt` values should be set to the null string (`alt=""`). In the case of text browsers and screen readers this will remove all evidence of those images, as if they had been assigned a `display` value of `none`.

Image Dimensions and Borders

In the earliest browsers, the inclusion of `width`, `height`, and `border` values became best practice with respect to publishing images. This habit evolved from the fact that early browsers were unable to display any part of the page until its entire layout had been computed—a process that could not be completed without explicit data for image dimensions. In the absence of workable `width`, `height`, and `border` values, all images needed to finish downloading before the page could be displayed, a wait that could take several minutes on the 56 kbps connections that were once common.

Improvements in rendering technology spare site visitors from having to wait for the browser canvas to be displayed. Even so it's a good idea to provide image size data in your markup or CSS so that layouts don't shift about unexpectedly while the page loads. The results can be jarring, regardless of connection speed.

The question for a developer is how to *reference* those values: in the stylesheet, or the markup? The advantages and disadvantages of each approach are summarized in Table 11-1.

Table 11-1. Advantages and disadvantages of setting image dimensions in markup and CSS

Modality	Advantages	Disadvantages
Markup	• Layout behavior remains intact regardless of network or server reliability issues • Attribute/value pairs serve as wholly appropriate metadata	• Markup must be altered directly after images are changed • Markup values override any desirable styles that contradict those values
Stylesheet	• Detail-conscious art direction is rewarded with reduced production time • Image layouts are more easily exposed to the cascade	• Separation of image characteristics from rendered image data can make images less usable in different contexts • Poor art direction necessitates the use of heaps of `class` and/or `id` tokens

A close reading of Table 11-1 raises the profile of solid art direction. Perhaps more so than any other web-related technology, CSS rewards consistency of design. Consider a design in which all images with a common subject grouping, or within a single section of the page share characteristics of presentation. Rather than heaping on all kinds of `width`, `height`, `class`, and `id` values, one can take shortcuts and write rules like:

```
#bodyCopy img {
    float: right;
    clear: right;
    width: 288px;
   height: 144px;
   border: 0;
    }
```

or:

```
body.annualReports .graph {
  display: block;
    width: 478px;
    height: 200px;
    margin: 1em auto 1em auto;
    border: 0;
    }
```

and then start uploading images with no need for further attention to image layout.

The mention of borders is also conspicuous in its own right, and is compounded by the fact that borders can usually be added to images directly. However, the habit that some user agents have of putting a five-pixel border around linked images cannot be ignored, so that the presence of:

```
a img ( border: 0; }
```

is usually welcome among the rules of any stylesheet.

Image Production

Images that stand on their own as page content usually benefit from the application of the same composition fundamentals as any other graphics of the same type (such as fine art, commercial art, or infographics). While the original assets you receive might well be excellent, you will often want to utilize any number of simple image production techniques before uploading images to a site repository, staging environment, or production environment. The following passages about composition and production are aimed principally at readers with a strong bias toward technical experience.

Cropping

You'll often be dealing with a folder of images that all differ with respect to aspect ratios, quality of composition, or both. To fit all of these into a design, you will likely need to perform a considerable amount of cropping.

The following instructions reference detailed workflows used in Adobe Photoshop. For the sake of brevity, the transformation functions provided by the Crop Tool, Edit → Transform, and Image → Rotate Image are not included.

In this situation it's best to use the Rectangular Marquee Tool (the uppermost item in the left column of the two-column toolbar, and the second item in the one-column toolbar) to select an area constrained to the Fixed Aspect Ratio that will be retained. If possible, the selection should be dragged so that the retained image will gain the greatest benefit from the Rule of Thirds, which is discussed on this book's companion site (*http://www.htmlcssgoodparts.net*).

Once the selection of the retained area is complete, the crop can be finished by selecting Image → Crop from the application menu.

In this situation, it's best to use the Rectangular Marquee Tool Options palette as it appears when the tool is set to a Fixed Aspect Ratio (as shown in Figure 11-1).

Figure 11-1. Photoshop's Rectangular Marquee Tool Options palette with an active Fixed Aspect Ratio

The Rectangular Marquee Tool is preferred to the Crop Tool because the latter's Snap To behavior is unforgiving of slight user input errors.

Matting: Creating a Virtual "Frame"

If an image cannot be cropped without removing important details, it can be matted to a desired aspect ratio by using the Canvas Size dialog, shown in Figure 11-2.

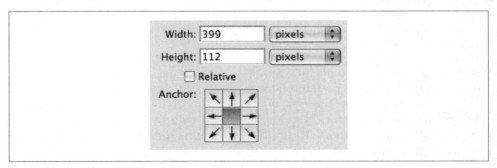

Figure 11-2. Detail of the Canvas Size dialog used for matting

To mat an image using the Canvas Size dialog, take the following steps:

1. Verify that the current background color displayed on the toolbar is the desired matte color of your image.
2. Taking into account the desired aspect ratio of the image, calculate its new dimensions.
3. Use Image → Canvas Size... to open the Canvas Size dialog, and replace the displayed (current) values with the new values.
4. Anchor the existing image area to the appropriate corner or edge, if necessary.
5. Repeat steps 2–4 as needed until the desired matting has been added to the image.

The Canvas Size dialog can also be used to add a border to an image. To obtain that result, set the desired background color, activate the "Relative" checkbox, and supply values equal to the weight of the border that you want to apply.

Resampling: Altering the Absolute Size of an Image

The Image Size dialog is similar to the Canvas Size dialog, except that it effectively alters the resolution of an image. I offer the following guidelines for its use:

- Unless you intend to "squish" an image, leave the Constrain Proportions option selected.
- Alter the Width and Height values in the dialog, not the Resolution value.
- Avoid upsampling (enlarging) images whenever possible. If you *must* upsample an image, minimize the upsampling factor. Any factor greater than +10% will create obvious blurring in areas of high contrast.
- If you downsample an image by a factor more than –20%, use the Unsharp Mask Filter (Filters → Sharpen → Unsharp Mask) to reduce the blurring that will occur in regions of high contrast, as demonstrated in Figure 11-3. With experimentation, you'll hit upon an appropriate combination of Amount, Radius, and Levels values.
- If you're working with an image that is free of obvious compression artifacts, use the bicubic algorithm for resampling images. When there *are* obvious compression artifacts, use the bilinear algorithm instead. The Nearest Neighbor algorithm is provided *specifically* for creating a "zoomed" (and thus pixellated) appearance at nonfractional factors of amplification.

Figure 11-2 shows these guidelines in action. In all cases, it's best to create a copy of an image resampled to the resolution at which you expect to display it on a site, instead of letting the browser or the server do that work for you. Offline image processing tools allow you to set output quality as the guiding parameter for resampling an image, while both browsers and servers will instead attempt to resample images at the lowest possible resource cost at the expense of quality.

Figure 11-3. Three views of a single inset: at original size, at one-third original size, and at one-third original size after an application of the Unsharp Mask filter

Level Changes: Optimizing the Contrast of Photographs

A perfect photograph straight from the camera is a rarity, because at the moment the shutter opens, there are so many environmental factors at work that are beyond the photographer's control.

One of the most important tools used to correct flaws in Photoshop is the Levels dialog (Image → Levels), which is used to directly alter the channel balance of digital photos. There are five sliders on the dialog, each of which alters the gamut (i.e., range) of a given channel: the upper three by increasing it, and the lower two by reducing it. These are functional contrast and brightness controls, but the presence of the histogram in the dialog makes it possible to discover exactly where the limits of a photo's color gamut *should* lie, instead of applying changes on a static (and essentially arbitrary) scale.

Levels dialog examples are shown in Figure 11-4. The first instance shows the levels histogram of an unaltered photograph, the second shows the gamut adjustments made with the guidance of the first histogram, and the third shows the appearance of the histogram after the gamut adjustments have been applied. The banding in the last capture is owed to the rounding used to apply the gamut increase, and the best way to

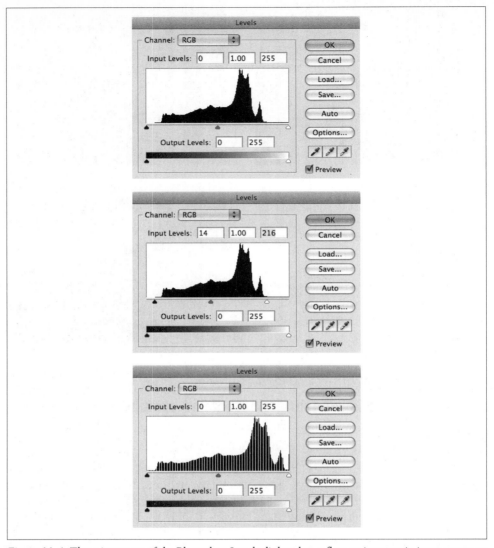

Figure 11-4. Three instances of the Photoshop Levels dialog that reflect an increase in image contrast

correct that is to resample the photo. When the photo is resampled regions of high contrast are interpolated, which tends to fill in the empty bands.

A good guideline for optimizing photo contrast can be stated as follows:

> When a levels histogram peaks somewhere in the middle, the most effective contrast adjustments are made by pinching the graph by its "shoulders."

Applying Multiple Adjustments

When more than one of the adjustments described earlier need to be applied to an image, they should be applied in the following order:

1. *Cropping:* If the levels of an image are adjusted *before* it is cropped, the adjustments will be made to fit to a different histogram than the one that describes the cropped image.

2. *Levels:* Without subsequent resampling, the gaps in a photo's gamut will simply be shuffled around, not removed.

3. *Resampling:* Resampling an image after a level adjustment allows an image processing program to interpolate high-contrast regions of an image, an opportunity that is lost if resampling is done first.

4. *Matting:* The same interpolation that fills gaps in a resampled image's histogram will also blur the interior edges of a matted image, unless the resampling is the first of those two actions to occur.

Working with Color Profiles

As was pointed out in Chapter 9, what you see when creating or implementing a site design is *not necessarily* what your visitors will see. Hardware quality is the most significant contributor to such deviations, but the *assumptions* under which hardware is configured also play a role.

Every medium commonly used to display web documents—e.g., liquid crystal diode (LCD) screens, cathode ray tube (CRT, TV-type) screens, projectors, sheets of multipurpose paper, coated paper—has different physical characteristics that define how it displays color. These media are all manufactured under certain assumptions about the gamut of colors they will display, and the level of ambient light available to the viewer. *All* of these factors (and others) affect the colors seen by the consumer of your content, so graphics files often contain *color profiles* that define the color reproduction characteristics of the tools used to create them. Figure 11-5 describes the relationship between device and media color profiles.

In the mid-1990s, Microsoft and Hewlett-Packard approached the challenge of differing display media by publishing the *sRGB color space*, a physical description of color that can be used in the design and calibration of electronic display hardware. The sRGB color space is endorsed by the W3C, and is incorporated into the specification of Scalable Vector Graphics (SVG), one of two graphics file formats created in the course of the W3C's activities.

sRGB is not the only color space in use, but it's the most common one on the Web. Apple's Safari browser applies International Color Consortium (ICC) profiles as a matter of course, and Firefox 3 offers ICC profile support that ships in a disabled state.

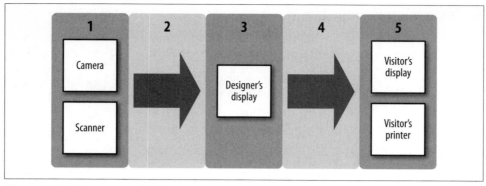

Figure 11-5. Five stages of color management: creation, upload, alteration, transmission, and consumption

Consider the following guidelines when working with color profiles:

- If your display includes an sRGB color setting in addition to a list of white points, set the sRGB option. Otherwise, maintain the white point set at the factory.
- If an original image file contains an embedded profile, convert its color space to sRGB when you open the image for manipulation.
- In Photoshop, the Save for Web dialog strips color profile data before writing an image to disk. Avoid its use if image quality takes priority over file size.

It's safe to assume that an image without color profile data will be displayed in the sRGB color space. This is why images should always be converted to the sRGB color space before they're uploaded to a web server.

Image Optimization

Choosing the Right Image Format

Three image file formats are reliably supported on the Web:

Graphics Interchange Format (GIF)
GIF is the oldest of three file formats in use on the Web, and is typically used for images with large areas of flat color.

Joint Photographic Experts Group (JPEG) File Interchange Format
As suggested by its name, the JPEG format is especially well-suited to photographs, and is supported by all digital still cameras. The JPEG format is also the only popular format that reliably supports embedded color profile data.

Portable Network Graphics (PNG)
The PNG specification was drafted and approved by the W3C as a direct response to the technical and patent limitations of GIF. In fact, PNG is superior to GIF in

nearly all respects except for one—Internet Explorer 6 does not support PNG alpha channels as a matter of course. This issue is discussed in Chapter 14.

A fourth format, called Scalable Vector Graphics (SVG), is actually a dialect of XML. While SVG offers a number of impressive features—and, like PNG, is a categorically open format—it's incompletely supported by common web browsers (and in Internet Explorer's case, not at all).

If an image is a line drawing, or contains large areas of flat color, it should be saved in GIF or PNG format. PNG is preferable if more than one level of transparency (i.e., on or off) is required.

Photos should always be saved in JPEG format. Applying JFIF encoding to nonphotorealistic images is a trickier proposition, as JFIF is a "lossy" compression format that assumes gradual but large contrast gradients between regions of an image. An image that fails to meet these assumptions will be populated with jarring compression artifacts.

Finding the Happy Medium Between Size and Quality

Before compression is applied, there are two easy ways to reduce an image's file size: by reducing its footprint (downsampling), and by reducing its contrast. Both of these have a direct and almost universally negative effect on image quality, so they should be applied carefully.

The two methods reduce image file size in different ways. In downsampling, the number of pixels that need to be compressed are reduced logarithmically—in other words, quickly in relation to the incremental decrease in an image's dimensions. Reducing contrast *slightly to moderately* is also effective because it reduces the brightness range of the image, which is suited to the strengths of both lossy (JPEG) and lossless (GIF, PNG) compression formats. This assertion is discussed at greater length on this book's companion website.

Given a running instance of Photoshop and a stack of images that need to be manipulated for site production, the remaining question is one of the quality index of the output. In the case of JPEG images, quality indices are controlled transparently by the JFIF codec. In the case of GIF and PNG images, quality is more subjective; a technician reduces the quality of these images by reducing color depth and indexing the colors that remain, which may introduce a requirement to dither an image. *Generally speaking*, the best settings for GIF and low-quality PNG images are to be found in an Indexed Color mode, at a depth of 2, 16, 64, or 256 colors.

Once you choose a color depth for a production image that will be subjected to lossless compression, you'll then need to choose a dithering method. Photoshop offers four options when you index an image's colors, listed here in typical rank of output quality at low color depth:

1. Pattern
2. Diffusion
3. Noise
4. None

These rankings are somewhat subjective; the lower an image's contrast or number of significant colors, the less likely a casual visitor will be to notice an apparent misjudgment of palette and dithering settings.

Publishing Images

Publishing images might seem like a straightforward task, but that's not always the case. Destination folders, filenaming conventions, and Content Management System (CMS) behavior are relevant to image publication, to degrees that vary on a per-project basis.

Keeping Images Organized

If a site has reasonably high production values, it will likely incorporate dozens or hundreds of images. Larger sites, especially those operated by social networking services, often store hundreds of thousands or even *millions* of individual image files.

So if you're the one who needs to keep them all organized, what do you do?

In some ways, the organization of a site's image assets is a mirror of the organization of the site itself; the only major cognitive challenge of image management arises when you have so many images to organize that you need to spread them across multiple directories. For small sites, my approach is to upload files to an /images directory and name them with series of tokens, for example:

    /images/bg_sidebar_contact.jpg

When generalized, that comes across as:

    type_pagescope_sitescope.ext

There are other tokens you can add: subject descriptors, artist surnames, and production dates all offer legible clues about an image's content, at least to a maintainer who is familiar with the site.

Filename tokens can follow whatever order you feel is most appropriate. I choose to put a type token first, because in my experience it makes file listings easier to scan.

On larger sites, it may be better to create an *images* directory for each major section of the site. So that instead of */images/article_photo_reports_2009q2_factoryfloor.jpg*, you might instead use an src value like */reports/images/article_photo_2009q2_factory-floor.jpg* while reserving the root */images* directory for accents that are common to multiple sections of the site.

Another challenge is handling the disposition of content that's been revised. On large sites your best choice is to store all content in a Revision Control System (RCS) such as Subversion or Git. When revising smaller sites, you can usually manage by creating a directory that includes some kind of time reference (such as a datestamp or an iteration codename), copying the "old" files into that directory, and uploading the "new" files in their place.

Image Publishing and Management in a CMS

Many images on user-managed sites will be stored in a location that can only be accessed safely from a Content Management System (CMS) control panel. At first glance this doesn't seem like a bad outcome; when image manipulation extensions are installed, the CMS can automate `src` values and create image previews on demand. However, there are a number of downsides that site operators need to take into account:

- Preview gallery interfaces are tedious to use.
- File naming conventions are either too strict or too lax, compounding the tedium of management via preview galleries.
- Implementation and behavior vary from one site to the next, depending upon the underlying CMS and its installed extensions.
- Image styling is unforgivingly strict out of necessity, a reality that many casual users are unable or unwilling to accept.

Managing these downsides calls for a number of strategies:

When possible, use publishing tools that store images themselves in an accessible directory of the host filesystem
> This approach poses its own share of drawbacks, and in fact the question of how to store images within a CMS is one of the most contentious among CMS developers. However, storing images in the filesystem makes it far easier for professional maintainers to update images quickly and on short notice.

Use publishing tools with control panels that support fulltext search against image names and descriptions
> In practice, such search tools are slow and often return badly sorted or unreliable results, but when the alternative is constantly paging through hundreds of gallery preview pages, you take what you can get.

Develop expertise in one CMS platform in preference to others
> Such a step is a matter of developing good habits; every tool has its bugs and peculiarities, and your best weapon is experience.

Write a strict guide for house style, and ensure its enforcement
> For many readers this is impractical, but others will discover that educating casual users about the "Garbage In, Garbage Out" principle to site presentation will reap benefits far out of proportion to the time invested. The concept of style guides is

introduced in Chapter 5, and discussed in greater detail on this book's companion site.

Maintaining the production values of user-managed content is among the more daunting tasks faced by the conscientious developer, and it's best done in cooperation with trained users and reasonably powerful Content Management Systems. In less carefully managed environments it might be necessary to let things lie, which usually means letting users correct their own mistakes whenever possible.

Image Publication Etiquette

Since images fall in the same access regime as pages, the practice of assigning `src` values is no different from the practice of assigning `href` values. The simplicity of this implementation beguiles the inexperienced and unscrupulous into publishing images on their own sites that are actually hosted on the sites of others.

When it comes to images, be sure that you're neither unscrupulous nor naive.

Best practice of image publication *requires* that the following conditions be met:

1. Permission, whether expressed or implied, to publish an image in the context of a URI under your control has been granted by its rights holder.
2. Appropriately conspicuous credit is given to images' creators, or at least to their rights holders.
3. Image files published in the context of URIs under your control are also *hosted from* URIs under your control.

Failure to meet the first condition violates copyright law, failure to meet the second is supremely rude, and failure to meet the third consumes network resources that someone else is paying for (which amounts to theft).

The request header of any image requested via the `img` element includes the relevant document URI in its referrer field. If you find yourself the victim of a site operator who is violating the third condition, you can reconfigure the web server to check the referrers of image requests, and issue a 3xx–5xx series reply to requests not referred by URIs under your control.

Styling Images and Plug-in Content

The layout behavior of inline-block elements, such as images, makes it rarely ideal to publish images without the benefit of at least *some* styling.

Composing Image Layout Within a Column

In practice, it will become a habit to justify images to column margins, or center them within their parent column; the styles used are shown in Figure 11-6.

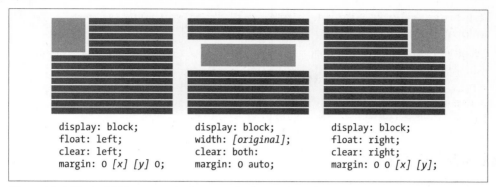

```
display: block;        display: block;        display: block;
float: left;           width: [original];     float: right;
clear: left;           clear: both:           clear: right;
margin: 0 [x] [y] 0;   margin: 0 auto;        margin: 0 0 [x] [y];
```

Figure 11-6. Typical CSS property/value pairs for formatting inline images

The property/value pairs shown include an explicit reference to `display: block`, which is provided to normalize layout behavior. When used with a class selector, it can also reduce the work required to style accompanying captions.

Captioning Images

Adding a caption to images formatted like those suggested by Figure 11-6 is most easily done in one of two ways:

- Mat the original image, set bitmapped type in the new negative space, and supply values for the `alt` and `title` attributes that reflect the caption text.
- Follow the image with the caption text, and enclose both in a `div` element (or less often a paragraph) that's supplied with layout styles similar to those suggested in the figure.

The first of these captioning implementations requires less markup than the alternative, and ensures that the image will always be presented in an apparent context. Its principal drawback is that it increases bandwidth use out of proportion to the amount of added content. That bandwidth increase is worse with respect to photos compared to other types of images, because the mixture of flat color and photorealism means that you'll need to use a higher-quality index than you would for the photo alone.

In the event that a caption integrated with an image needs to be *hidden*, the image as a whole can be enclosed in an element that has its `height` and `overflow` values set to truncate the caption. For example:

```
div#altProductPhoto {
 float: left;
 width: auto;
 height: 176px;
 overflow: hidden;
}
```

If instead you choose to provide a caption in plain text, you would assign styles like the following:

```
div#productPhotoWithCaption {
  float: left;
  width: 176px;
  margin: 0 9px 9px 0;
  font-size: small;
  font-style: italic;
}
```

In all cases where a plain-text caption is published, its parent `div` should be assigned a `class` or `id` value that reflects the presence of a caption.

Working with Previews (Thumbnail Images) in a Gallery or Slideshow Setting

There are two common resource types that offer similar layout challenges: gallery/slideshow previews, and application interfaces. Their implementation poses challenges at both the theoretical and practical levels, mostly because of the peculiar behavior of replaced elements. There are plenty of solutions to these challenges; you can use `div` elements with `class`es, lists, or even tables, and not go (too) wrong.

In my experience, the best compromise between anonymity and brevity utilizes ordered or unordered lists, especially if the page design intends an entirely arbitrary number of images within a given set of previews. Definition lists are also a possibility for captioned images, if you can predict the exact dimensions of your layout in advance. By relatively positioning the containing `dl` and absolutely positioning its various `dt` and `dd` elements, you can nail down each image and caption to precise coordinates with little trouble.

However, before you can act on this, you need to consider your conditions:

- Do all of the images have the same dimensions?
- If images are differently sized, can they be matted or cropped to force them all to the same size?
- If not, how do the images and their labels need to be aligned?

The first two questions hint at the desirability of ensuring that all of your preview images are the same size. Images of the same size create shared margins, which make the resulting layout more legible. Furthermore, ImageMagick, GD2, or other image manipulation libraries can be used to handle the process of cropping or matting images on the server. The use of ImageMagick for exactly this purpose is discussed in Shelley Powers's *Painting the Web (http://oreilly.com/catalog/9780596515096/)* (O'Reilly).

In general, sound layout of image previews and other `float`-heavy content follow a simple guideline:

> When working with contiguous, `float`ed elements, you'll be forced to choose between predictable dimensions and empty clearing elements to control vertical composition.

Clearing elements are discussed at length in "Canceling float Values with Corresponding clear Values" on page 87.

By way of illustration, assuming an unordered list and thumbnail images consistently sized at 240×180, we wind up with styles not unlike those discussed just discussed:

```
ul#thumbs { margin: 0; padding: 0; list-style-type: none; }
   ... li { display: block; float: left; width: auto; padding: 15px; }
   ... li img { display: block; width: 240px; height: 180px; }
```

As suggested, identically sized previews are worth the effort when it comes to element styling; regardless of the size of the images themselves, you should be certain that all image *containers* share either a common height or a common width. This is due to the behavior of elements to which `float: left` has been applied, as demonstrated in Figure 11-7.

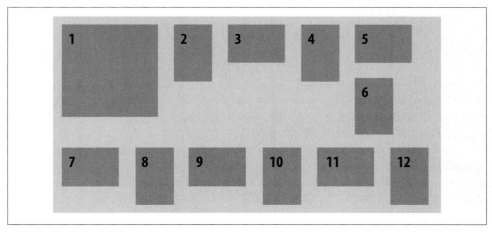

Figure 11-7. Float behavior demo

In the figure, element 6 is pushed below element 5 because otherwise it would overflow its container. If it were wider than the space available between element 4's element box and the right margin of their shared container, it would be pushed below element 2 instead.

Element 7 would overflow its container if placed adjacent to element 6 in the default flow, so it's instead placed immediately below element 6 and pushed as far to the left as necessary under the circumstances—all the way to the left margin of its container. In the absence of an overflow or overlap condition, an element box must share a top margin with a `float`ed predecessor, which explains the location of elements 2–5 and 8–12.

By ensuring that series of contiguous `float`ed elements share common dimensions, their layout behavior can be reliably predicted, which minimizes the difficulty of trying to avoid layouts like the one shown in the figure.

Lightbox: Previews, Galleries, and Slideshows

Content specialists and designers who are bereft of JavaScript skills or who require a third-party tool to manage large numbers of image-heavy content should investigate a tool called Lightbox (*http://www.huddletogether.com/projects/lightbox2/*). Lightbox is an ongoing project undertaken by an independent designer/developer Lokesh Dhakar.

There's a good chance that you've seen Lightbox (or one of its imitators or spinoffs) used on other sites. If you've ever clicked on a preview image to see a windowshade effect open onto an image over a darkened canvas, you were likely interacting with a production instance of Lightbox.

Lightbox runs entirely within the browser, and its current version also relies on public JavaScript libraries. Implementing Lightbox is straightforward:

1. Upload your full-size images to the directory of your choice.
2. Upload and reference the various CSS and JavaScript files associated with Lightbox as directed.
3. Insert the markup for your previews as a series of `a` elements that link to the images uploaded in step 1, specifying `rel="lightbox"` on each.

Lightbox is not an ideal solution for all projects, but if you have a need for shiny effects, a lack of JavaScript knowledge, and a tight deadline, it can be an excellent tool for presenting previews, galleries, and slideshows.

SlideShowPro

If Lightbox and custom-built slideshow code libraries are inadequate your needs—for example, in the face of a requirement to make slides maintainable by nonspecialist users—you can take things a step further by licensing and installing a tool called SlideShowPro, a popular slideshow presentation platform for enterprise sites.

Created by Todd Dominey and marketed through his company Dominey Design, SlideShowPro plays to the strengths of Flash by providing a simplified platform for the kinds of transitions and effects that are especially appropriate to slide presentations. It's true that vendor extensions to JavaScript provide much of the same functionality, but usually at a higher resource cost, since JavaScript deployment requires that each browsing platform be tested separately and at length. By comparison, SlideShowPro is exhaustively documented and on average easier to use for slideshow and gallery presentations. In the face of these benefits, the only justification for using a pure JavaScript solution is to reduce dependencies (i.e., on Flash in addition to the various browser platforms on which you develop your sites).

Successful implementation of SlideShowPro requires that you are able to create or obtain a Flash file and load SlideShowPro-specific assets into it. Once those steps have been taken, there are a number of ways to create and reference slides:

- Upload the files directly to your site via FTP and reference them via XML
- Use a Really Simple Syndication (RSS) vocabulary to reference materials that are already online
- Install a sister application called SlideShowPro Director that will accept web uploads, insert your images into a database, and generate the needed XML files on demand

Adding Motion and Sound: Using SWFObject to Insert Flash Videos and Presentations

Apart from the traditional web stack, Adobe's Shockwave Flash platform is currently the most popular tool used to integrate audio and video with traditional web content.

Those who want to simplify the process of publishing compiled Flash presentations on their sites should consider using a piece of openly available JavaScript called SWFObject, created by Geoff Stearns. SWFObject uses the DOM API and other interfaces to work around the hassles that accompany Flash content, in particular version detection.

Given production-ready Flash content and the current *swfobject.js* file on the web server, a developer need only call the *swfobject.js* file via a `script` element in the `head` of the document, insert a line of markup into the production document, and follow that markup with another brief fragment of JavaScript that creates an application-specific `SWFObject` object. That object in its turn modifies the preceding markup to create and populate the element that contains the desired Flash presentation.

It is also possible to write your own standards-compliant `object` markup and execute the SWFObject script *solely* to gain access to version detection and other features.

As you'll see near the end of the chapter, HTML5 is introducing new solutions to address audio and video more directly, without Flash.

If you have a bare video file that needs to be placed online and you choose Flash as your playback environment, simply using SWFObject to publish a presentation isn't enough. You'll need to take the following additional steps to prepare your footage:

1. Store to disk
2. Resample
3. Re-encode
4. Create or license the SWF used for playback
5. Upload both the finished FLV and its SWF playback container as needed

At a practical level, many of the particulars of steps 1–3 are governed by your choice of postproduction software. The subject of web video postproduction easily warrants a book of its own (which I look forward to seeing in bookstores someday).

In most professional settings, you will use an SWF file that can serve as a wrapper for multiple FLV files; the details of how to fit *those* together also differ from one setting to the next.

Inserting Unwrapped Multimedia

If you look around the Web, you'll notice that every site offers its own instructions for embedding multimedia into your own content. YouTube offers markup like this:

```
<object width="425" height="344">
 <param name="movie"
  value="http://www.youtube.com/v/iG9CE55wbtY&amp;hl=en&amp;fs=1&amp;rel=0"></param>
 <param name="allowFullScreen" value="true"></param>
 <param name="allowscriptaccess" value="always"></param>
 <embed src="http://www.youtube.com/v/iG9CE55wbtY&amp;hl=en&amp;fs=1&amp;rel=0"
  type="application/x-shockwave-flash" allowscriptaccess="always" allowfullscreen=
  "true"
  width="425" height="344"></embed>
</object>
```

Vimeo offers markup like this:

```
<object width="400" height="270">
 <param name="allowfullscreen" value="true" />
 <param name="allowscriptaccess" value="always" />
 <param name="movie" value="http://vimeo.com/moogaloop.swf?clip_id=4841397&amp;
  server=vimeo.com&amp;show_title=1&amp;show_byline=1&amp;show_portrait=
  0&amp;color=&amp;
  fullscreen=1" />
 <embed src="http://vimeo.com/moogaloop.swf?clip_id=4841397&amp;server=vimeo.com&amp;
  show_title=1&amp;show_byline=1&amp;show_portrait=0&amp;color=&amp;fullscreen=1"
  type="application/x-shockwave-flash" allowfullscreen="true" allowscriptaccess=
  "always"
  width="400" height="270"></embed>
</object>
```

And Odeo offers markup like this:

```
<object type="application/x-shockwave-flash"
 data="http://static.odeo.com/flash/player_audio_embed_v2.swf" width="325"
 height="60"
 id="odeo_audio">
 <param name="movie" value=
 "http://static.odeo.com/flash/player_audio_embed_v2.swf" />
 <param name="FlashVars" value="jStr=[{'id': 24363363}]" />
</object>
```

All three examples nest an **embed** element (which lies entirely beyond the scope of the HTML 4 specification) within an **object** element (which doesn't). This is done because in addition to **param** elements, **object** elements can contain fallback content that will be loaded if the browser cannot load the content specified in an `object` element. Ideally this fallback content will be nothing more than an image with a touch of explanatory text, but thanks to the application of Postel's Law (be conservative in what you send, and liberal in what you accept), there's no practical reason why `embed` elements cannot also be used for fallback purposes.

A Tale of Three Companies

In the founding era of the Web, one browser vendor—Netscape—came out especially strong, while Microsoft and smaller players took their time getting up to speed. The role of CSS in the resulting battle for market share was discussed in "Vendor Priorities" on page 44; a similar schism developed with respect to multimedia embedding, with a similar result: Microsoft's implementation won the day on paper, but Netscape's proposal (or rather its consequences) hung on for the next several years. Only recently has the W3C-defined element for multimedia publishing—`object`—enjoyed anything remotely like a workable level of cross-browser support. The `embed` element, on the other hand, was the first out of the gate, and was the only multimedia-embedding element supported on Netscape's original rendering platform.

Atop the hassles of cross-browser support, a corporation called Eolas, which exists solely to obtain intellectual property and license its use, successfully sued Microsoft in 1999, on the grounds that Microsoft's implementation of the `object` element infringed on Eolas's corporate rights. That litigation further clouded the issue, and forced Microsoft to change the way that Internet Explorer behaved when loading multimedia content.

Finally, Microsoft's support for the `object` and `param` elements is closely tied to its own APIs, so that in practice developers who are called upon to rely on Windows Media Player for playback facilities are best off subscribing to Microsoft vendor programs for the sake of gaining access to complete documentation. Larger shops can easily afford that degree of support, but individual freelancers who need to spread their focus across multiple operating system platforms cannot necessarily justify such costs, which can run into the hundreds of dollars per year.

Enter Flash

Most problems with audio/video content on the Web are exposed to the end user in terms of encoding, which is almost, but not entirely, synonymous with compression. Imagine how much grief would be caused if each operating system vendor had its own peculiar approach to compressing image content; this is why video is such a burden to implement. There's exactly one A/V encoding format (MPEG1) that's broadly supported on all systems out of the box, and it happens to be the oldest and least efficient encoding format in popular use. All other encoding formats are supported by specific software titles, and one of those is Adobe Shockwave Flash.

The virtue of Flash is that it has an uncommonly high penetration rate—roughly 99% on desktop platforms, according to Adobe. No other single software title is nearly as ubiquitous on personal computers; even Microsoft Windows (without respect to its versions or accompanying web browsers) has a U.S. market share that can be generously estimated in the 90–95th percentile at the time of publication.

YouTube and other sites built to capitalize on the demand for opportunities to publish and view user-generated A/V content served to demonstrate that Flash video was not only practicable but easy, which more or less vaulted Flash to its preeminent position among A/V playback platforms.

SWFObject (which was originally written by one of YouTube's engineers) gets Flash into web documents without any trouble—but what about other programs such as QuickTime and Windows Media Player? What's to be done when you don't have access to an appropriate SWF container for a Flash video? How do you embed plug-in content without writing invalid markup?

Using Bare Markup to Publish Multimedia Content

Avoiding the `embed` element when embedding A/V content is difficult when you're working from scratch, but as it turns out, someone has already done the testing-and-tweaking required to work with plug-in content *and* write valid markup.

Our benefactor is a gentleman by the name of Simon Jessey, who since 2006 has been maintaining a set of tested and *valid* `object` markup examples at the Dreamhost wiki. The samples available at the time of publication include markup appropriate to:

- Flash
- QuickTime
- Windows Media Player

This list might seem short at first, but those three playback environments manage in aggregate to cover nearly the entire web user population.

The current iteration of Jessey's work is available at *http://wiki.dreamhost.com/Object_Embedding*.

A Caveat of Plug-in Content Styling

The problem with plug-in styling is that by their very nature, plug-in instances resemble modal dialogs more than typical elements; a plug-in instance is more like a window inside of a window, and less like normal web content. If you decide to use advanced layout techniques on pages that display plug-in content, the best way to deal with that peculiarity is to ensure that in *all cases* the plug-in content does not overlap onto other elements or `select` controls. Otherwise, you might well discover that your other content is hidden without recourse.

Sidestepping Plug-ins with the HTTP Content-Disposition Header Field

It's not unheard of for a site operator to recommend that visitors use their context menu options to initiate a file-saving action. This option is called "Save Target As…" in Internet Explorer, "Save Link As…" in Firefox, and "Save Linked File As…" in Safari. Better yet, situations like this can be handled without the need to provide user instructions.

If you don't want to annoy your users or stumble into support issues, you can *force* a file download dialog in lieu of presenting content for playback in the browser canvas. This is accomplished by sending a line like the following in a reply header:

```
Content-Disposition: attachment; file=/video/developers.avi
```

As with other custom header data like `Content-Type`, this is usually best handled by using the HTTP API of your preferred server scripting language. The result is that along with a normal page, the browser will begin to save an additional file (*developers.avi* in these case) in the preferred destination folder specified by the visitor's browsing preferences, or will present a Save As dialog. One extremely popular site that presents this behavior is *download.com*.

With careful planning, you can also use the return value of an `XMLHttpRequest` function to obtain this behavior without forcing a complete page redraw; the critical action is to add a proper `Content-Disposition` field to the HTTP response.

Keeping an Open Mind

Despite its obvious value, multimedia publishing has been the target of significant venom throughout the Web's history. Much of that is owed to the ubiquity of poor presentation design practices. Even so, the people who order the work and write the checks tend to be fond of the bells and whistles found in multimedia presentations. It is the web developer's job to ensure that multimedia content is published with compatible standards of usability, resource cost, production values, and forward-compatibility.

The video and audio Elements (HTML5)

The `video` and `audio` elements finally make video and audio first-class citizens of the Web. Elevating video and audio to first-class citizenship means:

- It's as easy to put video and audio content into web documents as it is to put in text, hyperlinks, and images.
- It's possible to use video and audio in combination with other core web technologies; for example, applying SVG filters and CSS styling to video content.

The `video` and `audio` elements help achieve these goals by enabling video and audio content to be directly embedded in web documents without needing to rely on plug-ins. And the associated `HTMLMediaElement` interface that both elements share allows audio and video content to be programmatically manipulated through DOM scripting, just as other first-class web content can be.

Embedding a video

The following example shows how you can insert video into an HTML5 document, complete with a set of playback controls:

```
<video src="video.foo" controls="controls"></video>
```

In this example, the purpose of the `src` attribute is analogous to the purpose of the `src` attribute on the `img` element: it provides the URL of the video file to embed. The purpose of the `controls` attribute is also straightforward: it tells the browser to expose a set of playback controls to enable users to play and pause the video, as well as actions like changing the audio volume level, seeking through the video to any arbitrary point, and having it play in full-screen mode or in a separate window. In short, the purpose of the `controls` attribute is to offer exactly the same kind of controls as a typical embedded media player provided by a third-party plug-in. The difference is that in the case of the `video` element, the browser itself generates the controls and directly interacts with the video content, rather than handing off those tasks to a plug-in.

Supporting alternative video formats

If you're a particularly sharp reader, you may have noticed that the previous example uses a video file named *parrot.foo*, and in your experience there is no commonly used video format that has a *.foo* file extension. And you would be right. You are meant to imagine that instead of *.foo*, the file ends in some other extension that corresponds to a standard video format that's supported across all current browsers.

The problem is that in reality, there currently is no single video format that's supported across all browsers—Firefox supports Theora-encoded Ogg Vorbis files, while Safari appears likely to settle on support for H.264-encoded MPEG4 files. There are some ongoing efforts among vendors to try to get agreement on a standard video format, but such efforts will take quite a while to reach resolution.

Making video available to the widest number of users will require encoding the video in multiple formats and, in place of using the `src` attribute on the `video` element itself, putting `source` elements as its contents, as in the following example:

```
<video controls="controls">
 <source src="parrot.ogg"/>
 <source src="parrot.mov"/>
 <source src="parrot.wmv"/>
 <source src="parrot.3gp"/>
</video>
```

A browser will look through each `source` element provided until it finds a video file in a format that it's capable of playing.

Providing video content for browsers that don't support the video element

Another case you'll need to consider is how to provide video content to older browsers that don't support the video element. One way is to also include an object element that embeds content by way of a third-party plug-in, as in the following example:

```
<video controls="controls">
 <source src="parrot.ogg"/>
 <source src="parrot.mov"/>
 <source src="parrot.wmv"/>
 <source src="parrot.3gp"/>
 <object data="parrot.swf" type="application/x-shockwave-flash">
  <param name="movie" value="parrot.swf"/>
 </object>
</video>
```

Of course, users who don't have the necessary plug-in installed (or have it disabled) won't be able to view the content referenced by the object element either.

The canvas Element (HTML5)

No introduction to HTML5 would be complete without some mention of the canvas element.

The canvas element is essentially an img element that's dynamic instead of static. It is a particular place in a page, with specific dimensions, where you can dynamically (which is to say, programmatically) draw images and display animations and so on. It can be used for things like dynamically generating charts and graphs, making in-browser drawing/painting applications (or even in-browser text-editing applications), and creating in-browser games—basically, the kinds of things that various browser plug-in runtime environments like Flash currently deliver.

The CanvasRenderingContext2D API

Another way to look at the canvas element is essentially as one part of a two-part "Canvas feature" that also includes a programming interface, the CanvasRenderingContext2D API, which in practice is a necessary part of actually making use of the feature. Contrast that with the case of other interactive elements that are new to HTML5, such as the video element, which can be perfectly useful without needing to be scripted using their related APIs. But you really can't do anything with the canvas element, without using it in conjunction with the CanvasRenderingContext2D API.

The details of actually developing canvas content basically boil down to details about programming with the CanvasRenderingContext2D API in JavaScript, which is beyond this scope of this book. The canvas element is less of a markup feature and more of markup "hook" for hanging some programming on. There are plenty of examples and write-ups elsewhere to help you get started, including a chapter in *Painting the Web*.

SVG as an alternative to canvas

If you're not already an experienced JavaScript programmer, canvas should perhaps not be your first choice for delivering animations and interactive images as part of your content. Instead, you might want to consider looking into SVG, and seeing if that does the trick. If you're primarily a markup author or designer, you'll probably find the declarative-programming approach that SVG uses—which is actually quite similar to the declarative approach of CSS—much more familiar than the imperative-programming approach on which canvas relies.

Web Typography

While certain parts of CSS—especially the `float` property—can be charitably described as difficult, there are other parts that offer a terrific return on the investment of time required to learn them. Font and text properties are among these easier aspects.

 The material that follows is not intended as a complete property survey. For a full overview of CSS properties and values, please consult this book's companion website (*http://www.htmlcssgoodparts.net*). The following O'Reilly books, both by Eric Meyer, might also prove useful:

- *CSS: The Definitive Guide* (*http://oreilly.com/catalog/ 9780596527334/*)
- *CSS Pocket Reference* (*http://oreilly.com/catalog/9780596515058/*)

This chapter starts with an introduction to the art of traditional Western printing, which will go a long way to helping you understand why untrained stakeholders often develop unrealistic expectations of the Web's capacity for controlling presentation.

A Brief History of Letterforms

In the present day, when functional literacy lies within the reach of all but the most impoverished and isolated, it's easy to take writing for granted. In fact, writing systems claim 5,000 years of steady evolution, and much of that change has taken place within living memory.

The history of writing and printing teaches *control*—artists and designers have centuries-long traditions of being able to exercise complete control over the impressions that make their way onto the printed page. This is a far cry from the state of the Web, which places many absolute limits on design control. The use of Adobe Flash to create web content can lessen design constraints, but imposes burdens of its own, and no technology can make up for the fact that user environments vary widely.

Given the influence of formally trained graphic designers on the Web, it's helpful to know how their product has evolved, particularly with respect to type.

Origins of Modern Western Letterforms

Most of the world's ancient civilizations developed writing independently, working to preserve a permanent record of events—in effect, to augment memory.

 This discussion of printing history blithely neglects Asian contributions, due to a paucity of high-quality English language sources, ignorance on the part of the author, and the fact that industrial-scale printing was largely a European invention.

The Western alphabets in use today can be traced back ultimately to the diffusion of Egyptian hieroglyphs to the Levant, about 3,500 years ago. This diffusion led to the Phoenician alphabet, which in its turn formed the basis of the Greek alphabet. Greek eventually led to Latin and Cyrillic.

The form of the classical Latin alphabet chiseled into Roman monuments is a subset of modern print majuscules (uppercase or "capital" letters), while the later miniscules (lowercase letters) evolved from Roman cursive in the early Middle Ages.

Written literature as we know it today did not start to take shape in the West until the late Middle Ages, not long before Johannes Gutenberg invented his printing press. Until then, writing continued to be performed almost exclusively by hand, mostly for making and copying records.

Gutenberg's Press and the Art of Typography

Gutenberg's construction of the first mechanical press designed to use movable cast-metal type changed the economics of publishing and led directly to the practice of *typography*: the design of letterforms designed for specific purposes and specific duplication methods, usually according to the ebb and flow of artistic tastes among the well-read. Among its many benefits, cast-metal type afforded a previously unheard-of degree of consistency in the appearance of printed matter—consistency that we take for granted today.

Press design, papermaking, and bookbinding enjoyed their share of innovations in the centuries after the introduction of Gutenberg's press, but innovation in typography was slower: in the last quarter of the 19th century, printers were setting type just as Gutenberg did.

The pace of innovation picked up with the introduction of hot type, which is cast in lines on demand from molten lead ingots in a machine built for that purpose, then arranged on the working surface of the press. The term "leading," which is still commonly used by contemporary graphic designers and prepress techs, is directly comparable to the CSS `line-height` attribute, and takes its etymology from the strips of cold lead inserted between fresh type castings to create negative space between lines of type—a practice inherited from earlier centuries.

Later in the 20th century came the introduction of phototypesetting, which uses photosensitive compounds to create printing plates—an innovation of the lithography process that by then had been used by printmakers for several centuries.

The Emergence of Digital Typesetting

The development of workable computerized typesetting happened within a few years of the invention of the laser printer, and those two innovations were followed shortly by the appearance of affordable computers that were capable of running software to compose type.

The final pieces of the digital type puzzle were put in place by affordable laser printers and user-friendly word processing titles with graphical user interfaces, which were followed a few years later by full-featured desktop publishing suites. In the space of 20 years, computerized typesetting had evolved from single-column systems for cold type—which did little more than duplicate the (rare) skills of an experienced hot type operator—to off-the-shelf software suites that could run on broadly capable computers and compose entire page layouts with graphics. By the early 1990s, both workstations and printers were capable enough to set not only film-ready type, but film-ready graphics as well.

In current offset printing practice, these digitally typeset layouts are exported directly to a machine called a *platesetter* that creates resinous printing plates from the exported raster data. Less frequently, layouts are laser-printed, photographed—thus the term "film-ready"—and then fed manually as photographic negatives into a platesetter.

The accents of today's digital typesetting landscape were added in 1991, when the TrueType font format was licensed for use in Microsoft Windows. The TrueType format has since been joined in common use by the OpenType format, though as of this writing, the distinction between the two is minimal with respect to web design.

Different Limitations Without Changed Expectations

For centuries, typesetting and printing have been *tangible* processes, and during most of that time design limitations have been imposed far more by *tools* than by *media*. The assumptions of web browser engineering turn this paradigm on its head: now the medium itself poses nearly all of the limitations, while tools in the hands of an experienced operator can produce almost anything imaginable.

A Visual Glossary of Typography

Figure 12-1 shows a heap of terms that describe the parts and varieties of type, exploring the physiognomy of individual letters.

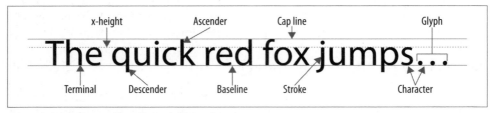

Figure 12-1. Typography jargon for letterforms

There are many more terms site stylists should be aware of:

Blackletter
> A style of type inspired by German calligraphy of the late Middle Ages, and strongly identified with Germany to the present day. Sometimes called "Gothic," but this is an anachronism (see the entry for *Gothic*).

Condensed
> A style of sans-serif font distinguished from others in its typeface by its narrow and tightly spaced nature. Opposite of *extended*.

Copy
> The generic term for a writer's work product. Different from "text" since the latter refers only to nonnumeric data in the most general sense; all copy is text, but not all text is copy.

Diacritic
> A glyph added to a letter to indicate altered inflection or pronunciation. Commonly encountered examples include the acute accent (´), umlaut (¨), and cedilla (¸).

Dingbats
> A collection (usually comprising a well-populated font) of characters that are simple drawings (e.g., musical notes, circuitry symbols) rather than members of a standardized orthography.

Extended
> The complement to condensed fonts. Letters are wider than in the normal fonts, and letterspacing is usually more generous. Also referred to as "wide" and/or "extra wide."

Glyph
> The atomic unit of a font, a single mark that contributes some degree of meaning. (Many characters are composed of a single glyph, while others combine more than one.)

Gothic

For the past century, reliably synonymous with *sans-serif*, so named because most of the early sans-serif typefaces originated in Germany and the German-speaking regions of Switzerland.

Gutter

Negative space between a text margin and rule, between two columns, or between two passages of text, in many cases, controlled with the CSS padding properties.

Italic

A font evolved from its upright serif counterpart, through the addition of calligraphic accents. Usually skewed 5–10° clockwise from the upright. (*cf. oblique*). So named because the earliest designs for these fonts were developed in Italy. Italic fonts are drawn more narrowly than their "Roman" counterparts with the intent of increasing the number of words that can be placed on one line.

Kerning

Atypical letterspacing in the middle of specific pairs of glyphs, particularly ones that include A, f, j, J, L, T, V, W, w, and y. When neglected, enforces an illusion that the letters in a given pair seem uncommonly (and distressingly) far apart. Some combinations of operating systems, software, and fonts call for frequent manual kerning of high-quality rasterized type.

Justification

Refers to the margin (or margins) to which lines of type are hewed. A left-justified column starts all lines at a common left margin, a right-justified column ends all lines at a common right margin, and all lines of a fully justified paragraph except the last begin *and* end at common margins. This aspect of layout is controlled in CSS with the `text-align` property. Oppose *ragging*.

Leading

As described earlier, the negative space between lines of type, so named and pronounced because hot type castings were separated on the press by strips of cold *lead* to create that space. Cognate (but not identical) to the CSS `line-height` property.

Letterspacing

Consistent space inserted between individual glyphs within a passage of text. Controlled by the CSS `letter-spacing` property (and to a degree by the `word-spacing` property).

Lower-/uppercase

Synonymous with miniscule and majuscule letterforms, respectively. So called because printers once stored individual letters of a given cast type font in upper (majuscule) and lower (miniscule) drawers.

Mono

An appellation used to distinguish fixed-width typefaces from their variable-width counterparts.

Negative space (whitespace)
> Any space on a page or canvas not occupied by type, illustrations, or rules. The use of "whitespace" as a design term illuminates, but is a generalization, of its use as a computing term.

Oblique
> The sans-serif counterpart to *italic*, without calligraphic accents.

Orthography
> The study and practice of writing; a single system of writing.

Ragging
> The practice of removing all letter and word spacing from a passage so that text does *not* justify to a margin. By default, web text that is left-justified is right-ragged, and vice versa.

Roman
> When used to refer to a typeface, "Roman" is generally synonymous with *serif*.

Rule
> A line placed to one side of a block of text. Usually controlled with the CSS border properties.

Sans-serif
> A class of typefaces distinguished by their reliance on obviously geometric shapes, consistently weighted strokes, and unadorned terminals.

Script
> A class of typeface also referred to as *cursive* and designed to resemble continuous handwriting; usually decorative.

Serif
> Inspired by classical incised letters, serif typefaces are characterized by variable weight strokes and the presence of *serifs*—slight feet or flanges, if you will—on terminals.

Weight
> The width of a rule, stroke, or font. When applied to text, weight is controlled by the CSS `font-weight` property. Common font weights for print applications range from hairline (lightest) to extra black (heaviest); the typical body copy weight is sometimes assigned the appellation of "Medium" or "Book," but usually takes no special appellation at all. Figures 12-2 and 12-3 display specimens of these font components in use. Figure 12-2 shows the Microsoft Core Fonts for the Web, while Figure 12-3 shows the Safari/Macintosh and IE7/Windows system defaults for the various `font-family` keyword values.

 The nomenclature of character encoding is discussed later in this chapter.

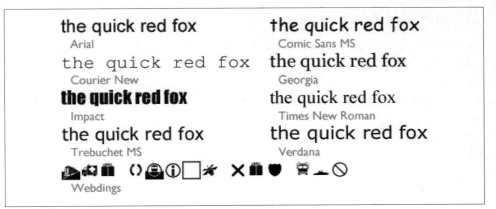

the quick red fox
Arial

the quick red fox
Comic Sans MS

the quick red fox
Courier New

the quick red fox
Georgia

the quick red fox
Impact

the quick red fox
Times New Roman

the quick red fox
Trebuchet MS

the quick red fox
Verdana

Webdings

Figure 12-2. Commonly available Microsoft core font families

Mac: Safari 4 and Firefox 3.5	Windows: Firefox 3.5
the quick red fox Times	the quick red fox Times New Roman
the quick red fox Helvetica	the quick red fox Arial
the quick red fox Courier	the quick red fox Courier New
the quick red fox Apple Chancery	the quick red fox ComicSans MS
the quick red fox Papyrus	

Figure 12-3. Defaults in various browsers for the serif, sans-serif, monospace, cursive, and fantasy font-family keywords

Aliasing and Anti-Aliasing

The good news is that for centuries, typography has been a cornerstone of high aesthetic standards.

The bad news is that during those centuries, it never occurred to anyone that their work might *need* to be pixellated, as on an electronic display.

To make a long story extremely short, that means that most traditional typefaces look awful on-screen. This is caused by *aliasing*, which is described visually in Figure 12-4.

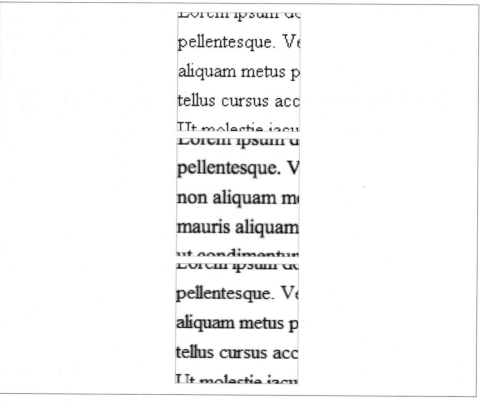

Figure 12-4. An illustration of aliasing and anti-aliasing applied to 16px/12pt Helvetica: (1) original against a pixel grid, (2) aliased, (3) anti-aliased at the OSX Medium setting, and (4) anti-aliased in ClearType/Vista

Aliasing *approximates* the strokes of a letterform, which leads to an obviously "blocky" appearance. For this reason, fonts that are not designed to account for aliasing tend to look much different—and frankly uglier—than their print counterparts, an effect exacerbated by the fact that human eyesight is keyed to differences in brightness.

Anti-aliasing attempts to undo some of aliasing's damage to the ideal appearance of on-screen lettering by smoothing edges, as shown in Figure 12-4. Anti-aliasing algorithms create regions along the edges of letters where the difference between foreground and background is interpolated *gradually*, which obscures the true degree of contrast and allows more of the type's hinting to be applied.

Hinting is the introduction of slight deviations to the outlines of letters. In print typography, the most obvious hinting is applied to the crotches of letters like "k" and "v" that would otherwise become obscured by bleeding ink during printing. By comparison, type designed for screen display is usually hinted to account for the effects of aliasing and anti-aliasing.

The strongest disadvantage of anti-aliasing is that it tends to make small type nearly illegible. Just as a downsampled image is subjected to considerable blurring, small type with its low resolution becomes nothing but regions of contrast, as shown in Figure 12-5.

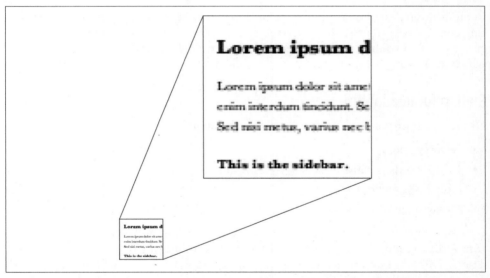

Figure 12-5. The functional result of reducing type size to decrease its resolution on electronic displays; when anti-aliasing is applied to type at these small sizes, the results can be illegible

One drawback of fonts designed for screen display is that they tend to be more attractive at smaller sizes than larger ones. The reason for this is revealed by common sense: since most copy is set at 12-point/16-pixel and similar sizes, it makes the most sense to ensure that a typeface is most readable at those sizes. For this reason the hinting, interior curves, and stroke variations of screen-optimized type tend to be less complex.

On the other hand, optimization for display at smaller sizes makes screen-optimized fonts seem excessively simple when rendered at larger sizes and compared to their traditional counterparts. So goes one of the principal reasons why designers often choose to use bitmapped headings set in traditional fonts: the increased detail of print-originated typefaces is preserved (and in some cases, actually enhanced) at larger sizes, making them more attractive than their screen-optimized counterparts.

Type Styles, Readability, and Legibility

In publication design there are two complementary concepts that drive many typesetting choices: readability and legibility. *Readability* is the quality of copy that makes it easy to read in volume, for extended periods of time; *legibility* refers to the ease with which data, words, and short phrases can picked out while a passage is being scanned.

Styling for Readability

Our expectations of book design illuminate the definition of readability:

- Serif typefaces
- 12–15 words per line
- Fully justified lines
- Moderate and consistent letterspacing

Upmarket press runs also often employ increased leading (20% or more of the body copy size) and more detailed fonts, to ease the task of making out margins, lines, and letters. This is due to the fact that profit margins on downmarket editions range from poor to outright lousy, which creates a strong incentive to minimize manufacturing and distribution costs—in other words, to reduce net paper costs.

In their turn, paper costs are reduced by using lower grades of paper in smaller quantities. That being the case, there are more lines on each page, smaller page margins, and—on account of paper quality—less-detailed fonts, which suffer less from the ink bleeds that occur when lower grades of paper are used.

Paper costs aren't a concern on the Web, so we can use the full arsenal of available tools to enhance readability. For screen display, the result might be something like the following:

```
#bodycopy p {
  width: 50em;
  font-family: Georgia,'Times New Roman',serif;
  font-size: 14px;
  line-height: 17px;
  text-align: justify;
}
```

However, the screen environment presents a challenge not found in books: the requirement to scroll content means that lines of text actually *move* up the canvas. For that reason, the default left-justification of body copy is usually maintained on websites; when ragged right margins are used, it's easier to pick out specific lines, a necessity for tracking lines that actually move around.

Styling for Legibility

While readability is desirable for long passages of text, legibility is better suited to things like headlines, brief passages, and data. Newspaper infographic (table) design provides us with an excellent case study of legibility, and tends to obey some or all of the following principles:

- Sans-serif typefaces
- Larger type for headlines, smaller type for data
- Strict adherence to a grid
- Extensive use of rules at the margins of text/data, on one or both axes
- Row (or less often, column) background banding
- Flush justification—related columns of content are justified on their shared margin

Chapters 10 and 13 offer a number of detailed recommendations for styling legible content in table and form contexts.

When working with left-to-right writing systems (as in English and European languages), the most legible text is typically left-justified and right-ragged, except in cases where there's a significant difference between the right margins of lines within a particular block of text. In such cases, legibility can be enforced by breaking lines with the white-space attribute (explained in more detail shortly), right-justifying text, or applying both solutions at once.

"The Fold" and Tiny Type

Imagine, if you will, a folded newspaper, displayed in a vending box or a newsstand rack with the top half of the front page oriented toward the purchaser. The assured visibility of the headlines and content to be found there force careful layout choices, and stories "above the fold" are agreed to carry special cachet.

The analogous space on a website is the immediately visible fraction of a home page or landing page (see Figure 12-6), also called "above the fold" by many web user experience professionals.

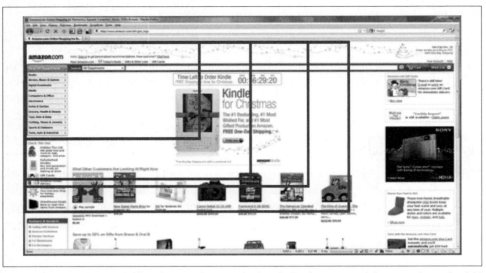

Figure 12-6. A 1920×1080 browser window overlaid with the footprints of the area above the fold under differing circumstances of browser window geometry

Many people consider the space above the fold to be the most valuable on a website, and it can be tempting to crowd it—the logic being that with more content above the fold, the more opportunities to entice a visitor.

This conclusion is misguided for the following reasons:

Clutter actually discourages visitors who are seeking specific information
The above-the-fold paradigm supposes that the typical visitor would rather leave than scroll, a position that is sometimes carried to absurd extremes like ensuring that none of the pages on a site require vertical scroll bars. However, scrolling is a function of *effort*, and attempting to find the proverbial needle in a haystack of home page clutter can easily consume *more* effort than scrolling.

Clutter reduces content differentiation
The presence of so many items within a layout ultimately leaves *color* as the only means by which content can be differentiated. The founding attitude of the above-the-fold paradigm may well lead to the use of many equally saturated colors, resulting in epic ugliness.

The use of small type to cram content above the fold renders pages unusable to those without excellent eyesight

You don't even need to go online to test this assertion: just read through an entire page of fine print on a contract, and ask yourself if the result is any more acceptable on a website.

The variance in popular display resolutions means that content above the fold for one group of users will be a thin strip for other groups

For visitors viewing higher-resolution displays, attempts to emphasize the area above the fold at lower resolutions are completely overwhelmed by the surrounding canvas space.

The insight gained from an examination of the above-the-fold fallacy is that smaller body copy type should never be made part of a design, except for carefully considered aesthetic reasons that will resonate with a majority of the site's audience. Put more directly, itsy-bitsy letters are neither cool nor useful, except in situations few and far between.

Of course, this does *not* mean that content shouldn't be carefully prioritized, with the most important still at the top. Instead, the effort should be made to "layer" content in levels on a grid.

Sizing Type

If there's one thing that gets trained designers excited, it's control over type. CSS delivers, for the most part; if a font can be rendered by a visitor's browser, its characteristics can be controlled by the stylist. This is especially important with respect to the *size* of type, which follows some fairly basic rules:

- Trained designers who are stuck in a print-media mindset fail to grasp the degree of control that most users have over type sizes. For this reason, it's usually best to set your baseline type size in pixels, for example:

  ```
  body { font-size: 14px; ... }
  ```

  and then control type size down the cascade with `em` or percentage units (which are functionally identical). Stylists who work on sites targeted at large numbers of IE 6 users may need to disregard this recommendation for usability reasons, which become important because of IE 6's complete inability to zoom text ultimately set in `px` units.

- Heading sizes are set by the browser as a proportion of the base font size. It's usually best to preserve this behavior by relying on a comparable approach when assigning heading resets, a step that allows headings to better withstand layout changes. If you're implementing bitmapped headings, you might find yourself adding `background-position` values to your image replacement rules to account for this change in approach.

- If you need *absolute* control over the dimensions of an element, set its content as an image and supply the actual text in that image's `alt` value. Such situations are best avoided, but are sometimes inevitable in the real world.

- Avoid setting `line-height` values in pixels, unless you intend to pair each instance of `font-size` with a companion that references `line-height`. Heading size values are handled automatically in the cascade, and so are `line-height` values. This means that if you set a `line-height` value in pixels for the benefit of your body copy, the same static leading might be applied to larger type and produce illegibly solid typesetting.

Choosing the Right Units for Sizing Type

When styling type for display in the browser, you can use one of four units to set its size: pixels, ems, percentages, or keywords.

- Pixels (`px`) are absolute units, to a point; under normal circumstances, text sized in pixels will have the same footprint in all environments regardless of the user's default text size or values established higher in the cascade. There are two pitfalls to using pixel units: the first has to do with the limitations of Internet Explorer 6, and the second is the risk of blowouts when text size is increased by the user beyond the footprint of underlying background images or element boxes.

- Ems (`em`) and percentages (`%`) are *relative*; the value specified will be applied multiplicatively according to the value that is next highest in the cascade, even if that value is the browser default. These multiplicative results are explained next for the benefit of the math-impaired.

- Keywords can take one of seven values, and are related to default heading sizes. The important thing to remember about size keywords is that they always render type at sizes relative to the browser default established in the browser's preferences pane, with `medium` being equal to the explicit default (usually 16 pixels).

Em/Percentage Size Telescoping

When a `font-size` value expressed in ems or percentages is subject to the cascade, the value applied is a *multiple* of the inherited size. Consider:

```
body { font-size: 15px; }
.lede { font-size: 1.4em; }
.note { font-size: .667em; }
```

In the absence of intervening `font-size` values, the functional size of copy in `.lede` will be `21px`, and `10px` in the context of `.note`.

For the sake of demonstration, suppose there's another rule like this:

```
.lede em { font-size: 1.429em; font-style: normal; }
```

The suggested effect is to *enlarge* rather than *italicize* emphasized passages—the sort of art direction that might be applied if the intent of the design is to convey whimsy or brashness. Aesthetics and psychology aside, the two `font-size` values are *multiplied* rather than *added*:

$$(15 \times 1.4 \times 1.429) \approx (15 \times 2) \approx 30$$

The same telescoping effect works with respect to decreasing values as well. For that reason, when I participate in forum discussions with newcomers to CSS, I intently (and controversially) discourage people from using `em` or `%` units for `font-size` values of the `body` element, because careless additions of progressively smaller `font-size` values to descending stylesheet rules can lead quickly to illegible copy.

Size Keywords

According to the CSS 2.1 Specification, the seven `font-size` values relate to heading sizes as described in Table 12-1.

Table 12-1. The relationship between font-size keyword values and heading sizes

Keyword	xx-small	x-small	small	medium (default)	large	x-large	xx-large
Heading	h6	—	h5	h4	h3	h2	h1

Support for `font-size` keyword values evokes the `size` attribute of the legacy `font` element, and the two share cognate values in practice.

Given vendor default text size settings in Firefox 3, Internet Explorer 8, and Safari 3/4, the sizes of text set using `font-size` keyword values are described in Table 12-2.

Table 12-2. Default sizes (in px) of text set with font-size keyword values

xx-small	x-small	small	medium	large	x-large	xx-large
9	10	13	16	18	24	32

Working with Typefaces and Fonts

The ability to specify typefaces outside of markup is one of the greatest strengths of CSS. On account of this, presentation of typography on the web medium is now a far cry from where it was in its infancy, when all pages were set in a single typeface chosen by the visitor.

The Challenge of Limited Choices

To make another long story extremely short, there are all of 16 typefaces available to Windows XP that are appropriate for web use—and of those, 3 are functionally useless, each for its own reasons. OS X offers a broader range of choices, but given its market share, the best thing a designer can do is choose one of the XP typefaces as a fallback, in addition to choosing an OS X font, as shown in Table 12-3.

The ubiquity of Microsoft Office (and its bundled fonts) is a bright spot in this otherwise bleak typography landscape, but most of those fonts are intended for print use, not web use.

Table 12-3. Latin typefaces [a] commonly available to web users, according to operating system. Broadly available fonts are highlighted; fallbacks [b] are spelled out.

Typeface	Operating system			
	Windows XP	Windows Vista & 7	Mac OS X 10.3	Mac OS X 10.5
American Typewriter	Courier New	Courier New	✓	✓
Andale Mono [c]	✓	✓	Monaco	✓
Apple Gothic	Microsoft Sans Serif	Microsoft Sans Serif	✓	✓
Arial [c]	✓	✓	✓	✓
Arial Black [d]	✓	✓	✓	✓
Arial Narrow [d]	✓	✓	✓	✓
Arial Rounded	Arial	Arial	✓	✓
Arial Unicode	Arial Unicode MS	Arial Unicode MS	Arial	✕
Arial Unicode MS	✓	✓	Arial Unicode	✓
Baskerville	Palatino Linotype	Palatino Linotype	✓	✓
Big Caslon	Bookman Old Style	✕	✓	✓
Book Antiqua [d]	✓	✓	✓	✓
Bookman Old Style [d]	✓	✓	✓	✓
Brush Script	cursive	cursive	✓	✓
Calibri	Trebuchet MS	✓	Trebuchet MS	Trebuchet MS
Century Gothic [d]	✓	✓	✓	✓
Cambria	serif	✓	serif	Plantagenet Cherokee
Cambria Math	✕	✓	✕	✕
Candara	Tahoma	✓	Tahoma	Tahoma
Chalkboard	Comic Sans MS	Comic Sans MS	✓	✓
Cochin	serif	serif	✓	✓
Comic Sans MS [c]	✓	✓	✓	✓
Consolas	Lucida Console	✓	Monaco	✕
Constantia	Book Antiqua	✓	Book Antiqua	✕
Corbel	Tahoma	✓	Tahoma	✕
Courier New [c]	✓	✓	✓	✓

Typeface	Operating system			
	Windows XP	Windows Vista & 7	Mac OS X 10.3	Mac OS X 10.5
Didot	serif	serif	✓	✓
Franklin Gothic	sans-serif	✓	Gill Sans	Gill Sans
Futura	Century Gothic	Century Gothic	✓	✓
Garamond [d]	✓	✓	✓	✓
Georgia[c]	✓	✓	✓	✓
Gill Sans [e]	sans-serif	Franklin Gothic	✓	✓
Helvetica	Arial	Arial	✓	✓
Helvetica Neue	Arial	Arial	✓	✓
Herculanum	fantasy	fantasy	✓	✓
Hoefler Text	Georgia	Georgia	✓	✓
Impact[c]	✓	✗	✓	✗
Lucida Console	✓	✓	Monaco	Monaco
Lucida Grande	Lucida Sans Unicode	Lucida Sans Unicode	✓	✓
Lucida Handwriting[d]	✓	✓	✓	✓
Lucida Sans Unicode	✓	✓	Lucida Grande	Lucida Grande
Marker Felt	cursive	cursive	✓	✓
Microsoft Sans Serif	✓	✓	Apple Gothic	✓
Mistral	cursive	✓	Brush Script	Brush Script
Monaco	Lucida Console	Lucida Console	✓	✓
Monotype Corsiva [d]	✓	✓	✓	✓
Nyala	fantasy	✓	Papyrus	Papyrus
Optima	sans-serif	sans-serif	✓	✓
Palatino Linotype	✓	✓	Baskerville	Baskerville
Papyrus[d]	✓	✓	✓	✓
Plantagenet Cherokee [f]	serif	✓	serif	✓
Segoe Print	Lucida Handwriting	✓	Lucida Handwriting	Lucida Handwriting
Segoe Script	cursive	✓	cursive	cursive
Segoe UI	sans-serif	✓	Gill Sans	Gill Sans
Skia	sans-serif	sans-serif	✓	✓
Sylfaen	✓	✓	Baskerville	Baskerville
Tahoma	✓	✓	✓	✓
Times	Times New Roman	Times New Roman	✓	✓
Times New Roman[c]	✓	✓	✓	✓

Typeface	Operating system			
	Windows XP	Windows Vista & 7	Mac OS X 10.3	Mac OS X 10.5
Trebuchet MS [c]	✓	✓	✓	✓
Verdana[c]	✓	✓	✓	✓
Zapfino	cursive	cursive	✕	✓
Dingbats				
Apple Symbols	✕	✕	✓	✓
Marlett [g]	✓	✓	✕	✕
Symbol	✓	✓	✓	✓
Webdings[c]	✓	✓	✓	✓
Wingdings	✓	✓	✕	✕
Zapf Dingbats	✕	✕	✓	✓

[a] All of the operating systems described include a number of Cyrillic and Asian fonts that also provide limited Latin support. In addition, not all faces listed are supported with a complete collection of fonts.

[b] The fallbacks suggested here are entirely subjective. Some, though not all, of these fallbacks work across operating systems.

[c] Included in the Microsoft Core Fonts for the Web collection: Arial, Arial Black, Comic Sans MS, Courier New, Georgia, Impact, Tahoma, Times, New Roman, Trebuchet MS, and Verdana.

[d] Some of the typefaces listed in this table are provided not with Windows, but instead with Microsoft Office, which is installed as trial software on most OEM (i.e., "brand-name") systems, including Macs. Even when the Office trial ends or is uninstalled, the associated fonts are left behind on the system—in the case of Macs, if the trial software was run at least once. Since many of these fonts are better suited✕ to print, their use should be considered with care.

[e] Gill Sans is the typeface used by OS X for user interface text labels.

[f] Includes Latin, symbol (e.g., currency), and Cherokee syllabary glyphs.

[g] Includes many of the glyphs used to label Windows interface controls.

Representative specimens of the typefaces listed in Table 12-3 are available at a number of sources, including this book's companion website.

Applying Type Choices: the font-family Property

If you've taken a close look at CSS source, the `font-family` property seems pretty straightforward: property, colon, face, comma, face, comma, face, comma. It seems like something an especially bright chimpanzee with touch-typing skills could manage.

In fact, `font-family` has many rules:

1. All typefaces specified should refer to the *exact* family names found in the font libraries of client hosts, including initial capitalization and any foundry name or encoding designation that's present. For example, `Arial` is an entirely different family from `'Arial Unicode MS'`, which refers to both its licensor and its encoding scheme. Bear in mind that this requirement may force you to name multiple instances of the same typeface.

2. If a family name includes spaces, it must enclosed by single or double quotes.

3. A full comma-separated list of family names should be ordered from most to least desirable, even if a given font in that list is likely unavailable. Therefore, if you want visitors with capable systems to see text set in Futura, you should specify `font-family: Futura,'Century Gothic',sans-serif` in the applicable stylesheet rule.

4. All `font-family` values should end with the desired generic name. Valid generic family names (refer to Figure 12-3, shown earlier) include:

    serif
    > Roman faces; designated as "Latin," "Old Style," "Antiqua," and "Copperplate."

    sans-serif
    > Gothic faces; designated as "Geometric" and "Grotesk."

    monospace
    > Fixed-width faces such as Courier New; sometimes found with the appellation "Mono" or "Typewriter." Fonts with names that end in "10," "12," and "15" are usually fixed-width fonts; those numbers refer to the character pitch per inch at a 12-point size.

    cursive
    > Calligraphic or continuous faces, which often include "Calligraphic" or "Cursive" in their names. To be distinguished from italic fonts, which can be continuous, but usually aren't.

    fantasy
    > Decorative faces apart from calligraphic/cursive faces.

5. Newer browsers that encounter valid `Content-Type`, `Content-Language`, and `charset` HTTP header values can be counted upon to render properly implemented fonts as desired. Such is not the case with legacy browsers—developers stuck supporting legacy browsers should specify fonts that are encoded out of the box for their declared `charset` (if any) (see "What Is Character Encoding?" on page 224). For pages written in Latin alphabets, the safest "legacy" approach is to deliberately identify and serve content that's encoded according to the appropriate ISO 8859-x code page.

 Although outstanding in many respects, Internet Explorer 8 produces unpredictable—and often unacceptable—results when forced to rely on a generic `font-family` value. For this reason, the wisest course of action is to ensure that every list of font names used in a `font-family` or `font` value precedes the generic name with at least one appropriate font that will render as intended on Windows systems. See this book's companion website for more details on this evolving issue.

Finding Canonical Typeface Names

Rule 1 stipulates that `font-family` values need to refer exactly to the name of the typeface used by the client host. To find this name on a Windows system:

1. Open the system Control Panel, which is found in the Start menu under the heading "Settings" or "Control Panel." Alternatively, go to *C:\WINDOWS* in Windows Explorer.

2. In both the Control Panel and the *\\%WINDOWS* folder there is an item labeled Fonts (the former is a hard link to the latter). Open it and browse to one of the font files you expect to use to render type in your document.

3. Open the desired font. The first line of the viewer record will describe the parent family name.

On Macs, the process is even easier. Open Font Book from the Applications folder, select "All Fonts" in the leftmost pane, and browse the items listed in the middle pane until you find your desired typeface. The name displayed is the one that should be referenced in your stylesheet rules.

Figure 12-7 displays captures of the system UI in the final steps of these procedures.

Accessing System Default Type with the font Property

I usually discourage use of the `font` property, because it can force the stylist to apply otherwise unnecessary typesetting values that might need to be countermanded in other rules, effectively increasing the complexity of the stylesheet. The most significant exception occurs when you need to reference system default fonts, which can only be accessed via the `font` property.

The structure of a valid `font` value is as follows:

```
font-style font-variant font-weight font-size/line-height
 [font-family|UI text type designation]
```

Fragments of `font` values, where present, should be arranged in the order shown. In cases where an explicit `line-height` value is unnecessary, the slash that would separate it from its companion `font-size` value can be omitted.

The `font-family` fragment should be supplied just as it would be for a normal `font-family` instance, or replaced with a keyword relating to an object type within the client host's user interface. These keywords are described in Table 12-4 according to corresponding form controls and browser window geometry.

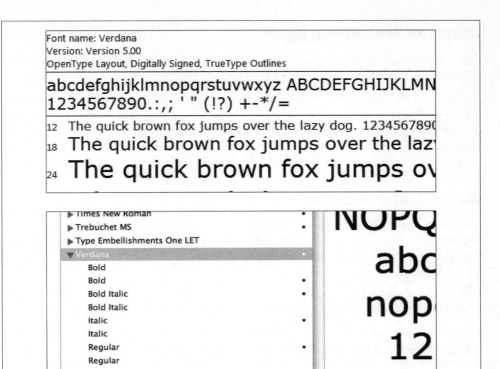

Figure 12-7. A canonical type name

Table 12-4. Font UI keyword fragment values, corresponding to browser controls that use them by default

Keyword	Corresponding form control or browser window label type
caption	input type="submit"
icon	Toolbar button labels; sidebar item text
menu	option
message-box	window.alert() arguments
small-caption	Window geometry matter; usually dingbats
status-bar	Self-explanatory

As of this writing, it's not entirely certain that UI font keyword support will be maintained in CSS3.

Character Encoding in Brief

The last rule for applying `font-family` values can create some confusion, as HTTP response headers aren't always under the control of stylists.

Every properly configured web server that runs an adequate implementation of HTTP—which is to say, nearly all of them—specifies the language and character set of each document that it sends to client hosts. Additional interfaces such as the `meta` element and the PHP `Header()` function allow developers to alter or override those assignments on a case-by-case basis.

What Is Character Encoding?

Hopefully you're familiar with the concept of bits and bytes; a bit ultimately represents the state of a single circuit in system RAM, and a byte is equal to eight of those in a logical row, which can arranged in one of 256 ways.

The technicians of the English-speaking world have grown accustomed to the representation of a single Latin character—or *glyph*, in typography jargon—within a single byte. That example has been followed for other alphabets as well.

Consider the example of Morse Code: its character representations are composed of variable-length series of dits (analogous to unset bits) and dahs (analogous to set bits). In this case, the assignment of a character's unique sequence of dits and dahs is informed by its typical frequency in telegraphic messages.

In the guts of a computer, however, a more systematic means of assignment can be afforded. The definition of "systematic" encompasses the following questions:

- Should the uppercase letters be placed before or after the lowercase letters?
- Do control signals belong at the beginning or end of the character set?
- Does the encoding scheme specify that the first bit of a given character references code positions zero and one, or the entire lower or upper half of the 0–255 range?
- What host system constraints might affect the final encoding scheme?
- Which code positions should remain unassigned to account for future developments, like the introduction of new currency symbols?
- What assignment logic should be used for logographic writing systems like hanzi and kanji, or complex syllabaries like Hangul?
- Will a given encoding be practical for all users of a given orthography?

The profusion of character sets in use today can be explained by the many different answers engineers have to these questions. On the Web, many of these need to be supported as a matter of course.

ASCII, ISO 8859-1, Unicode, and UTF-8

In the mid-1960s several parties collaborated to develop a basic, static-width, 7-bit (128-position) encoding scheme for Latin characters as used in American English, called ASCII (American Standard Code for Information Interchange) and based on earlier teleprinter encoding schemes. A few years later, it was mandated that all computers, storage, and transmission hardware configurations purchased by the U.S. government support ASCII—and in fairly short order, ASCII was ubiquitous in the English-speaking world.

In the 1980s, the International Standards Organization (ISO) published a standard for encoding several European and Near Eastern alphabets, many of which were variants of the basic Latin alphabet. All of these encoding schemes—which remain in popular use today as the ISO 8859 code pages—were half-populated by ASCII.

While all of this activity was transpiring in the West, comparable work was being undertaken to advance standard encoding schemes for writing systems used elsewhere, particularly in Japan. In the early 1990s all of this work was independently amended and amalgamated into the Unicode standard, which has since been progressively expanded with the goal of representing all known writing systems, including dead systems that are used in historical records.

The Unicode code charts presently comprise a total of more than 100,000 characters. On the Web, the characters needed in any given document are usually encoded using a scheme called UTF-8 (8-bit Unicode Transformation Format), a variable-width scheme that encodes all ASCII characters in a single byte (out of a maximum of four), thus ensuring backward data compatibility with all but the earliest ASCII-reliant systems.

Choosing an Encoding Scheme

By default, web server software typically serves documents encoded as UTF-8. If your content is written in English and you use HTML entities (discussed later in this section) to declare instances of characters outside the ASCII character set, there is no need to manipulate the server configuration, or add custom HTTP header output to server-side scripts for the sole purpose of declaring an appropriate character set. This is true for two reasons.

The first reason has to do with the efficiency of the encoding scheme: ASCII-reliant content uses one byte per character, and the added load of entity references is negligible when compared to the hassle of including high-bit characters of uncertain encoding.

The second reason why UTF-8 is acceptable for primarily English-language content is owed to the way that modern browsers handle fonts. The default encoding setting of modern browsers is "Auto," which in the case of ASCII characters means little. However, that same setting allows the browser to render entities regardless of the native encoding of the specified fonts, since the relationships between Unicode code positions and code positions in other schemes are well documented. The browser transparently translates code positions as needed, and the desired character is rendered.

UTF-8 and the "Auto" setting are not the beginning and end of type rendering, however.

A number of scenarios result in the insertion of odd characters into a document. The most common are form submissions from user agents that are set to a custom text encoding setting, and publication of content pasted directly from word processing programs (which tends to be encoded as static-length, 8-bit characters when written in the Latin alphabet).

When these "odd" characters make their way into production, they present proverbial "bumps" in the character stream that a visitor's browser may fail to render properly. If such bumps are a frequent occurrence, you should consider changing the encoding of documents to ISO 8859-x or Windows-1252 (which are almost identical). Developers who work with content written in Asian languages should consider a comparable course of action.

Inserting Entities to Provide Non-ASCII Characters

There are a number of diacritics used in European languages. The only one used in English (for English words) is the umlaut (¨), which was briefly popular in the 1960s and 1970s as a signal to the reader that the second vowel in a pair should be pronounced distinctly as a short vowel, e.g., "coördination." That usage has since been supplanted by the practice of inserting a hyphen in the midst of such pairs, and only then as a matter of house style.

Many house styles also require that loanwords with English homographs (among which "résumé" is a familiar example) include the diacritics used in the originating language.

Many common European diacritics are referenced in the HTML 4 character entity reference list, and displayed alphabetically by English name in Table 12-5.

Table 12-5. Common Western European diacritics referenced by HTML 4

Name	Diacritic glyph	Entity pattern	Example
acute	´	&?acute;	é, í
cedilla	،	&?cedil;	ç
circumflex	^	&?circ;	ô
grave	`	&?grave;	à
tilde	~	&?tilde;	ñ, ã
umlaut; diaresis	¨	&?uml;	ö

Not all diacritics will combine with all letters; those that do combine with a given letter can be applied to both the lower- and uppercase instances. Consult this book's companion website for a link to a complete table of HTML entities. That list, compiled by Adrian Roselli (*http://adrianroselli.com/*), also includes the decimal codes for the high-bit ISO 8859-x glyphs that are not supported by properly served XHTML. In addition to letters with diacritics, there are a number of specialized characters that will be of value to stylists required to produce content adhering to a high standard of typography. Many of these are displayed in Table 12-6.

Table 12-6. Useful HTML entities, listed by common English name in alphabetical order

Character(s)	Literal(s)	Alphanumeric value(s)	Unicode value(s)[a]	Prefer to
Approximately equal to	≈	&asymp;	&#8776;	~
Bullet	•	&bull;	• (U+2022)	*
Cent (currency)	¢	&cent;	&#162;	
Copyright	©	&copy;	&#169;	(c)
Daggers, single and double	† ‡	† ‡	† ‡	* and ** for some annotations
Degree(s)	°	&deg;	° (U+00B0)	
Division sign	÷	&divide;	&#247;	/ in noncomputing contexts
Ellipsis	…	&hellip;	… (U+2026)	...
Em dash	—	&mdash;	&#8212;	- enclosed by spaces, or - -
En dash	–	&ndash;	&#8211;	- for ranges
Eszett	ß	&szlig;	&#223;	"ss" substitution (German language)
Euro sign	€	&euro;	€ (U+20AC)	
Fractional half[b]	½	&frac12;	&#188;	1/2
Guillemets	« »	« »	« » (U+00AB, U+00BB)	" in some languages
Inequality (not equal to)	≠	&ne;	&#8800;	!=
Inverted exclamation point and question mark	¡ ¿	¡ ¿	¡ ¿	
Less than/greater than or equal to	≤ ≥	≤ ≥	≤ ≥	<=, >= in noncomputing contexts
Middle dot	·	&middot;	&#183;	
Multiplication sign	×	&times;	&#215;	x, X; * in noncomputing contexts
Per mille[c]	‰	&permil;	&#8240;	
Pilcrow (paragraph)	¶	&para;	¶ (U+00B6)	
Plus/minus	±	&plusmn;	&#177;	+/-
Pound (currency)	£	&pound;	£ (U+00A3)	

Character(s)	Literal(s)	Alphanumeric value(s)	Unicode value(s)[a]	Prefer to
Primes, single and double	′ ″	′ ″	′ ″	', '', ', ", m:s elapsed
Quote, double low	„	&bdquo;	&#8222;	" or ,, in some languages
Quote, single low	‚	&sbquo;	&#8218;	' or comma in some languages
Quotes, double	" "	“ ”	“ ” (U+201C, U+201D)	", '', or ``
Quote, double [generic][d]	"	&quot;	" (U+0022)	
Quotes, single	'	‘ ’	‘ ’ (U+2018, U+2019)	' or '
Registered trademark	®	&reg;	&#174;	(R)
Section	§	&sect;	§ (U+00A7)	
Space, nonbreaking[d]				
Trademark	™	&trade;	&#8482;	(tm), etc.
Yen; yuan; renminbi	¥	&yen;	¥ (U+00A5)	RMB for PRC currency amounts

[a] Some symbols might find their way into content values associated with English-language content; these are annotated with both decimal entity and hexadecimal Unicode code position values. For more details, consult the discussion of the content property in the Bad Parts.

[b] One-quarter and three-quarters fractions can also be referenced with the same pattern as the one shown here.

[c] The permyriad (basis point) symbol (‰₀) is found at the next code point, but isn't referenced in the HTML 4 specification.

[d] The only named entities supported by XML are &, <, and > (&, <, and >, respectively). All of the entities described in this table should be referenced by their decimal value when served as XML.

Finally, note that the Unicode code point references provided in the fourth column of Table 12-6 are unreliable when the declared document encoding is anything other than UTF-8.

Creating Balanced Type Treatments

If you've designed or produced documents for any length of time, you almost certainly know to avoid what has been called the "ransom note effect"—the juxtaposition of too many typefaces in a given document.

However, the ransom note effect on the Web is not a matter of font abuse alone; it's also a function of the colors, sizes, and styles in which you set type.

Predictability, Preference, and Panic

A site is arranged into sections, and each section contains one or more pages. The ease with which web documents can be organized hierarchically means that it's not only possible but *easy* to enforce a degree of consistency in a site's presentation that pays ongoing dividends. The workload of the designer and stylist can be reduced, and it becomes easy to identify and stake out the parts of the site's page layouts that serve as signposts for visitors.

The bad news is that like most aspects of the Web, this consistency has limits: in many cases, particularly those involving user-generated content, it becomes impossible to predict the amount of content that will be present on a given page. With that unpredictability comes a certain loss of control—and from that follows panicked attempts to manipulate the presence, behavior, and content coverage of a site's layouts.

One common reaction to this panic is to make slight adjustments to gutters, rules, and type size throughout the site, which at first glance makes it easier to resolve each "special" layout case as it comes up.

Assessing Content Scope

The first step in the process of tightening control over typesetting is to scope your content using the cascade. On a given site, you might have some or all of the following elements:

- Site identity
- Body copy
- Titles/headings
- Ledes
- Sidebar content
- Asides
- Navigation:
  — Primary
  — Secondary
  — Outgoing/tertiary
  — "Breadcrumbs"
- Attractors and/or advertising (multimedia content that encourages visitors to follow a link to a landing page elsewhere)
- Forms
- Application functionality
- Last but not least, hypertext links

When presented with so many different functional elements, designers are vulnerable to two colossal mistakes. The first of these has already been mentioned: surrendering to the desire to "tweak" on a case-by-case basis, which turns the stylist's job into a mockery of the intent behind CSS. So many `ids`, `class`es, and junk elements wind up being added that the resulting work product is a hash of nonsense.

The second mistake is to design for the requirement that each significant element of the design needs its own type, which tends *not* to be the case.

In practice, you have six notional classes of type on a site that *must* be made distinct from one another:

- Identity
- Titles (A-heads)
- Subsidiary headings
- Body copy
- Navigation
- Hypertext links

Many designs also call for secondary content—such as long quotes and sidebars—to be set in different fonts.

When considering this list, much less adding to it, the question to ask is:

> *Why* does this item need to be different?

In the list, each case represents a fundamental part of a site, providing vital intrapage or intrasite signposts, or serving as primary content—thus accounting for its need to stand out.

Distinguishing Type: Face, Size, Weight, Style, Color

 While the information covered in this section may seem obvious, its inclusion is meant to provide a framework for the process of making design decisions.

Once you've worked out your content classification as it relates to typesetting, you need to decide how to execute and implement your design decisions.

Face, size, weight, style, and color: when you need to make text stand out, these modalities are the ones that you can choose from. The opportunity to stake out specific areas of a layout with a distinct background color (or shade) can aid your decision, but doesn't actually make that decision for you.

In light of tradition and other factors, these modalities all signal different cues to the casual reader:

Face

Differing typefaces provide cues for content classification; for example, some newspapers set headlines in sans-serif type and body copy in serif type. However, this approach isn't as popular as you might think, either for headlines nor ancillary content, or for reasons both arbitrary (tradition) and practical (differences in font metrics).

Size

Enlarged or reduced type offers an idea of a passage's relative importance. It's also the origin of most stylesheet edge cases. Each case that calls for differing type sizes also calls for changes to composition, which in turn create many of the edge cases that keep stylists awake far past bedtime.

Weight

Setting bold text amplifies content, but only when its boldness is discernible relative to that of neighboring content. Increased weight is best framed as a half-step increase, while obvious size changes signal full steps.

Style

The use of an italic/oblique font signals momentary changes in editorial voice, usually in the form of emphasis. These fonts are also used to set apart some proper nouns, such as titles of periodicals, titles of creative works, ships, named aircraft, and very rarely famous accommodations. Small-caps fonts and wide letterspacing are also used for emphasis, but far more rarely.

Color

Using color to style type for contrast is a far easier task on the Web than in other media, but it puts visitors with impaired color perception at a disadvantage. For this reason, color use should rely on brightness as well as hue, whether it's applied to links or to other text in need of emphasis. Ideally, the use of color in type styling will be paired with other forms of differentiation. Chapter 9 examines these considerations in detail.

Generally, it's preferable to reduce the number of tools you use to differentiate your type, as well as the range of presentations that will result from their use. When too many changes are applied in combination to the same passage, the result tends to overwhelm the visitor.

Once you've narrowed down your tool choices, your next task is to work out the details of composition. Most of the difficulty of this task lies in addressing what happens when unusual cases are encountered:

- What happens to content that takes up more space than expected, particularly with respect to any grid that's being used?
- How do you distinguish passages of content with similar levels of priority but differing function, such as the title of a body copy passage and the title of a sidebar item?

- If the designer has taken a print-inspired approach to the comps and introduced slight differences from each comp to the next, how does the stylist corral the resulting herd of rules?

Setting Type Around Blowouts

The latter two of the three questions just posed can be answered in a well-written stylesheet.

The *easiest* solution to the problem of potential blowouts is to set text and box properties on the target elements with the fewest possible rules, then add `overflow: hidden` to the box properties with the understanding that avoiding blowouts becomes the responsibility of content producers. In settings where the absence of reasonable constraints on content is a frequent but avoidable fact, I actually advocate this approach. (Constraining the amount of space available for content tends to encourage simplicity and clarity, a fact that every habitual user of Twitter knows well.)

If that easy solution to avoiding blowouts is either impractical or impossible—which is sadly often the case—then it becomes the stylist's responsibility to account for deviation from what was comped. Take a heading that was comped to one line; how do you deal with headings that are two lines long? Reducing type size probably isn't an option, but altering `line-height` to fit the long heading into the grid very well might be.

Another case is a hyphenated word that is too long to fit into a column; Internet Explorer will break the line on the hyphen, but other browsers will not. The insertion of a zero-width nonjoiner (`&zwnj;`, most commonly used to indicate logical but invisible space between two glyphs) also fails to yield a break.

In all cases, typesetting to avoid blowouts should:

- Follow the grid laid down for the layout as a whole
- Fit logically within the sizes set in the existing styles and/or type treatment
- Respect the space available, with a minimum of process changes

Styling Passages of Similar Priority

The stylist's job is easiest when the designer starts out with one basic style for type and "branches out" from that baseline; CSS itself is tailored to that approach. In a simple two-column site, the result might be something like this:

Body copy
>   12px Georgia; black

Headings
>   Increased from `h4` (usually sized identically to default text) in four-pixel increments

Sidebar
>   All copy lightened to 75% black

Navigation
Four-pixel size increase for primary navigation, normal text size for secondary navigation; colors handled via link pseudoelements

A stylesheet reflecting this approach would contain the following rules and property/value pairs:

```
body { color: rgb(0,0,0); font-size: 12px; font-family: Georgia, serif; }

h1 { font-size: 2em; }
h2 { font-size: 1.667em; }
h3 { font-size: 1.333em; }

#sidebar { color: rgb(64,64,64); }

 #navPrimary a:link { color: rgb(0,0,192); }
#navSecondary a:link { color: rgb(0,192,0); }

 #navPrimary a:active,
#navSecondary a:active { color: rgb(192,0,0); }
```

Additional work and additional selectors are usually required to differentiate the various sections of a site, but the basic principle should be clear.

The challenges start to spiral out of control when a print-trained designer starts tweaking things. Suppose that the title of a column can't be made any shorter horizontally, so the designer reduces the type size on the headings in that column to preserve consistency.

Duplicate that event three or four times on the same site. Before long, you're forced to write rules with selectors that look like this:

```
body.about#contact #sidebar h3.telephoneContact
```

It's also quite likely that if you're writing selectors like *that*, you're also writing selectors for many of the elements in between `body` and `body.about#contact #sidebar h3.telephoneContact`.

Enter Type Treatments

The scenario just described could have been avoided if it had been agreed upon in advance that sidebar headings could grow onto two lines. This is the sort of thing handled in a style guide. Adjunct to a style guide is a *type treatment*, which basically displays *all* of the type used in a project.

When I create a type treatment, the result usually looks something like Figure 12-8, a chart divided into three columns as follows:

1. The function, and perhaps the selector(s), of a given type choice (e.g., identity, A-head, lede, body copy)
2. A specimen of the type in its intended state

Logotype	**ACME WIDGETS, INC.**	Copperplate Gothic Bold, 48px, #000000
A-head	This is a headline.	Helvetica Neue, 36px, #404040
B-head	Quick red fox	Helvetica Neue, 36px, #808080
C-head	Lazy brown dog	Helvetica Neue Bold, 16px, #404040, 24px line-height
Body copy	Lorem ipsum dolor sit amet, onsectetur adipiscing elit. Curabitur id lectus	Helvetica Neue, 16px, #404040, 24px line-height
Navigation	PRODUCTS	Copperplate Gothic Bold, 24px, #404040
Inline links	visit one of our locations	Helvetica Neue, 16px, #000000, 24px line-height, underlined

Figure 12-8. An inset of a type treatment formatted in three columns (created by the author)

3. The actual metrics of the type, either in English or in the form of CSS property/value pairs

If a site's designer has weighed down the product with exceptions and outliers, the type treatment will run to several pages in length and illuminate the fact that certain aspects of the design process have gone out of control.

Even more importantly, an effective type treatment documents many design decisions in a more human-readable format than what's found in the stylesheet, and can become a tremendous time-saver in the face of challenges like staff turnover and neglect of site maintenance.

Typographical Miscellany in CSS

There are a number of obscure CSS properties that demonstrate the limits of what designers can control with CSS, but also introduce many of the accents that stand between the plain and the elegant.

The line-height Property

As suggested earlier, the line-height property inserts negative space between lines, making it analogous to leading in print. However, as shown in Figure 12-9, the result is applied equally to *both* sides of each line of type to which it applies. The good news

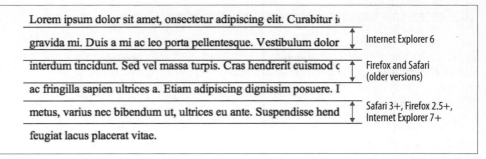

Figure 12-9. Behavior of the line-height property in various browsers (specimen used is 16px Times New Roman at a line-height value of 32px)

is that in current browsers this behavior is consistent; older versions placed *all* of the additional negative space above the type (as in Internet Explorer 6), or below it, as shown in Figure 12-9.

The other notable detail of the `line-height` property is that its range of valid values includes numbers without units, such as:

```
line-height: 1.5;
```

which is functionally similar to a value of `150%` or `1.5em`.

For the sake of consistency and discipline, I find that it's usually better to use the same size units for `line-height` values that you apply to the rest of your font and text properties.

Default `line-height` values are specified with a `normal` value, vary from one font/platform combination to the next, and tend to be very small, in the range of `120%–125%`.

The font-variant and text-transform Properties

The most common functional purpose of the `font-variant` and `text-transform` properties is to provide odd forms of emphasis—for example, for capitalizing a trademark or a quoted passage delivered in a raised voice.

The `text-transform` property is uncommonly used, and its values (among which `uppercase` is the most common) are unremarkable. The `font-variant` property and its single nondefault value—`small-caps`—are another story.

Actual *fonts* that render uppercase letterforms at varying sizes to indicate capitalization are often redrawn so that the strokes of capital letters are comparable to others in the same font. When instead the `font-variant` property is used, the normal lowercase letterforms are replaced with appropriately smaller uppercase letterforms, so that the capitals appear to be a bit on the "fat" side. The same result is visible with some normal fonts, especially those designed exclusively for print use, but is particularly obvious in text to which `font-variant: small-caps` has been applied.

The letter-spacing and word-spacing Properties

Letterspacing and wordspacing are typically best avoided, but sometimes a design requires their use to ensure that a bit of composition is just right. Another uncommon use of these properties is to provide emphasis—as if the speaker was *dr-a-a-a-w-i-i-i-ng* out every syllable of a word. Letterspacing helps convey the same voice outside passages of dialogue.

`letter-spacing` and `word-spacing` values are typically provided in tiny fractions of ems, but there's a hitch: on the Mac, that value is rounded to whole pixels before it's applied to the rendered page. Windows is more flexible when ClearType is enabled, however.

The white-space Property

The `pre` element is unusual in that it can indicate content with semantically important characteristics of appearance—for example, email excerpts. On the other hand, its capacity to control linebreak behavior without requiring the insertion of `br` or child `div` elements is too easily abused.

When applied to an element, the `white-space` property and its `pre` value cause content to render as if they were placed within a `pre` element. The use of that property/value pair also offers additional flexibility for developers who distinguish true preformatted content from content that needs to be subjected to a high degree of presentation control.

Apart from `normal` (the default), the `white-space` property has three other values, which vary from `pre` in the way they handle soft and hard linebreaks in content.

The Practice of Good Web Typography

Once visitors take in the color palette of a site (see the section "Creating Your Own Palettes" on page 149), their next strongest impression is formed around the appearance of its copy. In response to the high expectations of modern-day visitors, the web platform finally offers the tools to adjust a broad variety of type characteristics, and raises the reality of web typography far closer to visitors' expectations of aesthetic quality than was previously the case.

The bad news about these raised expectations is that first-rate practice of web typography requires considerable knowledge of theory...and the good news is that once the theory is out of the way, the practice is easy to master!

Clean and Accessible Forms

Web application development requires more than CSS layout and typography. While sites may simply present information *to* their visitors, applications need to get information *from* their visitors. Web applications thrive or wither on the strength of their form design and implementation.

Wherever there's a need for user-generated content, there's a form—and wherever there's a form, there are ample opportunities to foul the user experience.

This chapter introduces form design and implementation techniques that minimize the risk of ruinous mistakes.

Building Effective Forms

Creating useful forms requires more than knowing form markup. Understanding what makes a form work for its users is a critical part of the web developer's skill set.

Web Applications, User Perspective, and Design Choices

Imagine a heap of data—say, a collection of poetry.

A website that presents these poems will likely store them in an SQL database, which by design offers countless ways to sort and arrange its contents on demand. The heart of that imaginary site is described in the following MySQL table creation command, shared here because it's more or less human-readable:

```
CREATE TABLE poems(
            id SERIAL,
     author_id MEDIUMINT,
    date_added DATETIME,
      date_pub DATETIME,
    discussion TEXT,
     editor_id SMALLINT,
      folio_id MEDIUMINT,
       lang_id SMALLINT,
lang_source_id SMALLINT,
```

```
   marginalia TEXT,
        title VARCHAR(1024),
   translator_id MEDIUMINT,
        verse MEDIUMTEXT
);
```

For the sake of further readability, additional constraints have been omitted from this table structure.

Just by examining the table structure, a skilled application developer can discern some of the assumptions underlying the design of the site's backend—for example, that data about authors, translators, and site maintainers is stored in other tables within the same database.

When considered with respect to user experience design, the structure reveals the *views* that can be taken on the hypothetical site's content without imposing high resource demands. Those views will then influence everything else to do with the site, especially its information architecture and development process.

The views that can be taken on the site's primary content with simple SELECT queries can be framed in terms of:

- Author
- Original publication date
- Original folio/collection
- Display language
- Source language
- Title
- Translator

In addition to these views, the date_pub field allows new content to be exported to RSS easily, and other fields—particularly verse, the field containing the actual poetry—provide their own scopes for full-text search.

For each of those views, there are several ways to build the forms and tables of contents that might be used to find content. If the content in question is user-generated, the design choices that can be made for the forms needed to publish it will be just as varied.

The simplest approach to design is to organize the CRUD.

Organizing User Interfaces by Function

When we consider content in terms of *records*—the smallest collections of data that can be presented out of context—tradition offers four actions that can taken on each. CRUD stands for create, read, update, and delete; the corresponding literal SQL queries for each action follow in parentheses:

Create (`INSERT, CREATE`*)*

Instantiate records or collections of records that previously did not exist. Forms designed around this function will have fields that are empty or filled with default values.

Read (`SELECT`*)*

Retrieve and display extant records in a read-only state. The simplest forms designed around this function are provided for the sake of full-text search; on sites that are designed to be browsed but not searched, the user interface to this function is provided entirely by hypertext links.

Update (`UPDATE`*)*

Change the contents of a record partially or entirely. Well-designed applications, whether system-resident or based on the client-server architecture, will present forms similar or identical to those used for the "Create" function, but will first read the existing record and insert its values into those forms.

Delete (`DELETE, DROP`*)*

Remove a record or collection of records entirely. Web applications rarely expose *true* Delete functions to members of the general public, but instead mark "deleted" records as out-of-view for legal and practical reasons, while leaving actual deletion to the discretion of the site operator's data retention and privacy policies. A common (but not universal) user interface design for this function is a list of records, each with its own `input type="checkbox"` control, assembled into a table that is accompanied by a link or button labeled "Delete" or "Remove."

There is common sense to heed when designing applications and forms around these functions. Several of the following guidelines relate directly to interface design and implementation; any stylesheet that addresses forms should take at least some of the issues raised into account.

Ten Rules for Effective Web Forms and Applications

Effective web applications uphold three virtues above all others: security, simplicity, and transparency. The 10 rules listed here are essential to realizing those virtues in production:

1. *Don't request, much less require, more information than you absolutely need.* A visitor might have plenty of bandwidth and system memory, but the resource likely in shortest supply is *time*. Respect visitors' time (and enhance security) by emphasizing brevity in your form design. Additional forms can be visited later, and user records updated as needed.

2. *Distinguish required fields from optional fields.* Use two cues, one visual and the other text-based, to indicate that a particular field *must* be properly filled in to ensure successful submission of a form. If *all* fields need to be filled, state that clearly in the instructions.

3. *Provide clear instructions and failure/error messages.* If your web application—even the simplest mail form—fails when the visitor doesn't respect submission constraints, describe those constraints prominently and in the clearest language possible.

4. *Explain the consequences of a successful form submission in advance.* In many cases, particularly search, the consequences of a successful form submission are implied, or can be inferred from common practice. Unless you are designing for one of those common visitor objectives—and *especially* if you are asking for information of value—the visitor will want to know in advance, "what's in it for me?" Answer that question clearly. For the same reason, you should provide advance warning if the results of a submission are atypical.

5. *Be RESTful: don't base your application on unreliable assumptions about the state of the visitor's browser and session.* HTTP, as described in the appendix, is a stateless protocol; REST (REpresentational State Transfer) is a practice around which HTTP-based services can be engineered to respect that statelessness. In particular, don't assume that the visitor has been to other parts of an application during the current session, unless you first provide a mechanism (such as a session hash) by which such assumptions can be proven in advance.

6. *Choose field types that minimize the demands placed upon a visitor's fine motor control.* Use `select`, `checkbox`, and `radio` input for nonarbitrary values like Booleans and region lists. When using a `checkbox` control to supply a Boolean value, use only one. Lay out your controls so that all nonarbitrary choices are visible, unless the list of choices is long (and predictable) enough to justify the use of the scroll wheel or Page Down key to navigate to a specific `option` field. Avoid `select multiple` altogether.

7. *Always use labels in tandem with form controls.* The `label` element goes well beyond semantic nonsense: it is an active part of the interface associated with a specific form control via the `for` attribute. When a user interacts with a `label` by clicking on it with a mouse, the form control with the `id` corresponding to that `label`'s `for` value is brought into focus.

8. *Make user input as legible as possible.* Keep forms as short as possible, style text controls to fit the greatest practicable amount of input, and style text within the form at sizes equal to or larger than the size of your body copy. On the other hand, do not paginate your form amidst required fields—doing so introduces unnecessary dependencies into your application that lead to abandoned sessions.

9. *Obey rigidly consistent field sizes, justification, and column stops.* When controls are consistently sized and justified, the typical user's need to visually scan and mouse around a form is kept to a minimum. Small sets of field lengths and styles are preferable, by way of enhancing input legibility.

10. *Focus user activity on one of the four basic actions: Create, Read, Update, Delete.* By confining each application interface to specific combinations of action and

scope, the risk of user error is greatly reduced, as is the need for confirmation dialogs.

These 10 rules are not the only rules worth following; they're just the ones that can be applied to nearly all cases.

For deeper insight about improving the user experience of visitors who use the forms that you build, I suggest the following books:

- *Web Form Design: Filling in the Blanks*, by Luke Wrobleski (Rosenfeld Media)
- *Don't Make Me Think: A Common Sense Approach to Web Usability* (Second Edition), by Steve Krug (New Riders Press)

Assessment and Structure

Excellent form implementations exemplify priority and simplicity.

To move toward this goal, the first step is to define exactly *what* a form needs to request from the visitor. In some cases these requirements and the design patterns used to fulfill them are well established by tradition and common sense, but in others there are too many mitigating factors—such as institutional culture, legal requirements, visitor expectations, and the use or neglect of Ajax—to rush directly into implementation.

I point all this out in order to encourage *thoughtfulness* and *caution* in design; the critical importance of forms does not easily tolerate foolish design choices made while leaping blindly.

Application security is beyond the scope of this book, but well worth addressing in detail. Please be certain to follow common security practices, especially sanitizing form input against SQL injection attacks.

Establishing Requirements

Before attempting to design visual assets such as wireframes or composites, you need first to determine the form and function (if you will) of a form interface. The tasks involved can be divided and ordered as follows:

Assessment
Determine the benefits and requirements of the form, for both visitor and operator. It may seem ingenuous to point this out, but in fact it's far too easy for developers to consider forms only from their own perspective. When visitor requirements are taken into account, an entirely different set of design choices might be illuminated.

Scoping

In the case of web applications and other assets that demand large amounts of information from the visitor, it becomes necessary to divide tasks into manageable pieces or steps. By providing a well-defined scope for each form on your site, you improve your chances of achieving the "Goldilocks zone" of form length: not too long, not too short, but *just right*.

Triage

Ask the question:

Who benefits by receiving the requested information, and how?

This process defines three possible beneficiaries: the visitor, the site operator, or both. Fields that request information of benefit only to the site operator should be removed, paired with an incentive, or relegated.

Prioritization

In most cases, the visitor's objective can be stated as a simple imperative with a single object. "Send the message," "create the account," and "get the promo code" are all examples of common visitor objectives. If a form includes fields that don't relate clearly to the primary visitor objective, define the benefits of filling them and put them nearer to the bottom of the form.

Typing

Establish the type of data that needs to be provided in each field and assign the element to be used. Table 13-1 provides some guidance for this task.

Table 13-1. Form elements described by data type

Type	Element	Additional considerations
Arbitrary text or numbers (short)	`input type="text"`	Best for words, phrases, and string fragments (e.g., URIs).
Arbitrary text (long)	`textarea`	Best for sentences, paragraphs, and arbitrarily long lists of newline-separated reference data such as URIs and tracking numbers; ampersands must be escaped to `&amp;amp;` before serving `textarea` content in an update context.
Passwords	`input type="password"`	Styled like `input type="text"`; data is submitted in the clear and must be encrypted through a separate mechanism.
Identities	`input type="checkbox"`	`checked="checked"` required for activated element in XHTML; opt-out choices should always be reflected by an unactivated element.
Binary/trinary choices	`input type="radio"`	Contained within a single `fieldset`; `checked="checked"` required for activated element in XHTML; mutually exclusive choices must have the same name value.

Type	Element	Additional considerations
Large static domain (single value)	select	selected="selected" required for activated option in XHTML; value domains unfamiliar to the visitor should be immediately legible without scrolling.
Large static domain (multiple values)	select multiple input type="checkbox"	Best contained within a single fieldset, which may benefit from carefully chosen width and overflow values; cf. "Identities" and "Large static domain (single value)" entries above.
File uploads	input type="file"	See "The post Method and File Uploads" on page 249.
Static, ASCII-encoded, session- or user-specific data	input type="hidden"	Alternative to session cookies, with the caveat that data does not completely expire until the browser window is closed and the cached page is deleted.
Interface manipulation buttons	input type="button", button	Best inserted via client-side script, since it can only fire events; benefits from assignment to a class reserved for button-style controls; CSS background properties can be assigned to present an image in lieu of a button; button has more granular support for presentation than its counterparts, but is unreliably supported.
Plain-text submit controls	input type="submit"	Benefits from assignment to a class reserved for button-style controls.
Rasterized submit controls	input type="image"	Use alt values with these elements as you would with normal inline images; when activated in a graphical web browser, this element encodes x and y values corresponding to the pixel coordinates that received the button's onclick event, and scripts that utilize those values should include a default case to serve users of assistive technology and text-only platforms (if you don't take the more-accessible course of avoiding that feature altogether).

There are exceptions to the guidance provided in Table 13-1. For example, the mechanism for making a rating on a 7- or 10-point scale could be implemented with input type="radio" elements instead of a select element.

Markup and Structure

Once you establish the identity and source order of the fields to be used in a particular form, you can move on to the markup.

In addition to form and the field elements described in Table 13-1, you'll be using four other elements:

fieldset
    fieldset only validates in the context of a form. Its purpose is in line with its name: to provide a specific context for similar sequential elements, to which detail is

added with the content of an accompanying legend element, only one of which *must* be present in a fieldset when obeying the requirements of a normal HTML document type. input type="radio" elements are an obvious candidate for fieldset content; other possibilities include related checkbox fields, date/time fields, and series of input type="text" fields that ask the user to provide multiple arbitrary choices.

legend

>legend only validates when inserted into a fieldset element, and is paired with clearly related label/control pairs in the same way that label is paired with a standalone control.

ul *and* li

>Most form markup exists in notional pairs: label paired with a single control, or a legend paired with a series of label and control elements. In the former case, there's usually a need to wrap the pair in a common parent element. Since any block element can be inserted into a form, the best choice for the binding element is li, and that choice in turn begs the inclusion of ul.

The last of these choices is controversial; some implementers prefer to contain form objects within an element that expresses some degree of content indivisibility, while others prefer to settle for *implying* that quality. Note that screen readers and other assistive technologies add functionality to lists that may increase the time needed for an impaired visitor to examine and use the form.

As a direct result of these element choices, the markup used for a simple login form might look like this:

```
<form id="loginForm" ... >
  <fieldset><legend><span>Sign In</span></legend></fieldset>
  <ul>
    <li>
      <label for="username">Username:</label>
      <input type="text" name="user" id="username" value="" />
    </li>
    <li>
      <label for="password">Password:</label>
      <input type="password" name="pass" id="password" value="" />
    </li>
  </ul>
  <input type="submit" class="button terminalButton" value="Log in" />
</form>
```

A more complicated form—say, one with a series of input type="radio" fields—will place such fields and their accompanying label elements within a fieldset, which is then placed within the source order where an unembellished input type="text" or select element would ordinarily go, as shown in Figure 13-1. A legend element will also be inserted into such fieldset elements, as explained shortly.

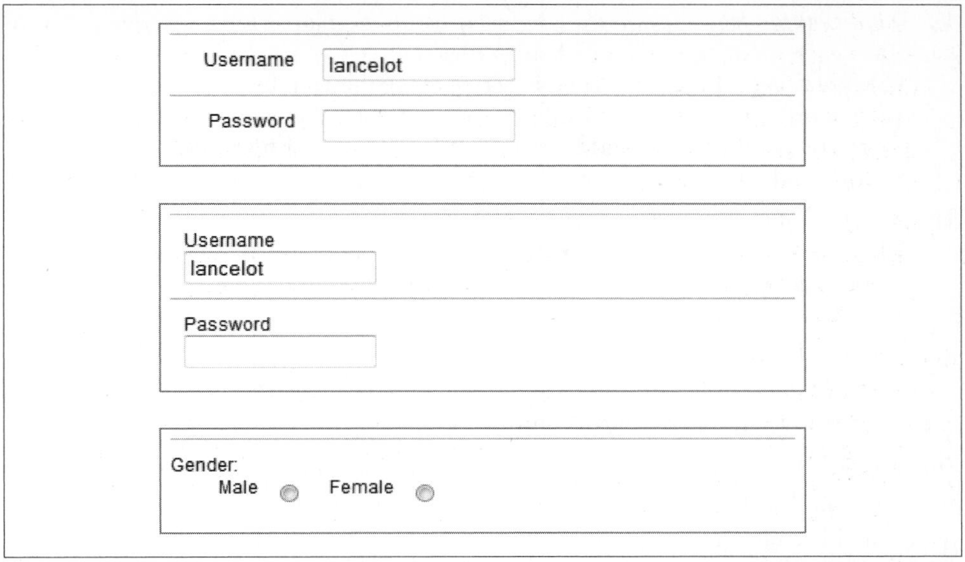

Figure 13-1. The arrangement of typical label/field pairs; contrast use cases that require the fieldset element

Online examples of this latter approach can be found on this book's companion website (*http://www.htmlcssgoodparts.net*), and at the Opera Web Standards Curriculum advanced forms tutorial, which can be found at *http://dev.opera.com/articles/view/34 -styling-forms/*.

In the previous markup example, there are several key details that may not be readily apparent to the casual reader:

The length *and* maxlength *attributes have been omitted*
> The use of the CSS width property supplants the length attribute on most platforms, and maxlength offers limited usefulness as a security measure. On the other hand, these attributes can be inserted into markup without harming the user experience, and may enhance it in some cases.

There is an anonymous span *within the form's* legend
> The legend element is infamously resistant to styling attempts, but fortunately span is not.

The form source is carefully formatted, which at first glance seems at odds with the behavior of the many inline and inline-block elements used
> On the other hand, source legibility is especially important with respect to forms, and the various elements are going to be assigned display: block during the stylesheet authoring process anyhow.

The submit button is not contained within the list markup used for scaffolding, and has two `class` values that point directly to its function

> The function of this element and its `value` make the `li`/`label`/control arrangement superfluous. However, special styles are needed to align such controls to the appropriate column stops, and Internet Explorer's poor support for attribute selectors demands an unusual degree of brute force to achieve ideal screen layout results.

The form itself has been assigned an `id` value

> The `id` associated with the form might well be unnecessary, but if you're using Ajax or placing more than one form on the page, including the `id` will reduce development time and code verbosity in the long run.

In some work environments, it might also be appropriate to add `id` values to the `li` elements and the submit button present in a form, especially if the design of the form's client-side error handling requires complex styles.

Forms that distinguish between required and optional data should also include `class` values on any `li` (container) elements that enclose fields intended for required data.

In summary, when you structure and mark up a form, you're trying to achieve the following for three goals:

- Ensure that each `label`/field pair has ample points of reference to the cascade, DOM API, and requirements for compatibility with assistive technology environments

- Overengineer the form to combat rendering bugs in Internet Explorer, particularly version 6

- Make it as easy as possible for application engineers to create normalized, modular output

The last of these goals is particularly difficult to achieve, but well worth the effort when the objective is to build a complete web application. Well-normalized and modular markup is far easier to process via object-oriented scripting code than are its ad hoc equivalents.

Before moving on to the presentation aspects of forms, there are some details—some obscure, some important—worth pointing out that relate directly to form markup and behavior.

Basic Form Structure, Presentation, and Behavior

Those of you coming to this book from a design or editorial background may be anxious to know: how the heck do forms work on a round-trip basis? (That was my first question when I started on my first big web application project in 1999, anyway.) There are also some oddities of form markup and behavior that are well known to experienced developers, but might not be familiar to all readers.

Form-Originated get Requests

If you've spent much time around form markup, you've surely noticed that every `form` element has an `action` attribute, and every field element has a `name` attribute. The latter are paired with their companion `value` values, and encoded by the browser in the following manner:

```
content=Hello+World%21
```

That's the literal submission to the web server, which in normal language reads "Hello World!"

There are two reliable methods for sending this data to the server: `get` and `post`. `get` appends the encoded data to the URI specified in the form's `action` attribute, resulting in a destination such as:

```
http://example.com/printmystuff.php?content=Hello+World%21
```

Note the literal `?` that separates the data submission from the name of the requested resource—in this case, a script named `printmystuff.php` in the root folder of the host's public filesystem.

Additional `name`/`value` pairs are separated by literal `&` (ampersand) characters, as follows:

```
http://example.com/printmystuff.php?content=Hello+World%21&color=red&size=xx-large
```

Even though the resulting URIs are substantively no different from URIs without form data, the advantage to submitting the data via a form is that the browser encodes the data without the need for tedious human intervention (like requiring the user to memorize half of the ASCII code table).

Because ampersands play a unique role, they must be escaped before they can be used as valid `href` and `src` values:

```
http://example.com/printmystuff.php?content=Hello+World%21&amp;color=red&amp;
size=xx-large
```

This odd requirement has led to the industry term "damnpersands." The genesis of that term is owed to the presence of unescaped ampersands in the content submissions of (understandably) clueless casual users, and the comparably wretched output of legacy third-party plug-ins...and these ampersands are often the only things standing between carefully written markup and the successful validation of a document.

If the script that accepts the encoded data as input is also set as the directory default resource (referenced as `DirectoryIndex` in Apache), and the appropriate server script interpreter is also properly configured, the name of the script can be dropped altogether:

```
http://example.com/?content=Hello+World%21&amp;color=red&amp;size=xx-large
```

Finally, Internet Explorer limits URIs to 2,083 characters, of which no more than 2,048 can refer to any combination of filesystem locations and encoded form data. When a URI overruns this limit, Internet Explorer reports an error to the user.

The Fine Print of URL Encoding: ASCII Entities

In the preceding examples you probably noticed the presence of the %21 encoding in lieu of !, which is listed in RFC 3986 as a reserved character. The full list of reserved characters is provided in Table 13-2.

Table 13-2. Reserved characters in URIs and their ASCII encodings

Literal character	Long name	Encoding	Decimal value
	space	%20	32
!	exclamation point	%21	33
#	pound sign	%23	35
%	percent sign	%25	37
&	ampersand	%26	38
$	dollar sign	%24	36
'	apostrophe	%27	39
(	left parenthesis	%28	40
)	right parenthesis	%29	41
*	asterisk	%2A	42
+	plus sign	%2B	43
,	comma	%2C	44
/	slash	%2F	47
:	colon	%3A	58
;	semicolon	%3B	59
=	equals sign	%3D	61
?	question mark	%3F	63
@	commercial at	%40	64
[	left square bracket	%5B	91
]	right square bracket	%5D	93

Literal spaces are *always* encoded—with %20 in actual URI paths, and with a literal + in URL-encoded values like those shown above. This leads to some unfortunate but necessary mangling: for example, if one wanted to submit 2 + 2 = 4 from a form, that data would be encoded to 2+%2B+2+%3D+4 before submission.

Some of the other characters described in Table 13-2 are posed literally in paths, but encoded when submitted as form data.

Browsers URL-encode user input without the need for developer intervention. However, the various scripting languages in common use on the Web all include functions that will convert user input to or from a URL-encoded format.

The post Method and File Uploads

When the request method associated with a form is changed to post, encoded form data is appended to the request body instead of the URI. Apart from serving as a way of getting around the practical 2,083 character limit on URIs, post submissions are more difficult for users to manipulate in ways not accounted for by a form's design. For these reasons, post is the request method required for file uploads.

While the default enctype attribute of form elements is application/x-www-form-urlencoded, forms that support file uploads must instead have a declared enctype of multipart/form-data.

Unfortunately for stylists, the input type="file" element interacts inconsistently with CSS. Its most significant characteristic with respect to layout is that it actually draws *two* UI objects on the canvas: a text input analog and a button. For this reason, the only CSS properties that you can apply to a file upload control with any expectation of gaining the desired results are color, background-color, and the properties that affect layout flow (such as margin properties and position). This unyielding nature applies especially to the button control, which in most cases cannot be changed from its operating-system-dependent appearance.

If you apply custom visual styles to form elements, your composites and designs should take a conservative approach to file upload controls, by assuming that they cannot be altered from their default appearance.

Manipulating the Size and Appearance of Individual Controls

Form controls behave a little differently from other HTML components:

- Font and text property values in form controls are not inherited via the cascade, but instead must be assigned those values via selectors that reference form controls directly.
- Unlike normal elements, form controls are rendered according to "quirks mode"—all box properties (except margins) lie within the control's specified width and height (if any).
- Form controls (except textarea) tend to disregard any line-height value that is assigned to them.
- With the exception of input type="file" elements and the contents of select elements, form controls can take on transparent backgrounds and custom background colors.
- The computed width of input type="text" is suggested by any length value it's been supplied. The best control of presentation is afforded by avoiding length and instead applying width values in the stylesheet, as in the source examples provided earlier.

- The apparent size of checkbox/radio controls is controlled not by `width` or `height` values, but instead by `font-size` values.

It's easy to resolve the box-model deviation in current browsers, all of which support the CSS3 `box-sizing` property (albeit as extensions in Firefox and Safari). It can be set to one of two values:

`content-box`
> Forces the element to be defined according to the "Strict" box model: the element's width value does not include its border or padding values. If you intend for form controls to be rendered according to the "Normal" box model, they should be assigned this value.

`border-box`
> The element is rendered according to the "Quirks" box model: its computed width includes any borders and padding that are set.

Finally, the `select` element has its own peculiarities:

- Under normal circumstances, a `select` control with a `width` value of `auto` will expand to the width of its longest `option`.

- If the width of a `select` control is less than that of its longest `option`, the "drop-down" box will still expand to that greater width when the control is activated, provided that it can do so without overflowing its parent viewport.

- The `width` and `font-size` values of `select` controls can be assigned in Safari, but all other aspects of their appearance are influenced by the specifics of their underlying interface library and cannot be altered.

- `option` elements can be grouped within `optgroup` elements, as shown in Figure 13-2. Especially long lists of `option`s should rely on `optgroup` to provide separators, instead of including meaningless `option` elements where group separators are desired.

- If an `option` that lacks a nonnull `value` is selected by the user, the user-facing content of that `option` will be encoded and sent to the server instead.

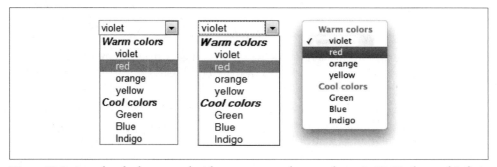

Figure 13-2. A rendered select control with optgroup members, as shown in IE, Firefox, and Safari

This book's companion website includes a test suite that demonstrates the behavior of `select` in greater detail.

Prototyping and Layout

Once a form has been designed at the functional level and implemented, the next step is to lay out the form so that it can be tested as a prototype.

Prototyping 101

A web application prototype serves the same function as any tangible product of an engineer's labor: to ensure that the product works as its designers intended. Much of the effort of prototyping an application goes into ensuring that executable code is bug- and hassle-free, but prototyping is also an opportunity to verify the usability of that application's human interface.

The user-facing aspects of prototype testing should answer the following questions:

- Are the application's forms adequately easy for the target users to follow?
- Does the draft design of any form appear to lead to any habitual or typical user errors?
- Do users routinely neglect certain fields, or intuitively invest extraordinary effort in others?
- Are there any aspects of the application's visual design and layout that require a labor investment out of proportion to the benefits gained from the resulting production values?

All of the information gleaned from the prototype testing process can have effects on the user experience of an application, but the aspects discussed here focus on markup and CSS.

Stylists need to avoid creating situations in which:

- The relationship between a form's fields and their associated `label`s is unclear or inadequate.
- Fields have been assigned a source or presentation order that poorly reflects user priorities.
- Instructions and warnings are poorly laid out, obtusely written, or lacking necessary detail.
- Specific design requirements expose egregious rendering bugs.

For a form to serve as an effective prototype, it needs to meet the following presentation requirements:

- The layout of the form should follow the conventions defined by the wireframes and composites.
- While accents are unnecessary, the foreground and background colors should supply adequate contrast.
- Instructions and required-data cues should be presented as similarly as possible to their intended appearance on the production site.
- If Ajax is to be used in the production application, it should be implemented in the prototypes as well, at least with respect to critical tasks. It falls to the stylist to ensure that Ajax output meets the requirements described here.

Some basic design patterns for form layout are described in the next section.

Design Patterns, Style Resets, and Form Layout

By default, form controls follow inline-block flow, and labels follow inline flow. Because these elements will in many cases be assigned `float` values, and since the presence of whitespace within source markup alters the layout of inline-block elements, these elements are usually far easier to work with when they're assigned a `display` value of `block`. Once other elements are taken into consideration, conservative reset rules for forms will look something like this:

```
form, form ul, form li,
    fieldset, textarea { margin: 0; padding: 0; }
  label, input, select,
textarea, form li span { display: block; }
      form ul, form li { list-style-type: none; }
              form li { clear: both; height: 1%; overflow: auto; }
            fieldset { border: 0; }
```

The layout patterns recommended for web forms are listed below, in order of desirability. Each pattern is accompanied by sample styles that rely on the markup patterns discussed in "Assessment and Structure" on page 241.

 In the following style examples, the `width` and box values were chosen for demonstration purposes only. Note that field margin values tend to complement the `width` values of corresponding `label` elements.

Labels to the left of fields

```
label, form li span { float: left; width: 9em; padding-right: 1em; }
      input, select, textarea { float: left; margin-left: 10em; }
fieldset label, fieldset input { float: left; }
              fieldset label { clear: left; width: 4.25em; padding-right:
                                .75em; }
              fieldset input { margin-left: 5em; margin-right: 1.5em; }
```

Same as the previous, with labels and fields justified to a common margin, in addition to the previous set of rules

```
label, form li span { text-align: right; }
```

Fields below labels

```
form li { clear: both; height: auto !important;
                       overflow: visible !important; }
fieldset label, fieldset input { float: left; }
          fieldset label { clear: left; width: 4.25em; padding-right: .75em; }
          fieldset input { margin-left: 5em; margin-right: 1.5em; }
```

Labels to the right of fields

Use the same styles as those applied to make labels fall to the left of their associated fields, but invert applicable `float` and margin values.

Multiple columns of `label` control pairs

Divide your `label`/control sets into an appropriate number of separate lists, and rely on the properties already discussed to achieve the desired layout for each column. To achieve the best results, add the following rules to your reset styles:

```
form { height: 1%; overflow: auto; }
form ul { float: left; width: 45%; margin-right: 5%; }
```

When you try to apply these examples to a working prototype, you'll discover that things aren't quite grid-perfect, particularly with respect to `input type="radio"` and `input type="checkbox"` controls. This is due partly to the tendency of most browsers to borrow form control rendering from the user interface library of the underlying operating system. The implications of this are raised in Chapter 14.

The second—and more straightforward—reason why things never seem to go according to plan on the first styling pass involves the position of forms in the cascade: *at the top*, for all intents and purposes. In order to influence form control sizes, you'll be called upon to set their `width` and `height` values on a case-by-case basis, an effort that also requires you to set a custom `font-size` value for each form (or all forms) if you intend to use the `em`-based approach to atomic grids that's described in "Layout Types and Canvas Grids" on page 106.

In practice, the work required to implement a production-ready form layout will involve many adjustments and tests. You'll find yourself creating `class`-scoped rules, setting a lot of box values, and making minute adjustments to specific types of controls. Especially complex form layouts might demand that you make minute layout changes to specific fields, such as:

```
form#supportTicket li#severity input { padding-top: .333em; }
```

In this example, you can discern the function of the affected fields from the selector applied—a support ticket submission form containing a row of controls that allow the visitor to define the severity of the problem, most likely a row of `input type="radio"` controls (given the use of `input` rather than `select` in the selector).

Explaining every potential form layout challenge that you're likely to encounter would result in an extremely long book. Additional test suites, library rules, and advice can be found on this book's companion website.

Grouping Controls by Appearance

Forms present several layout challenges, some of which are posed with great frequency:

- `input type="text"`, `textarea`, and `select` elements that are meant to handle variable amounts of input, e.g., street addresses and zipcodes.
- `input type="submit"` elements at the end of forms
- Rules such as `input { border: 1px solid rgb(0,0,0); ... }`, which must then be reset for `input type="checkbox"` and `input type="radio"` controls
- Unlabeled (or oddly labeled) controls that appear in series, such as dates, rating scales, and telephone numbers divided into their constituent parts
- Margin resets for `input type="checkbox"` and `input type="radio"` controls

 Internet Explorer's lagging selector support, especially with respect to attribute, sibling, and immediate child selectors, is actually one of the Bad Parts. The consequences are particularly bad with respect to stylesheet authoring for form presentation.

The use cases just listed are best handled by choosing selectors named according to use or to the length of the data to be contained in a given field:

For Text/`select` *field dimensions, use:*

- `.short`
- `.medium`
- `.long`
- `.small`
- `.large`

Choose the dimensions of select/option content carefully; fields that are too narrow can obscure option content, in some cases irretrievably. For Submit button and image controls, use:

- `.terminalButton`
- `.submitButton`

To differentiate between text and pointer-toggled `input` *elements, apply the appropriate* `class` *to the less-frequent* `type` *of:*

- `.textControl`
- `.buttonControl`
- `.boolControl`

- `.enumControl`

And for the "hidden":

Hiding or omitting labels is a bad idea, but if they must not be visible to screen media users, use negative `left` values in tandem with `position: absolute;` to move them out of view of screen media users. To label fields that are meant to store arbitrary choices in series (e.g., after a `legend` that instructs visitors to list three of their favorite things), use `label` content that references ordinal values (1st, 2nd, 3rd...) without respect to `label` elements' visibility within the form interface.

The `fieldset` element appears in many of the cases described; use it wisely in both your markup and your stylesheets.

Required Fields and Other Submission Constraints

There are a few occasions when a field *needs* to be filled, and the need is self-evident: search and login forms obviously meet that description.

Most of the time, however, it's only obvious to the developer of a form or an application that a given field must be populated by the visitor prior to submission, even in common-sense cases such as forms to collect mailing addresses (and titled as such). In these cases, form elements need to be marked as "required," and the corresponding checks need to be written into the site logic.

In other cases, user-submitted data might fall within certain constraints, as is the case with telephone numbers and email addresses especially. Handling these cases will require the use of string value checks and regular expressions.

Stylists have their own work to do in these cases: required fields must be marked appropriately, submission constraints identified in the clear for the visitor, and errors styled (preferably with accompanying feedback on the nature of the error).

Identifying Required Fields

Consider one of the `label`/control pairs described earlier in Figure 13-1, which delineates the footprints of `li` container elements, `fieldset`s, `label`s, and actual form controls. Assuming that you're laying out your forms with the styles provided elsewhere in this section, you'll likely be adding rules comparable to the following:

```
                .required { position: relative; padding-right: 3.3em; }
.required label span.warning { position: absolute; right: 0; width:
auto; color: rgb(192,0,0); }
```

Styles like these correspond with markup such as:

```
...
<li id="ZIPControl" class="required">
  <label for="zipcode">ZIP Code<span class="warning"> [required]</span>:</label>
  <input type="text" name="zip" id="zipcode" length="5" value="" />
</li>
...
```

When used together, the result will be a "[required]" label on the right margin of the label/control pair, set in a color with an H/S/B value of 0°/100%/63% (trending toward maroon). The label is styled in such a way that the same rule can be applied to *all* required fields in the document with a reduced risk of blowouts, provided that li and fieldset elements have a functional width value of auto.

The drawback of this technique is that it can be missed by some screen magnifiers, particularly the one included with all installs of Windows. When designing for this case, the "required" tags should instead lie flush with the left margin of the associated field, and either above or below it. The effects of such a change are easy to work out, though it's likely to result in a layout grid with far more vertical negative space than the one implied here.

Many form designs will suggest required-field tagging that can be accomplished with more "natural" element flow, but in cases such as these it's helpful to know that positioning context (see "CSS Positioning Properties" on page 96) is there when you need it!

Discovering and Identifying User Input Errors

The next step in ensuring the validity of user input is to check it for errors, a task that is best accomplished with both client- and server-side logic. The pipeline works something like this:

1. User input is tested against the appropriate combination of checks against .length, indexOf(), parseInt(), and RegExp objects on the client side.

2. If JavaScript is enabled, user input that contains errors is flagged by the validation script; an appropriate class such as error is appended to the existing value (if any) of the appropriate li or fieldset container, and content is added to indicate the nature of the error. If the user input meets requirements, the extra round trips of transactions between client and server can be avoided.

3. The submission is received by the server and sanitized to prevent injection of malicious SQL statements, executable code, and markup.

4. The sanitized input is checked against server-side logic similar to that executed in the browser; if user input errors are found, the submission response includes the same altered markup that should have been effected by the browser.

5. Steps 1, 3, and 4 are repeated until user input is free of errors.

The error description should be appended either at the top of the form, or at the beginning of the li associated with the control that contains the erroneous user input. It's best to use *both* content positions, or else the latter alone; error messages placed solely at the top of the form will force many users to scroll back and forth between the notifications and the errors—if they can recognize the errors at all, under the circumstances.

To handle error descriptions, you can attempt rules like the following to complement the .required span.warning styles provided earlier:

```
.error .warning { display: block; background-color: rgb(160,0,0);
color: rgb(255,255,255); font-weight: bold; }
    .error input { border: 1px solid rgb(160,0,0); background-color: rgb(255,160,160);
}
```

In addition to these styles (which are provided entirely for the sake of illustration), clear, width, and margin values can be added to ensure that the error notification will lie horizontally flush to its associated input control or fieldset.

The disabled and readonly Attributes

If you've ever installed an operating system, especially one that requires a license key, you are familiar with the notion of disabled controls. In software installation scenarios configuration is often handled in several steps, each of which must be completed before the next can begin, and the "Next" control at the end of each step is "grayed out" until all parts of a step are completed.

You can impose similar bottlenecks on web forms with the disabled attribute, or less often with the readonly attribute. Both are supported by the various form elements as suggested in Table 13-3.

Table 13-3. Summary of disabled and readonly support

Attribute	button	input	option	select	textarea
disabled	✓	✓	✓	✓	✓
readonly		✓			✓

While the use of these attributes can lead to more elegant user experience designs—mostly by preventing a visitor from setting values on controls until dependencies have been satisfied—their values can only be changed with the assistance of JavaScript. For this reason, you should avoid applying these attributes in the absence of alternative solutions to the problem of satisfying dependencies within user input.

If you decide to obscure fields that need to be filled to satisfy intraform dependencies, preserve the space that those fields are meant to occupy when fully visible, loading them via Ajax or altering CSS properties *other than* display. Sole reliance upon display to effect field availability is jarring, and may reduce the quality of the user experience for users of assistive technology platforms.

Creating Accessible Forms

Since forms are the beginning and end of many sites' business objectives, it's important to consider the likelihood that a significant proportion of your visitors cope with reduced physical or mental function that complicates their efforts to use the Web. Impairments relevant to the design of websites can be grouped into several basic categories, each illustrated with common examples:

Motor dysfunction
> If users' range of motion is limited, so is their ability to use a mouse, keyboard, or perhaps both.
>
> - Broken arms and/or fingers
> - Chronic tendinitis or repetitive strain injury
> - Peripheral neuropathy
> - Paraplegia and quadriplegia

Impaired eyesight
> The user interface design of personal computers and mobile devices is largely predicated on users' ability to respond using their senses of sight, hearing, and touch. Of these, eyesight is most significant to the design of websites, particularly those that rely on forms to meet their business objectives. If users can't see a form or the data they're putting into it, their ability to use such sites is greatly reduced.
>
> - Myopia
> - Astigmatism
> - Age-related degeneration of visual acuity
> - Macular degeneration
> - Glaucoma
> - Di- and monochromaticity (color blindness)
> - Profound blindness

Cognitive dysfunction
> The perception of value in media content, including web content, is entirely a function of the brain and mind. A user who can't concentrate on a site or quickly comprehend its value is unlikely to stick around—thus the emphasis on brevity.
>
> - Attention deficit disorders
> - Dyslexia
> - Auditory processing disorder
> - Symptomatic brain injury

- Acute vitamin B deficiency

There are many other conditions that affect a person's ability to use the Web. Shortage of time, for example, is not among the types of impairment listed above, but is a common affliction.

It's almost certain that you and people you know are familiar with at least a few of the disorders listed here. I have extensive personal experience with three of them, two of which I cope with on a daily basis—yet I still use the Web.

How about that!

Implementing Forms for Accessibility

You can make your site usable by practically all visitors by following some basic practices:

Consult the Web Content Accessibility Guidelines (WCAG) during the design and test phases of each project
> This recommendation points more to habits than actual process; as you become more familiar with the techniques described in the WCAG, you'll get into the habit of implementing them with progressively less effort.

Never rely on a single modality for signaling context or accepting user input
> Where you use text, supply a purely visual cue as well (and vice versa). Ensure that a visitor can interact with your site with a pointing device or a keyboard *alone*, while still allowing the choice of using one device in preference to the other.

Always order source markup and content so that it reads coherently without the benefit of CSS support
> This goal requires that you consistently put the most important stuff first.

If you require a user to do something more demanding than "go wherever you want and provide whatever data you please," ensure that those requirements are clear and easy to understand
> Provide succinct instructions. You want to respect users' intelligence within reason, so don't "talk down" to your visitors. However, it can often damage the user experience when you assume that visitors share your depth of knowledge and your perspective.

Avoid applying `display: none` *and* `visibility: hidden` *at runtime, unless you're willing to accept that impaired users may never see the associated content*
> Since assistive technology platforms run on the assumption that the only styles available are written for screen media, those property/value pairs suggest that affected content should be ignored.

Do your best to ensure that users can read their own input under reasonable circumstances
Failure to style to this requirement results in unnecessary squinting, scrolling, and cursor manipulation on the part of the user, activities that are never easy for visitors with motor or visual impairments.

Consistency makes your site more predictable; design and implement layouts accordingly
Use steady margins and control sizes. Keep `label` content brief, without leaving it completely bereft of meaning. Place `label`/control pairs in columns, so that each control follows its predecessor in the same way that lines of copy flow from top to bottom.

Where you use techniques such as Ajax and `display` value toggles, implement WAI-ARIA (W3C Web Accessibility Initiative Accessible Rich Internet Applications) support via a JavaScript framework
More information about WAI-ARIA can be found on this book's companion website.

Write valid markup to the spirit, rather than the letter, of the HTML and CSS specifications
This means that you never use `table` elements to lay out page content, and that you always include `alt` attributes with your images. Furthermore, it means that you use the elements intended for your task if they're supported, and that you use `id` and `class` to impart context if they're not. Most importantly, you should structure *markup in general* to impart context, rather than using it to wrangle presentation.

Supporting Keyboard Navigation of Forms

Form elements and links in particular can be focused through the use of the Tab key alone; the Enter key can be used to follow links and submit forms. This functionality is exposed at the structural level through the `tabindex` attribute, which can be used to change the order in which elements are focused by pressing the Tab key.

Under normal circumstances, use of the Tab key moves focus from one element to the next in source order. When values are provided for applicable elements' `tabindex` attributes, the focusing order changes so that elements with a `tabindex` are focused from lowest value to highest, followed by unassigned attributes in source order. Elements with identical `tabindex` values are focused according their source order relative to one another.

However, the `tabindex` attribute has two drawbacks: first, when `tabindex` is poorly implemented on long pages, the scroll bar can leap great distances, leading to disorientation. And second, as a site goes through revisions, `tabindex` values are rarely updated in practice.

On the other hand, a page with proper source order can benefit from the addition of `tabindex="0"` to important elements that would not ordinarily receive focus early in the visit (or in some cases, under any circumstances). You can also add negative `tabindex` values to elements that you want to exclude from a document's tabbing order.

The `accesskey` attribute supplants tab order by allowing users to bypass it entirely. Valid values for the `accesskey` attribute are single characters, i.e., any normally unshifted, printable character. These values can be activated by the user when they are pressed in combination with one of the shift keys listed in Table 13-4.

Table 13-4. Activating accesskey assignments in the major browsers

Browser	Key combination
Firefox/Windows	Alt+Shift+?
Internet Explorer	Alt+?
Safari and Firefox/Mac	Ctrl+?

Two of the platforms described in the table carry special implications for user expectations. The first of these is the OS X environment, where Ctrl rather than Cmd is the key used to shift to an access key. Since Cmd is normally used to execute application commands from the keyboard of a Macintosh (and the Ctrl key is neglected outside of command-line environments), the assignment makes sense and poses reduced risk of conflicts.

In contrast to this happy situation, there is the matter of the Internet Explorer `accesskey` implementation. Windows applications focus their main application menus with a press of the Alt key, the same key used as the `accesskey` shift—thus, Alt+F activates the File menu, Alt+E activates the Edit menu, and so on. It's important to remember that if a conflicting value is supplied for an `accesskey` attribute, the corresponding *application* interface trigger is typically overridden and thus disabled.

Given Internet Explorer's preponderance of market share, use of the F, E, V, A, T, and H values for the `accesskey` attribute is strongly discouraged. Some toolbars and browser extensions may suggest similar exclusions for Windows browsers in general.

Form Features in HTML5

HTML5 initially focused on adding new features for HTML forms. It may be the area where HTML5 makes the largest changes, but it's still in development. This section gives an overview of the form features, and supplies details about a couple of features that, while currently not as well known as some other new features, nonetheless have great potential to have significant impact on end users.

New Input Types

HTML5 forms improve on HTML 4 forms through the addition of the following 13 new types of `input` controls:

- `datetime` (global date-and-time input)
- `datetime-local` (local date-and-time input)
- `date` (date)
- `month` (year-and-month input)
- `time` (time input)
- `week` (year-and-week input)
- `number` (number input)
- `range` (imprecise number input)
- `email` (email address input)
- `url` (URL input)
- `search` (search field)
- `tel` (telephone-number input)
- `color` (color-well control)

These new input types offer a major improvement to authors: in the case of any of the new types that have a special user interface associated with them, the user interface is handled natively by browsers, instead of requiring authors to write their own JavaScript code or use JavaScript libraries. For example, for color input, the browser generates a color picker that allows users to select a color by pointing and clicking; for date input, the browser generates a calendar picker. Providing users with a GUI control for those kinds of input types also provides a built-in (as opposed to bolt-on) mechanism to ensure that users can only enter valid values.

The big improvement for end users is also the provision of that kind of automatic client-side validation—to either ensure that users can't input invalid data to begin with, or to quickly alert users when they do. (In HTML5 form implementations, client-side form validation is always on by default, and can only be turned off by a user option in the browser or by a page author explicitly setting a `formnovalidate` attribute on the entire form or on a specific control.)

The required Attribute

The `required` attribute is a new form-related HTML5 feature whose purpose is relatively simple yet very powerful. Specifying `required` on an `input` or `textarea` element in a particular form indicates that users must provide a value for that element in order to submit the form.

For the case where proper processing of a form requires that certain fields have non-empty values such as the name field in an account-creation form, it's necessary to check the form contents and alert users when they attempt to submit the form with empty values for those fields. That checking is currently done in one of two ways. The first way is to do the check on the server side after the user submits the form; this is sub-optimal because it means an extra network pass, and extra time for the user. The second, better way is to do the checking on the client side, before the browser sends the form to the server. However, the current downside is that this requires authors to do the checking using custom JavaScript code or a JavaScript library of some kind.

Enter the `required` attribute. The benefit of the `required` attribute to you as an author is that it eliminates the need to rely on JavaScript code to do client-side checking of form fields for which values are required. Instead, all you need to do is set the `required` attribute on the form field, which causes the browser to automatically do the checking.

The benefit of the `required` attribute to end users is that it can save them time and trouble; it also gives them a consistent user experience, across all web applications, for being alerted in the case of a form with missing values for required fields. It also enables them to get localized "missing form value" messages from their browsers in their preferred languages (instead of being limited to the language a particular web application uses for its error messages).

The Bad Parts

The Web is a wonder of modern civilization. Unlike any other time in history, it's now possible for people to instantly publish without the need for external approval, and the Web is a key part of how we achieved that state of affairs.

Unfortunately, like any system, the Web has flaws, technical limitations, and vulnerabilities. These are the Bad Parts. I discuss a number of them in this chapter, along with a brief explanation of how they should be used, if at all.

This chapter concludes with "The Awful Parts" on page 286, which should be avoided almost without exception.

The Numbing Nature of Internet Explorer (Especially IE 6)

The trouble with Internet Explorer is less a flaw of HTML and CSS than of an implementation, but the flaws in that implementation cast very long shadows. When Internet Explorer 6 was released in 2001, it was *categorically* the best web browser available. Why?

- It offered more and better support for web standards than any of its predecessors, mated with what was then the best DOM API support.

- The rendering technology underlying Firefox, codenamed Gecko, was more than two years from maturity.

- Internet Explorer 5 for Macintosh claimed the most standards-compliant CSS implementation, but it used its own rendering engine and was hampered by a lack of market penetration and internal support.

- Netscape was dying...because its best was to be found in Netscape 4.

- Safari was unheard of at the time, and wouldn't reach full maturity for four years. It took another year beyond that for Safari to become functionally similar to its contemporaries with respect to rendering behavior and capability.

In other words, Internet Explorer 6 wasn't too shabby in its own right when it was first released, and it enjoyed a wide-open market.

Originally spurred on by Netscape's initial dominance in the web space, Microsoft did an incredible job of releasing terrific web browsers for four consecutive years, but in the end, it became the napping Hare.

Apple, Inc., and the Mozilla Foundation fell collectively into the role of the slow-yet-indefatigable Tortoise: they built and released their browsers, bit by painful bit, until in 2005 there was no denying that Internet Explorer was showing its age.

Browser Wars 2.0

In mid-2005 the U.S. Government recommended that web users avoid Internet Explorer altogether, for reasons of security. Open-software advocates and anti-monoculture gadflies enthusiastically began extolling the virtues of alternative browsing platforms, and the results of that effort nibbled at Internet Explorer's market share, month after month.

Shaken out of somnolence, Microsoft has since released two new versions of Internet Explorer that stand well above their offering of 2001, but that dinosaur—eight years old as I write this—continues to hold on. There are a number of reasons beyond simple network effects that explain the persistence of IE 6:

- When first released, the menu bar of Internet Explorer 7 was hidden by default, confusing and alienating many casual users.

- Since enterprise information technology shops (the beating heart of Microsoft's recurring revenue) are viewed as cost centers in spite of the efficiency they make possible, their best intentions are hobbled by the maxim "if it ain't broke, don't fix it." For this reason, Internet Explorer upgrade deployments are viewed by many as imposing unnecessary hassles.

- Since its release, Windows XP, which includes Internet Explorer 6 out of the box, has garnered more user goodwill than any of Microsoft's more recent operating system offerings. Windows 7 has been on the market since October 2009 and shows great promise of outclassing Windows XP, but it will claim a smaller market share than its predecessor for some time to come.

- It's quite easy to set low-pass filters for CSS, thus hiding many of Internet Explorer 6's flaws from casual users—at least to a point.

- Between 2001 and 2005, a number of service providers, especially banks, launched customer-facing sites that were tuned to Internet Explorer for Windows, or were perceived as such because the teams that built them didn't know any better. This profusion of platform-specific services created an unintended heap of Fear, Uncertainty, and Doubt (FUD) about the credibility of alternative browsers.

- Security, filters, and platform specificity notwithstanding, most casual users quite frankly don't give a damn *which* browser they use, as long as it's usable and seems to work.

That said, Internet Explorer 6 is considered a Bad Part unto itself not because it's a burden on the user experience, but instead because it's *ubiquitous*. Where it fails to support something, all web users are denied access to newer web technologies, since most commercial clients will not expend resources on products that can only be enjoyed by a fraction of their intended audience.

In other cases, Internet Explorer provides support for specific features, but only through methods so convoluted that developers consider it burdensome to implement them.

The following sections comprise a survey of Internet Explorer's flaws. Where workarounds can be applied, they are described as well.

Absent or Poor Selector Support

Table 14-1 describes the shortcomings of selector support in Internet Explorer.

Table 14-1. Significant shortcomings in Internet Explorer's selector support

Selector	Earliest supported version	Notes
> (direct descendant)	7	
[foo] (attribute)	8	Simple attribute selectors work in IE 8, but efforts to further narrow their scope fail to show results.
:first-child, :last-child	8	
:nth-child()	n/a	
:before	8	Counters are ignored.
:after	n/a	
.foo.bar	7	IE 6 reads this selector as .bar.
:hover	3	The :hover pseudoclass was only applied to elements *other than* a as of version 7; in the case of :active, as of version 8.

If top-tier support for IE 6 is a priority, it's generally best to avoid these selectors. Alternatively, their behavior can be duplicated with JavaScript, but that solution requires code that accomplishes the desired results through a different kind of brute force.

Verdict

Use these selectors where called for, but educate stakeholders and designers about what to expect. Replace :first-child, :last-child, and > selectors with classes where needed.

To track and solve layout issues caused by Internet Explorer rendering bugs, consult the following resources:

- "Position Is Everything," *http://www.positioniseverything.net/*
- The css-discuss mailing list's wiki and archive, *http://css-discuss.in cutio.com/*

hasLayout

hasLayout is an odd property, specific to Internet Explorer, that evaluates to true or false when queried via the DOM API. When hasLayout evaluates to true, the applicable element's presentation characteristics are defined somewhere within the rendering engine's logic, rather than being polled. The latter outcome leads to many of the layout bugs that stylists encounter when testing their work product in IE 6.

If you need to repair a layout bug by forcing the value of hasLayout to true, then you must ensure that the "blown" element will assume *defined* dimensions on at least one axis. This is most often accomplished by setting position and height values to anything other than static and auto, respectively. This technique is called the "Holly Hack" after Holly Bergevin, the developer who first popularized it.

Applying zoom: 1 is another way to force hasLayout = true and is preferred by many stylists, as it does not introduce the stacking issues inherent to positioned elements (see "Stacking" on page 101).

When used in tandem with a font-size value set in px higher in the cascade, use of flexible/grid layout techniques (see "Layout Types and Canvas Grids" on page 106) largely obviates these problems. The downside is that it can put vision-impaired users of Internet Explorer 6 at a severe disadvantage, since the text sizes in the IE 6 View menu are useless with respect to px-sized text.

Verdict
> Blowouts are sadly inevitable. Resolve them by whatever means necessary, preferably with a conditional stylesheet targeted to Internet Explorer and in combination with the * html low-pass filter.

Margin Doubling

Consider the following rule:

```
#someDiv { display: block; float: left; width: 20em; margin-left: 10em; }
```

Here, the margin and float values hew to the same edge of the parent element, and inexplicably, Internet Explorer *doubles* that margin-left value to 20em, precisely because the margin and float properties are applied to the same edge.

Half of the fix to this problem is documented by the W3C in Section 9.7 of the CSS 2.1 specification. The other half of the solution is counterintuitive: set the display value of the element to `inline`. This works because given `width` and `float` values, the display value of the applicable element will be `block` as a matter of course.

 Positioniseverything.net gives credit for this solution to Steve Clason (*http://www.steveclason.com/*).

Verdict

The fix to the margin doubling problem, while obscure and counterintuitive, is just the sort of unobtrusive business that we would wish from *all* workarounds. Move on. Nothing to see here.

expression() Values

Did you know that JavaScript can be inserted into stylesheets, and Internet Explorer will parse it?

If you set an `expression()` object as the value of a CSS property and provide a valid JavaScript expression as its sole argument, Internet Explorer will evaluate that expression and treat the result of this execution as the value assigned to the applicable property. This feature is eminently practical, but so thoroughly violates the spirit of progressive enhancement that I can't discourage its use vehemently enough.

Additional discouragement is offered by the fact that you cannot effectively reference document nodes in `expression()` statements unless you use the `defer` attribute on a script that in turn loads the stylesheet with the `expression()` value. This is tantamount to deliberate implementation of a Flash of Unstyled Content.

Verdict

Avoid this with great prejudice, for reasons of structural integrity and security. Filter it to a fare-thee-well when you can't avoid it. (This doesn't rate as an "Awful Part" only because somewhere, someday, it might well save your proverbial bacon.)

ActiveX Filters and Transitions

The ActiveX platform gives Internet Explorer access to a number of filters and transitions, most notably an `Alpha()` filter that serves as IE's analog to the `opacity`/`-moz-opacity` properties. A related filter is also critical to rendering the alpha channel of Portable Network Graphics (PNG) files in Internet Explorer 6, an issue discussed in the next section.

To effect any sort of transparency on an element in Internet Explorer, assign it the following style:

```
#foo { filter: progid:DXImageTransform.Microsoft.Alpha(opacity=xxx); }
```

In this case, opacity takes on an integer value between 0 and 100, rather than a floating-point value between 0 and 1 as with opacity and -moz-opacity.

Verdict

> Use of this feature—and its CSS3-derived counterparts—is best limited to two cases: scripted alpha channel transitions via the DOM API, and layout cases that disallow the possibility of visibly combining two overlapping background images into a parent element's background. In all other cases this feature should be avoided until the opacity property is *broadly* supported as defined in the CSS3 documentation.

PNG Support (or Lack Thereof)

In reality, all of the versions of Internet Explorer in common use *will* render PNGs. But with IE 6, there's a bit of a hitch.

At full bit depth, PNG images support 24 bits per pixel of color data (8 bits per channel, just like JPEG, Photoshop, web color, and sRGB) and an additional 8 bits per pixel (256 levels) of transparency.

However, when Internet Explorer 6 encounters a pixel with any alpha value other than FF (full opacity), it renders a gray pixel instead of the intended result.

The AlphaImageLoader "procedural surface" was introduced to help resolve this problem. In this case, it works by altering the relationship of inline images to the rest of their stacking context, and requires all manner of DOM API hacking be effective with background images.

The best solution to this problem (from a stylist's perspective) involves the use of an HTML Component file written by Angus Turnbull of *http://www.twinhelix.com/*. The documentation is linked (along with several alternatives, including JavaScript-framework-based solutions) from this book's companion website (*http://www .htmlcssgoodparts.net*).

Verdict

> Most of the time, most designs allow workarounds to this issue by other means, in other image encoding formats—happily, intellectual property disputes about image encoding formats no longer generate the furor that they did when Internet Explorer 6 was first released. Wait until IE 6's market share drops into the mid-to-low single digits, then use PNGs as desired and see what happens when you propose to let four-channel PNGs render as-is. (If enough vendors do this, stakeholders will finally start getting the hint that IE 6 is ancient in Internet years.)

Poor Property Support

There are a few property/value combinations that have been of particular interest to skilled stylists for a long time.

To put it bluntly, it's *just too bad* that IE 6 doesn't support these values as it should, but there's not much to be done.

Verdict
> Write alternative styles—without creating extra elements, if at all possible—that will reliably present the desired results on all platforms without the need for excessive filtering or other cerebral gymnastics. If support for `position: fixed` is particularly relevant, you're simply out of luck.

Issues with XHTML and XML

The lack of support for properly served XHTML is quite vexing, as it negates XHTML's practical advantages. To heap irony atop frustration, Microsoft was the first popular browser vendor to attempt useful support for XML *at all*.

The advantages that accrue to XHTML in the absence of proper platform support are still beneficial to developers' work habits. However, plain old web projects should be undertaken under the assumption that your visitors don't have support for all of XHTML's features. If you want to split the difference, you can parse the `User-Agent` field in the request header and send the most appropriate `Content-Type` in the reply, but this approach leads to unintended consequences of its own (e.g., sending the wrong `Content-Type` value to visitors who browse the Web from the far side of caching proxies).

Another drawback to serving your content as XML is that the XML specification is unforgiving in the treatment of malformed markup on the part of user agents; if you run a site or a datastore that relies to any degree on third-party content, you're *begging* for trouble if you serve your documents as `text/xhtml+xml`.

Verdict
> The ideal environment for XHTML opens the door to results of the shiniest kind—but unfortunately, the Web in everyday use is *not* that ideal environment. Darn. Use XHTML 1.0 and serve it with a `Content-Type` of `text/html`, or just revert to HTML.

Systemic Ugliness

People have adapted their habits and attitudes to the design of the Web and the Internet in general...up to a point. The world of the Web is a lot bigger than the subjective worlds in which most of its users live—it's worldwide, in fact!—which makes for some interesting quirks in the system.

Template Fragility and Third-Party Content

Given brokered advertising, blog comments, social media snippets, and the avalanche of third-party content that may well end up on your website, you can't realistically hope that documents will remain as pristine as they were when you put them into production.

Put more bluntly, not everybody has your chops.

Unfortunately, this is a challenge that cannot be avoided or solved, even though it can be attenuated by relying on Transitional document types. Sometimes garbage will find its way onto your sites. Live with it.

Verdict
> Educate as many visitors and third-party content providers as you can without damaging your workflow and lifestyle, and in the meantime use the sturdiest markdown tools you can find to process things like user comments.

Markup Validation As a Prerequisite to Proper Style Implementation

This is among the worst of the Bad Parts—not because it exemplifies a practice to be avoided, but because it illuminates one of the most intractable flaws of the HTML+CSS system.

Put simply, when you fail to insert a closing tag or foul an `id`/`class` value, you also inadvertently cause the working cascade to deviate from the one that you've designed. While vendors' obedience to Postel's Law (see "HTML Syntax" on page 7) often hides cascade flaws, you cannot reasonably expect that to happen in all cases...and if your markup is especially complex, the best way to find any flaws in your working cascade is to validate your markup.

Verdict
> This one's a necessary evil that some strict constructionists laud for being one of the few barriers to entry for novice web developers.

"Best Viewed with"

The platform specificity of the Web's infancy—when Netscape was far better than Mosaic, but was soon supplanted by Internet Explorer 3.0x, which had much better presentation support than anything Netscape was publishing at the time—isn't really common anymore. What's important is your development platform, which should be Firefox (thanks to its unequaled standards support) unless you build assets for an audience that uses Internet Explorer exclusively.

The good news is that nobody cares about your choice of development platform, and nobody needs to care.

Still, you will encounter stakeholders who want things to look *just so* at *their* workstations, even if they use ancient hardware and work with their backs to the sun in the afternoons.

Verdict

> Of the battles you'll be asked to fight, this one is probably worth it. Educate. Personally drag stakeholders away from their desks and ask them to look at your product in some other environment. Play at politics if necessary. Advocate graded support, which is discussed next. Don't be a doormat.

Graded Support

If you've been paying attention—or if you *really* care about Apple's design decisions—you've probably noticed that 64-bit personal computing is finally inching toward ubiquity. *This constitutes the first major leap in software design in several years.* On the other hand, even now web developers aren't confronted with the broad range of support requirements they faced as recently as 10 years ago, when a two-year-old workstation faced a good chance of being obsolescent.

The greatest variation stylists are likely to find among their audience relates to display resolutions. Some visitors might be browsing from dial-up connections or 2.5G mobile phones, but at least with respect to web browsing, most site visitors will be capable of running reasonably current software.

Even so, between the apathy of most casual web users and the comparatively slow progress of feature support, you will need to support a broad range of browsing platforms. Some stylists face greater challenges than others; internal site developers working in Windows shops don't need to worry about it at all, unless they use off-the-shelf software written by small publishers.

When it comes to variety, the companies that are forced to deal with the broadest range of browsing capabilities are the household names, such as Yahoo!; Amazon; major news sites; big social media networks like Facebook; and service providers like utilities, banks, and payment processors.

Yahoo! was mentioned first for a reason: they were the first organization to design, implement, and popularize a testing system that held *all* browsers to appropriate standards of performance.

Each combination of browser and operating system platform is tested by Yahoo!'s Quality Assurance department against one of three grades of performance:

"A" Grade

> These platforms are current, common, and capable of supporting popular-yet-recent features and offer comparatively excellent support for standards-compliant implementation techniques. They allow user experience to remain true to the intent of the original site design more or less perfectly.

"C" Grade

> Platforms receive the most significant benefit of progressive enhancement; while they lose access to the full depth of the intended user experience, they are still able to use the site effectively.

"X" Grade

> These platforms are kept out of the other grades *on purpose*. Many of them are capable, at least to a point. The most visible of their cohort tend to be recently released, and the ones that aren't have thin slices of market share. Support tickets for these platforms are ignored unless and until their market share grows to a level high enough to justify formal testing.

In addition to Yahoo!'s support grades, I introduce my prospective clients to a "B" Grade, which removes behavior support while preserving a reasonable amount of presentation support. Other shops might wish to reverse those priorities.

Since I've performed most of my work as a sole proprietor and usually enjoy little in the way of third-party support of my testing efforts, I place far more platforms in the "X" Grade than any large development shop might.

One point that I make in all of my project specifications, but that seems to be neglected in Yahoo!'s description of their graded support method, is that all user experience at a given support grade should be consistent for each individual visitor, and in the case of "A" Grade platforms, broadly consistent without respect to the platform used.

At this point, you may be asking: "Why is this a *Bad* Part?"

There are several reasons for the classification as a Bad Part. Most importantly, graded support legitimizes the market role of hangers-on like Internet Explorer 6 (and Netscape 4 before it)—browsers that are popular solely by virtue of inertia and network effects, rather than any merits they might have. The other major reason is the fact that quality assurance testing is the closest web teams get to making sausage: the customers like the results, but they'd never want to see it being done.

Verdict

> Apply support grades well and often, and act on test results with the best interests of your site visitors in mind. You may not like it, but your visitors do.

embed Versus object

The continued survival of the `embed` element is perhaps the most egregious example of applied network effects. Back when Windows Media Player was an afterthought, Flash was best known because of a site called Gabocorp, and RealNetworks' player was well on its way to helping pay for a United States Senate seat, Netscape was the first out of the gate with audio/video plug-in support. It merrily leapfrogged and disregarded the W3C's work on HTML 4.

At the same time, Microsoft was furiously trying to catch up, and took it upon itself to support the element the W3C had specified for supporting plug-in content.

The latecomers all got caught in the middle, and because Netscape's browsers had been *everywhere*, Mozilla and Apple focused on providing the best support for the existing population of `embed` media invocations—a choice that even Microsoft's ultimate market share could not undo.

Refer to Chapter 11 for an in-depth discussion of how to handle plug-in markup.

Verdict

> From a forward-compatibility perspective, `object` rules and `embed` drools. Avoid `embed` if you have any choice in the matter. Broad support for the `object` element has finally scraped its way to the point where it can be considered reliable in all likely use cases.

Form Controls, Plug-in Instances, and Element Stacking

The problem of plug-in instances and form controls appearing above all other elements in utter disregard of absolute positioning and `z-index` values is less prevalent than in the past, but still pops up (if you'll pardon the phrase) from time to time.

The unintended prominence of form controls and plug-in instances results from the way those elements are rendered by the browser. In many cases the user-facing objects are created and inserted not by the browser's rendering engine, but directly by operating system components. In the case of Internet Explorer, these include the .NET Framework and ActiveX, the latter of which inserts `object` elements into a page as if they were modal dialogs.

This problem borders on being an Awful Part because the incidents that do occur are intractable; `z-index` offers no respite.

The brute-force solutions are:

- Revise your layout so that nothing is called upon to stack over the offending element.
- Place the topmost content within an `iframe` that lies further down the source order than the offending element.

Verdict

> This problem is incrementally worse in Internet Explorer as compared to other browsers. Unfortunately, like many of the IE-derived Bad Parts, this one can't just be easily fixed without browser vendors changing their software.

Invalid Markup for Stupid Reasons

The most obvious Stupid Reason for a failure to validate is the appearance of a "damn-persand" in your markup, as discussed in Chapter 13.

However, there are other reasons that are far more frustrating. My favorite example of HTML's odd requirements comes from 2002, at the beginning of my tenure as the proverbial "utility pitcher" at Webstandards.org. I'd just followed up an incoming email with a related post on the site's blog, so naturally—given the mission and audience of the site—my next move was to validate my work.

It didn't validate, which is how the Stupid Reason made itself known.

Webstandards.org validates to a Strict document type, and my post contained a `blockquote` element. What I did *not* know (by virtue of being firmly attached to Transitional document types) was that in Strict document types, a `blockquote` must contain at least one block element—probably a paragraph, maybe a `div`.

Another obscure validation requirement was raised during the technical review of this book's draft manuscript: to be valid, `thead` and `tfoot` must *precede* `tbody` instead of being placed at either end of it.

These odd requirements and others are described in a comprehensive chart on this book's companion website.

Verdict
> Once you take it upon yourself to produce valid markup, you'll be introduced to some fairly strange requirements that impose limitations on element children, parents, siblings, attributes, values, and content. Save yourself the stress of being annoyed and *just fix it*.

HTML's Bad Neighborhoods and Cul-de-Sacs

HTML as we know it is almost 20 years old, and was originally designed to fulfill the objective of exchanging academic papers and other written matter. The circus of Flash, Ajax, podcasts, and social media was the furthest thing from anyone's mind.

As a result, features have been tacked on to the language, one piece at a time—and until the end of 1997, the "official" standing of contemporary additions to the language was provisional at best.

Between the evolution of HTML, the evolution of the infrastructure that delivers its content, and the changing expectations of web users, HTML shows off a fair share of vestigial bits and ideas-that-seemed-good-at-the-time. The Awful Parts are all vestigial bits of HTML (see the section "The Awful Parts" on page 286). The ones that might actually be useful on rare occasions are discussed next.

Frames

The Frameset Document Type Definitions refer to two elements that were all the rage in 1996, but are an embarrassment now: `frameset` and `frame`.

`frameset` is a substitute for `body` where it appears, and it supports the `rows` and `cols` attributes. Each of the rows or columns specified—as a comma-separated list of pixel or percentage values, of which there should always be at least one and preferably two or more—in turn corresponds to a `frame` within the same document. Each of those `frame` elements has an `src` attribute, which references another document. That child document will be either a typical page or another frameset.

Finally, each `frame` can be assigned a `name`, which can in turn be a `target` on any of the links that might appear within the `frameset`. This arrangement makes it possible for the content of one viewport to alter the content of other viewports.

A visual description of nested `frameset`s and their constituent documents is provided in Figure 14-1.

Frames are really quite whizzy and full of extra-special 20th-century flashiness, but that's not a feature—it's a bug. Assistive technology can't hope to offer the same view on framed content that typically functional visitors can take as a matter of course, and even more importantly, consider that the multidimensionality of web documents grows exponentially with each frame that's added. It's a rare designer who can impart anything useful to the complexity facing the visitor in that case; more likely than not, a designer who tries to make frames coherent will fail.

The one decent use of frames is to put your site navigation into one document and one frame, while the site's content is presented in the other frame. However, apart from the accessibility hassles, this approach also increases the complexity of the mechanisms required to preserve the "You Are Here" cues for all visitors. That's because you need to use JavaScript to convey the state of the "content" frame to the "navigation" frame, which in its turn must execute still more JavaScript to effect the appropriate cues.

There are also `iframe` (inline frame) elements, which are defined in the Transitional DTDs and distinguished from images at the markup level only by the fact that they can load documents of any MIME type that the browser recognizes. At the user interface level, they share with frames the capacity to display or deny scroll bars with the `scrolling` attribute.

You're much more likely to need inline frames than external frames, especially if you place brokered advertising on any of your sites. Inline frames also provide a platform for asynchronous transactions—a "poor man's Ajax," if you will. Instead of managing asynchronous transactions with `XMLHttpRequest` objects and copying new document nodes from their output, a developer can instead load serial documents into an offscreen `iframe` and then copy document nodes from that `iframe` for attachment to the user-facing document.

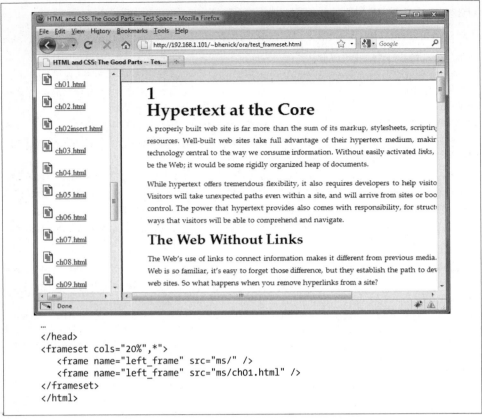

```
…
</head>
<frameset cols="20%","*">
    <frame name="left_frame" src="ms/" />
    <frame name="left_frame" src="ms/ch01.html" />
</frameset>
</html>
```

Figure 14-1. A working frameset and its corresponding markup

Verdict

Just *don't*—not today, not tomorrow, not ever. You can be excused (barely!) for deploying iframes if your ad vendors rely on them (and in so doing insist that you offer criminals another vector for attacking your site), but otherwise you can rely on server-side functionality and XMLHttpRequest to answer for the inoffensive functionality that frames and inline frames provide.

The strike Element

In short, the del element does what the strike element was always meant for, and it's consistently supported.

Verdict

Use the del element. Blogging platform developers take note.

The name Attribute

The name attribute turns up on many elements, as described in Table 14-2.

Table 14-2. Elements that take the name attribute, and their associated functions

Element	Function
a	Specifies a link destination in the midst of the document
form controls	Specifies the name of a given name/value pair; vital to effective encoding of form data
frame and iframe	Uniquely identifies a single frame object so that it can be accessed by the target attribute of a given link within the same presentation
link	Specifies a name by which the linked object (e.g., an alternate stylesheet) can be referenced from within the browser's persistent user interface
map	References the map element associated with a specific image
meta	The alternative to http-equiv, the value of this attribute specifies the name of an arbitrary name/value pair specifying document metadata such as keywords

Verdict

> The use of the name attribute is largely deprecated in preference to the techniques referenced in Table 14-3.
>
> These caveats leave link and form control elements as the only elements with which the name attribute reasonably can (in the case of link) or must (in the case of form controls) be used.

Table 14-3. Preferred alternatives to the name attribute

Element	Preferred alternative
a	id values are supported as link hash values in all current browsers.
iframe	Implement the desired behavior with JavaScript (in cases where the same-domain policy allows access to the object) and create a fallback implementation if possible.
map	Between consistent support of the x and y values of input type="submit" and other contemporary browser features, this element is deprecated altogether in practice.
meta	Avoid entirely, as the most popular name value of the meta element ("keywords") is completely disregarded by its primary "audience," search engines.

The noscript and noframes Elements

noscript content is only needed if you're up to a ton of no good by disregarding the virtues of progressive enhancement. You should instead design sites and applications on the assumption that scripting isn't available, and rely on scripting to enrich the user experience beyond what can be encountered at the notional "default" level of functionality. In fact, any other design philosophy begs you to violate the spirit of web accessibility guidelines and legislation.

In its turn, the `noframes` element channels just as much Inner Bunk as the elements it's intended to supplant.

Verdict

These elements exist to provide a fail-safe, which was good design practice on the part of the guys at Netscape who originally decided to implement the `script` and `frame` elements. However, you're leaning into bad design practice if you need either of these elements. If you *must* use them, do so for the sake of enriching the "low-fidelity" experience. In the case of `noframes`, the only acceptable use I can think of is to provide a link to a decent site map.

Semantic Contortions and the Limited Vocabulary of HTML

It's been pointed out that HTML has exploded far beyond its original design purpose, which often leaves semantically minded stylists struggling to shove square pegs into round holes.

The good news is that the folks in charge of HTML5 and the microformats advocates are all putting tremendous effort into making life easier for the semantically (and literally) minded.

In the meantime, the best we can do is get by with the tools we have; wring every drop of significance possible from the cascade, taxonomies, and universal attributes; and err on the side of overengineering our work product.

Verdict

Avoid inappropriate elements, lean hard on the universal attributes, and wait breathlessly for HTML5 to catch on.

Inline Presentation Elements

While HTML 4 might be semantically limited, its presentation elements are officially deprecated for good reason.

The `strong`, `em`, and `code` elements exist precisely to fulfill the typical functions of the inline presentation elements (`b`, `i`, `kbd`, `font`, etc.). The only remaining use of these elements is to follow typographic conventions of several generations' standing, for example the italicization of foreign words.

Verdict

Use these elements if and only if:

- The purpose of the markup is not better suited to semantically oriented elements as a matter of course.

- There are established typesetting conventions that categorically support your usage.

- You're happy to attach to the element the appropriate universal attributes that illuminate the relationship between the element, the applicable typesetting convention, and the element's content.

- You can get more benefit from the cascade by using presentation elements in preference to `span`.

  For its part, `font` is invalid in Strict document types and really shouldn't be used at all. If you encounter it in legacy content, you would do well to move its attributes, add a `class` value, and remove its presentation to the stylesheet (where it belongs).

Manipulating Vertical Space: hr and br

The `hr` (horizontal rule) and `br` (linebreak) elements are among the oldest in the commonly used HTML namespace, but they're artifacts of the era before stylesheets.

Even so, they turn up in some odd cases. `hr` is at times relatively positioned out of view and used to enforce a `clear` value other than `none`. `br` can very occasionally be useful in situations where application of the `white-space` property causes more problems than it solves, and the content in question can't be formatted as needed through `div` or `span` abuse.

Verdict

It's quite likely that you can find a better way to skin the proverbial cat, but there's always the possibility that sometime, somewhere you might need to call upon these elements as a last resort. Use a better way if you can find one, but don't think too hard about it if you don't have the time to spare.

The pre Element Versus the white-space Property

The highest virtue of the `pre` element is its user agent default style, which offers exactly the same benefit as inserting the following rule into your stylesheet:

```
p.preformatted { white-space: pre; }
```

In other words, it's less work to insert `pre` elements than it is to underscore their semantic meaninglessness by deploying the style just described.

Meanwhile, one purpose to which `pre` is frequently and inappropriately put is formatting the line/stanza structure of traditional poetry, for which it is disastrously ill-suited. Far better solutions to that objective exist, and I've even gone to the trouble of writing about one on this book's companion website.

Verdict

You really shouldn't use `pre`, unless you're monumentally lazy or so severely pressed for time that you're content to build crap and fix it later.

CSS Travesties

Those of us who were around and hard at work in the mid-1990s knew about CSS and prayed fervently for it to be implemented sooner and more effectively than it was. To make a long story extremely short, programming for the Web in the late '90s sucked because it wasn't.

Ten years on from the ultimate peak of "irrational exuberance," we now have better CSS. Still, it's not always so good at coping with the requirements of the contemporary Web. Its truly rough patches are described in the following sections.

@-Rules

As design elements go, @-rules are elegant. They provide an additional mechanism for narrowing scope via the cascade, which is awfully elegant on its own.

Unfortunately, they're poorly supported. Consider:

- `@import` rules might or might not be applied by a given browser, depending on how they're written and where they're located in the source order of a document or stylesheet.
- `@import` and `@media` rules can take on additional, vendor-defined, arbitrary attributes that usually want for clear documentation.
- Support for alternative media properties leaves a great deal to be desired, as discussed in Chapter 3.

Verdict
> When @-rules work, they're great, but when they don't, they...don't. Some of the features discussed here might pop serendipitously into your psyche and save you several hours of labor during a death march, but it's very unlikely that @-rules will ever be among them.

Computed Values and Rounding Differences

Every visual display medium has a fundamental unit of length, as was explained in detail in Chapter 3. During the rendering process, the browser needs to translate values expressed in other units, such as em, to baseline quantities (e.g., `px` in `screen` media). Particularly with respect to length measurements, the resulting values are referred to as being "computed." Odd rules can also cause stated values to be reflected by entirely different computed values, as in the case of the double margin bug discussed earlier in this chapter.

Variation among the visual characteristics and font rendering algorithms of the various popular browsing environments will occasionally result in rounding errors that are too obvious to ignore—for example, a fractional-pixel `letter-spacing` value will not be applied on the Mac, an outcome that carries implications for element dimensions.

When these variations lead to significant layout differences across platforms—as might be the case with designs that suffer from low fault tolerance—the outcome can be frustrating.

Verdict

When designs require a degree of precision that turns rounding errors into a burden, two habits can minimize the potential for damage. First, specify floating-point length values at high degrees of precision, like 10^{-3} if not 10^{-4}. Second, limit your stylesheets to a single medium and specify length units in a static unit suited to that medium, such as px for screen presentations and pt/in/cm for print presentations.

Vendor-Specific -moz and -webkit Property Prefixes

Because users of Firefox and Safari tend to be conscientious about their web use habits and are likely to be early adopters of new technologies, there are good reasons for the developers of these browsers to nudge their product toward the bleeding edge.

At the same time, proper support for CSS 2.1 and other "official" standards is top-billed in the marketing of these browsers, and the CSS3 properties supported by these browsers are still subject to change. In fact, most of the CSS3 modules haven't even achieved Last Call Working Draft status—the last stage of the W3C Recommendation (de facto standardization) process during which members of the general public can influence a web technology's development.

Because CSS3 is still maturing, its property support is best modularized into its own sandbox by browser engineers. This is why the -moz and -webkit prefixes exist.

The desirability of using those properties is another question. This is something that every development team must answer for itself, according to their development philosophies and the objectives of their projects.

Verdict

Use these if you want to, but be prepared for unintended consequences when you do—especially when new browser versions are released *after* CSS3 modules begin to pass the full W3C Recommendation milestone.

The inherit Value

Inheritance is a tricky matter. In most cases, foreground colors and type sizes are inherited by child elements from parent elements, but box properties and the like aren't. There *are* scenarios where you might want to force box values and other layout properties to be inherited, though they're rare.

On the other hand lies the travesty: browsers don't really support the inherit value.

Verdict
> This would be nice to have someday, though it will require a light touch to use well. In the meantime, we're stuck repeating literal values.

Hiding Stuff: z-index and clip

At first glance, the `z-index` and `clip` properties are both eminently useful. One changes an element's relationship in the vertical scheme of things, while the other affects its visibility to partial degrees.

In practice, both of these properties are far more difficult to use than you might think.

The trick to using `z-index` well is to remember that a document's stacking context is organized into strata; from bottom to top the layers are:

1. The page canvas
2. Block elements without `float` or `position` values
3. Elements with `float` values; and finally
4. Elements with `position` values other than `static`

Each element is overlaid by its background properties, then its content, and finally any overlapping elements in the same stratum that lie further down the document's source order. That stacking order is then repeated for each stratum.

The `clip` value, meanwhile, is broken. Its intent is laudable: to pad an element without shrinking its content box, leaving its values available for later manipulation via the DOM API. However, unlike the `padding` property, all of its values are measured from the top and left edges of the element, meaning that it's functionally useless unless you know all of the applicable element's dimensions at runtime.

Verdict
> Great in theory, lousy in practice, these properties are among the shortcomings that keep stylists working late into the night.

Counters

The prospect of automatic counting in CSS, while obscure, is still worth contemplating. The bad news is that the whole system is a wreck, because the use guidelines are impenetrable and the functionality isn't supported by Internet Explorer.

Verdict
> Rather than messing around with notional variables as the existing rules do, it would be far better if the functionality were replaced with a single `counter` value that is implied by its antecedent element's state and takes two arguments: a starting value and a level of significance. Most stylists—myself included—would rather

have *limited* automatic numbering, instead of powerful automatic numbering that's impossible to implement.

Element Flow Rules

Do you sometimes sit slackjawed in front of your display, wondering how the browser took your stylesheet and created *those* results? It's probably due to the heaps of intense lawyering in the CSS specifications. Consider the following:

> A line box is always tall enough for all of the boxes it contains. However, it may be taller than the tallest box it contains (if, for example, boxes are aligned so that baselines line up). When the height of a box B is less than the height of the line box containing it, the vertical alignment of B within the line box is determined by the 'vertical-align' property. When several inline boxes cannot fit horizontally within a single line box, they are distributed among two or more vertically-stacked line boxes. Thus, a paragraph is a vertical stack of line boxes. Line boxes are stacked with no vertical separation and they never overlap.
>
> In general, the left edge of a line box touches the left edge of its containing block and the right edge touches the right edge of its containing block. However, floating boxes may come between the containing block edge and the line box edge. Thus, although line boxes in the same inline formatting context generally have the same width (that of the containing block), they may vary in width if available horizontal space is reduced due to floats. Line boxes in the same inline formatting context generally vary in height (e.g., one line might contain a tall image while the others contain only text).
>
> —CSS 2.1 specification: Section 9.4.2, "Inline formatting context"

Got that?

Meanwhile, some unfortunate software engineer was forced to comprehend that passage and implement software that did what it said. You use that software every day.

This is one of the flaws in CSS that illustrates the virtue of communities—if you're able to join an active community of fellow practitioners, you'll likely encounter at least one person who has found the Zen in passages like the one quoted above.

Verdict
> Enlightenment is just as much a *process* as a state of being. Pursue your professional education accordingly, even if you're forced to grind your teeth and try again at times.

Unicode Code Position Values and the content Property

The content property, which was introduced in Chapter 7 and addressed again at the end of Chapter 8, has an odd shortcoming: it doesn't support entities. If :before/:after and content are present in your stylesheet, you have three "safe" ways to reference symbols outside of the 7-bit ASCII range:

- Ensure that both your production tool and your web server are set to the same character encoding before pasting in the literal character.

- Set the appropriate `@charset` declaration in your stylesheet and paste in the literal character.

- Use backslash-escaped Unicode code positions to indicate the desired content.

In current practice, all three of these choices have pitfalls. The first choice is dangerous unless you have absolute control over your editing environment and server, more than most people reliably have. The second is impractical because some extant versions of Internet Explorer and Safari choke on `@charset` declarations, each in its own annoying way. The third lacks reliable support, but has the virtue of being both forward compatible and immune to changes in server configuration and network conditions.

When you attempt to reference Unicode code position values in the `content` property, the value you want to supply is a Unicode code position expressed in base 16 preceded by a backslash; for example:

```
blockquote>p:before { content: '\201C'; }
```

This will cause a proper English open (double) quotation mark to be placed at the beginning of every paragraph that claims a `blockquote` element as a direct parent, since 0×201C = 8220.

Verdict
Paste UTF-8 characters as needed, and ensure that the server agrees with your approach.

The Awful Parts

It gets worse from here.

HTML and CSS are full of stuff that is deprecated, ill-considered, and pitilessly inevitable, each iota unto its own end...yet still with a strong claim on redeeming social value.

And then there's the misbegotten matter that inexplicably made it from the back of someone's mind, onto the back of a BevNap, through meetings, into the Action Item List of a manager's manager, around and within code, and finally came to life in the steaming bowels of a working web browser. *Never use the tools described in this final passage, unless your refusal will get you sacked.*

The marquee and blink Elements

These elements are really artifacts of the Web's late childhood—in fact the `blink` element is disabled by default in Firefox, if still supported—but they *force* visitors to divide their attention. As an added bonus, they also put some epileptics at risk for seizures.

Animations are different from content—and they're *behavior*, not structure or presentation. If you must animate, do so with JavaScript or Flash, and be a good citizen about it.

MSIE User Interface Properties

It so happens that Internet Explorer gives stylists access to scroll bars and the chrome of windows that they instantiate. This creates an opportunity to extend branding into other parts of the user experience, which might be seen as a win in the eyes of some people.

But it's not. When you mess around with the user interface that in every other application stays constant, you're violating user expectations and possibly leading your more skittish visitors to believe that their system has been infected with a virus.

Instead

Build a proper Adobe AIR app already. It'll force you to reinvent a number of wheels, but you'll definitely earn a living.

The align Attribute

Back in the Bad Old Days when CSS didn't exist—or couldn't be counted upon to work where it did—web producers had table markup and `align` to work with.

If you've been reading, you've probably noticed that the technology's improved a little in the years since.

Instead

Remove it where you find it, and use the appropriate `float`, `margin`, or `text-align` value instead.

The style Attribute

So...we have this universal attribute that allows you to apply CSS properties in the narrowest possible scope, in complete confidence that the specified values will be applied.

Some people probably also have a case of the flu. You don't see *them* going out of their way to propagate it.

When you use the `style` attribute, you destroy the cascade, media type declarations, and any hope of being able to maintain your deliverables.

Just don't.

Verdict

Sit down, leaf backward through this book, read "Rule Conflicts, Priority, and Precedence" on page 31, and finally apply what you learn. The `style` attribute might be easier to comprehend if you can't see past markup, but it's the web developer's analog to a thermonuclear bunker-buster.

div-itis

Developers unfamiliar with the idea of "CSS Zen" too often and too easily fall into the trap of wrangling their markup to their presentation, just as they would if they were using `table` markup for layout. This habit—called "`div`-itis" for obvious reasons—results in markup full of elements emplaced not for the sake of overbuilding, but instead to ensure a specific result in the presentation.

These elements are easy to spot because they usually have `class` or (more rarely) `id` values that refer not to the purpose of the content they contain, but instead to that content's presentation characteristics. `class` and `id` fragments that refer to relative bearings, such as `right` and `left`, make regular appearances in such markup.

Verdict

A number of techniques eliminate any call for `div`-itis. The fundamental practice of all such alternatives is to assign `class` and `id` values that reflect the *purpose* of a given element, rather than its relationship to the presentation of a document. Other important techniques include:

- Moderate structural overbuilding (see the section "The Four Habits of Effective Stylists" on page 49)
- Altered positioning context (see the section "CSS Positioning Properties" on page 96)
- Careful application of background images (see the section "Composing Background Images" on page 152)
- Effective use of *all* box properties (see the section "Margins, Borders, and Padding" on page 78)

Event Handler Attributes

Event handlers in markup are not so different from the `style` attribute, and they're even *more* unnecessary (if that's possible). When you attach them directly to tags, you thrust behavior into the structural layer of your work product, which begs trouble down the line (and makes your markup *much* harder to read). An "unobtrusive JavaScript" approach will be much easier to manage over the long run.

1. Assess the elements to which you want to attach events, and add any universal attributes necessary to ensure that you can access them via the DOM API according to your needs.

2. Create and reference a function that fires `onload`, e.g.:

   ```
   window.onload = assignEvents;
   ```

3. Within that `onload` function, walk through the various elements that you assessed in step 1, assigning event handlers and associated code as needed.

4. If your needs exist on a time line or have multiple dependencies, you might need to implement closures for the sake of handling your events. Links to discussions of JavaScript closures are provided on this book's companion website.

Gratuitous Underlining

If you like underlines, you need to do a reality check: underlines are for links, only links, and *nothing but* links. That's what visitors expect, and it's one of the more important expectations to meet—unless you want visitors who are randomly clicking around, trying to visit another page on your site.

Verdict

There are two meaningful uses for underlines beyond links: `ins` content (for which it is the user agent default style), and emphasis in copy that's styled to take on a typewritten appearance. In the first case, ensure at least that the underlined insertions have *entirely* different color and luminosity than any of your links; in the second, style the `em` element appropriately and place your "typewritten" content in a visual plane entirely separate from the rest of your page copy.

The http-equiv Attribute

 Some readers work with system administrators who take an extreme—and often counterproductive—approach to "locking down" every possible web server configuration option. If you're one of those readers, the following passage doesn't apply to you.

When members of the general public started publishing their own websites, virtual domains were a proverbial lightbulb over someone's head. Server-side scripting support was both expensive and difficult to utilize. At that time, some 15 years ago, web server APIs were guru-only territory.

The `http-equiv` attribute, like frames, was made available so that site publishers could mimic site behavior that otherwise could only be implemented after the expenditure of considerable money, time, and effort.

Verdict

Thankfully, the Web is well past the stone-knives-and-bearskins stage. If you want to influence the behavior of the web server that keeps your site going, you can just as easily use the HTTP API modules of the scripting languages that are supported by your hosting plan, or utilize Apache and its `.htaccess` platform. It's easier than it sounds, and there's plenty of sample code online; see this book's companion website for more.

Picking Up the Pieces

HTML and CSS have Good Parts that deliver terrific results. They have Bad Parts that you probably wish you didn't need to struggle with. Finally, like any technology, HTML and CSS have their share of outright Awful Parts that never should have seen the light of day.

By knowing which is which, and knowing when to use a given tool, you can sweep most of the damage out of your work product and get the best maintainability out of the sites that you build.

URIs, Client-Server Architecture, and HTTP

While hypertext brings into being a (virtual) landscape unlike anything else in human experience, its reliance on the underlying Internet often goes unnoticed. Web developers don't need to know much about the deep plumbing of the Internet—parts like TCP, IP, and DNS. Hypertext Transfer Protocol (HTTP), though, is critical to website construction, as it provides the foundation for all those http:// URIs scattered in links and references.

The Underlying Client-Server Architecture

Client-server protocols (including HTTP) typically work through the steps shown in Figure A-1 over the course of a transaction.

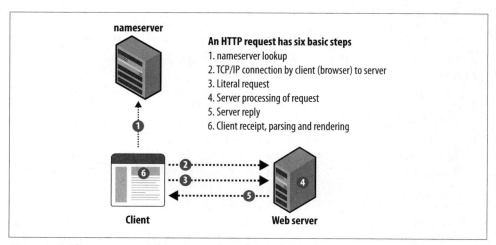

Figure A-1. Client-server architecture as a flow of six steps

1. The client looks up the IP address of the server from a nameserver if necessary.
2. The client looks up and opens a transport layer connection to the server; in the case of HTTP, this is done via TCP/IP.
3. The client then sends data to the server over that connection that is adequate to the requirements of receiving a reply from the server. That broadcast is usually termed a *request*.
4. The server receives the request and processes it by running all related executable code, then packaging the resulting output.
5. The server sends that packaged data back along the connection opened by the client in step 1. This is usually referred to as the *response*.
6. The client receives the data and—if it's sufficiently well-formed—stores and processes it locally. In the case of a web transaction, the "processing" often results in the rendering of a page.

This flow includes a number of opportunities for failure. The best-known such failure is HTTP's dreaded 404 Not Found error, which is caused by a problem encountered during step 3 of the process.

What Every Web Developer Should Know About HTTP

The finer points of HTTP and web server operation are beyond the scope of this book, but there are a few things about HTTP that every site builder should know, regardless of her particular specialty.

There are minimal provisions for excessive network latency, and the few that exist involve session termination (better known as a timeout)
> Since it's impossible to predict in all cases the state and extent of the network between server and browser, one can never assume the order in which page components will load, or the length of time it will take for a page to finish loading.

Any request for a single page will usually result in a series of requests pointed at multiple URIs
> Pages contain images, multimedia, code libraries, and other external resources, as shown in Figure A-2. In high-latency environments, delays can create or compound user experience issues, and in high-volume environments, improper resource management can overtax a web server. As a result, it's a good idea to actively seek the best trade-off between server resource utilization and network utilization—a search that is at least partly the responsibility of the HTML/CSS practitioner.

HTTP is functionally stateless
> "Stateless" in this case means that each transaction between web server and client takes place separately, without a surrounding context. Workarounds, such as cookies, make it possible for the server to keep track of context if desired. URIs can also be appended with session-specific encoded data, but at the cost of making

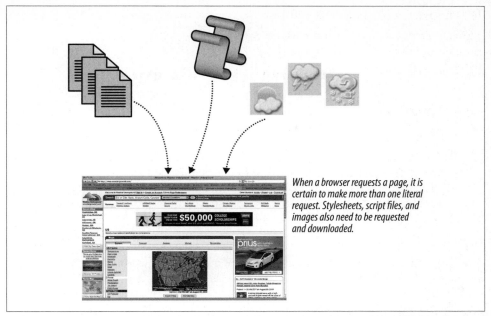

When a browser requests a page, it is certain to make more than one literal request. Stylesheets, script files, and images also need to be requested and downloaded.

Figure A-2. A page request including additional requests for stylesheets, script files, and images

those URIs extremely verbose. The biggest consequence of statelessness for the HTML/CSS practitioner is that it becomes impossible to predict with any certainty the state of a visitor's client environment. This makes it difficult to assume anything about the user's experience during the current session, which has broad implications for site optimization efforts.

An HTTP request typically takes one of two forms, called GET *and* POST

It's fair to say that most server requests are GET requests, but there are plenty of occasions—especially those involving form submissions containing visitor data—when a POST operation will be preferable for technical or security reasons. A more detailed explanation of the difference between GET and POST requests is presented in Chapter 13. (HTTP does support additional operations, but GET and POST do most of the work.)

MIME Types, in Brief

In addition to the document type declaration supplied by a page author at the top of a page's source, the server sends its own data about the formats it serves. This information is sent in MIME (Multipurpose Internet Mail Extensions) format, and it's included for security reasons. Some commonly encountered MIME types are described in Table A-1.

Table A-1. Commonly encountered MIME types

Resource type	Literal MIME type
HTML	text/html
Properly served XHTML	application/xhtml+xml
Images	image/gif, image/jpeg, image/png, image/svg+xml
Adobe Portable Document Format	application/pdf
Adobe Flash	application/x-shockwave-flash
MP3 audio	audio/mpeg
Windows Media	video/x-ms-wmv, audio/x-ms-wma

There are three universally meaningful ways to specify the MIME type of a file or server response:

Default server response header
> Web server configuration facilities provide mechanisms for mapping MIME types to filename extensions.

Custom scripted response header
> The HTTP functions of the major web server scripting languages provide interfaces for specifying MIME types on a case-by-case basis: for example, `Header("Content-Type: text/xhtml+xml\r\n");` in PHP.

Filename extension
> Web browsers make several checks on the content they receive, first by checking the MIME type specified in the response header, then by checking its filename extension, and finally by reading file headers.

Note that reliance on browser behavior is discouraged, because it offers no guidance about how to handle corrupted data like that occasionally found in video files and streams.

Controlling Request Volume

Overly complex stylesheets cause only *some* of the difficulties up to that are exposed when designers and developers fail to optimize their designs for the benefit of server and client host performance. Most relevant to stylists' work are the following considerations:

When possible, serve all of the files related to a single document request from a single server or local group of servers
> This advice is usually impossible to follow if your project includes advertising or third-party content (i.e., multimedia files and social media tools). However, concentrating a site's resources on a single server or network reduces the risk that a site might be rendered inoperable by failures beyond its operator's control.

In general, reduce the number of server requests

A properly configured server host with adequate connectivity can easily honor several hundred thousand HTTP requests per hour—but that's not the same as handling several hundred thousand *visitors* per hour. Even a simple, static page can imply dozens of requests for stylesheets, JavaScript files, and images. Techniques that can reduce request load include sprites, use of the `style` element for unique stylesheet rules, and *cached* concatenation of server-side markup and CSS resources via `include` and output buffer functions.

Place JavaScript files at the end of the page source order whenever possible

This allows all network requests and execution time required for JavaScript to be delayed until the page's actual *content* has loaded, which can lead to a significant improvement in page rendering time.

A second here, a second there, and pretty soon you're talking about some *real* time.

 O'Reilly Media offers several books that explore performance in greater depth:

- *High-Performance Web Sites (http://oreilly.com/catalog/9780596529307/)*, by Steve Souders
- *Even Faster Web Sites (http://oreilly.com/catalog/9780596522315/)*, by Steve Souders
- *Website Optimization: Speed, Search Engine, and Conversion Rate Secrets (http://oreilly.com/catalog/9780596515089/)*, by Andrew B. King

Glossary

Ancestor

An element higher in the document tree, possibly many levels higher, that contains the element in question. Cf. Child.

ANSI

American National Standards Institute. In the U.S. technology industries, ANSI can be considered an analog to Ecma International (formerly known as ECMA). Its name is raised in relation to fonts because the early Windows character encodings were based on a draft standard that was first advanced by ANSI before being taken up and published by the ISO (International Standards Organization). Cf. *Windows-1252* and *ISO 8859-x*.

ASCII

American Standard Code for Information Interchange: the earliest *character set* that had a viable claim to universal support in the English-speaking world, and ubiquitous almost 50 years after its introduction. Limited to simple Latin *glyphs* used in English, *whitespace* characters, and teletype-specific *control* and *transmission characters*. Practically all Latin letterforms and punctuation without diacritics are encoded to ASCII code positions.

Attribute

Additional information about an element, presented as name/value pairs within the opening tag.

Basic Multilingual Plane

The range of *Unicode code positions* from U+0000 to U+FFFF (0–65535 decimal). Contains nearly all orthography used on a daily basis, without regard to origin.

Blackletter

A style of type inspired by German calligraphy of the late Middle Ages, and strongly identified with Germany to the present day. Sometimes called "Gothic," but this is an anachronism.

See also Gothic.

Browser

The most common user interface to the web, software which presents web content on a computer's display.

Cascading Style Sheets (CSS)

The most commonly used stylesheet format for declaring how HTML documents should be presented.

Character

An encoded letter, number, symbol, or whitespace datum. The content of a single *code position* within a *character set*; can comprise a *glyph*, multiple glyphs, *whitespace*, a *control character*, or a *transmission character*.

Character encoding

The stream representation of character data, i.e., the bit sequence used to represent a character for transmission and/or storage. Cf. *code position*; one refers to the literal sequence of bits used to represent a character in a data stream, while the other refers to its position within a *character set*.

Child

An element directly contained by another element.

Client

The side of an HTTP transaction that makes requests and does something, typically rendering, with the response that comes back.

Code position

A single position in a given *character set*. The *character* referenced at a specific code position can change from one character set to the next, though in practice the initial 256 code positions used to identify a considerable fraction of the Web's text content are mostly or entirely identical across character sets. Even when the relationship between a character's code position and encoding is not 1:1, the transformation that defines that relationship is well documented.

Condensed

A style of sans-serif font distinguished from others in its typeface by its narrow and tightly spaced nature. Opposite of *extended*.

Control character

A sequence of bits representing a signal to be sent from a user interface device to a terminal or host, for the purpose of demanding action on the part of the destination device (e.g., Escape, Tab, Carriage Return).

Copy

The generic term for a writer's work product. Different from "text" since the latter refers only to nonnumeric data in the most general sense; all copy is text, but not all text is copy.

Descendant

An element contained by the element in question even if it is deeper in the document tree.

Diacritic

A glyph added to a letter to indicate altered inflection or pronunciation. Commonly en-

countered examples include the acute accent ('), umlaut ("), and cedilla (¸).

Dingbats

A collection (usually comprising a well-populated font) of characters that are simple drawings (e.g., musical notes, circuitry symbols) rather than members of a standardized orthography.

Document tree

The notional branching structure of all elements in a document. Synonymous with "Document Object Model" as applied to a specific document.

Document Type Definition (DTD)

A machine-readable formal definition of a given markup vocabulary.

Element

Structures in an HTML, XHTML, or XML document whose beginning and end are marked with tags.

Entity reference

A reference to a named piece of content, typically a special character, that begins with an ampersand (&) and ends with a semicolon.

Extended

The complement to condensed fonts. Letters are wider than in the normal fonts, and letterspacing is usually more generous. Also referred to as "Wide" and/or "Extra Wide."

File

A discrete node on a server host's native filesystem.

Font

A collection of *glyphs* in a consistent visual style; one component of a *typeface* or *font family*. Fonts are structured according to the details of the *character set* that they support.

Font family

A collection of fonts that vary only in respect to weight (e.g., light, medium, book, demi, bold, extra bold, black) and style (e.g., normal, italic, small caps). Raster font formats like those used by Windows and early laser printers also contain separate instances for each supported type size.

Glyph

The atomic unit of a font's human-readable contents. Usually, but not always, synonymous with *character* (and vice versa). Multiple glyphs are combined into single characters when required by the specification of the font's underlying *character set*, while multiple characters are combined into a single glyph through the use of zero-width nonjoiners and other esoteric interstitial characters.

Gothic

For the past century, reliably synonymous with *sans-serif*, so named because most of the early sans-serif typefaces originated in Germany and the German-speaking regions of Switzerland.

Gutter

Negative space between a text margin and rule, between two columns, or between two paragraphs. In many cases controlled with the CSS padding properties.

HyperText Markup Language (HTML)

The ubiquitous document markup format used to create web pages.

HyperText Transfer Protocol (HTTP)

The request-response network protocol underlying the Web.

ISO 8859-x

A series of character sets introduced after *Windows-1252* but prior to *Unicode*, supporting practically all contemporary European orthography and the orthography of Hebrew, Turkish, and Thai.

Italic

A font evolved from its upright serif counterpart, through the addition of calligraphic accents. Usually skewed 5–10° clockwise from the upright. *Cf. oblique.* So named because the earliest designs for these fonts were developed in Italy, made narrower than their "Roman" counterparts with the intent of increasing the number of words that could be placed on one line.

JavaScript

The most common programming language for data processing and interactivity within browsers.

Justification

Refers to the margin (or margins) to which lines of type are hewed. A left-justified column starts all lines at a common left margin, a right-justified column ends all lines at a common right margin, and all lines of a fully justified paragraph except the last begin *and* end at common margins. This aspect of layout is controlled in CSS with the `text-align` property. Oppose *ragging*.

Kerning

Atypical letterspacing in the middle of specific pairs of glyphs, particularly ones that include A, f, j, J, L, T, V, W, w, and y. When neglected, enforces an illusion by which the letters in a given pair seem uncommonly (and distressingly) far apart. Some combinations of operating systems, software, and fonts call for frequent manual kerning of high-quality bitmapped type.

Leading

The negative space between lines of type, so named and pronounced because hot type castings were separated on the press by strips of cold lead to create that space. Related (but not identical) to the `line-height` property.

Letterspacing

Consistent space inserted between individual glyphs within a passage of text. Controlled by the CSS `letter-spacing` property (and to a degree by the `word-spacing` property).

Lower-/uppercase

Synonymous with miniscule and majuscule letterforms, respectively. So called because printers once stored individual letters of a given cast type font in upper (majuscule) and lower (miniscule) drawers.

Markup
Structural information mixed with the content being structured. HTML, XHTML, and XML are all forms of markup.

Microsoft Core Fonts for the Web
In the late 1990s, Microsoft made available a collection of fonts, designed by Matthew Carter and others, that was distributed with Windows, Internet Explorer, and as a stand-alone, free-to-use download. These fonts have been broadly available for several years on Windows systems, and to a differing degree on Apple Macintosh systems as well; according to Apple's support documentation, OS X 10.5 is the first version of Mac OS to include all of them. The Core Fonts collection is not supported by Microsoft as a specific product at this time, but remains available for download on a variety of third-party websites.

Mind maps
They are a newly popular technique for visualizing this dimension of site design.

Mono
An appellation used to distinguish fixed-width typefaces from their variable-width counterparts.

Negative space (whitespace)
Any space on a page or canvas not occupied by type, illustrations, or rules. The use of "whitespace" as a design term illuminates but is a generalization of its use as a computing term.

Oblique
The sans-serif counterpart to *italic*—without calligraphic accents.

Orthography
The study and practice of writing; a single system of writing.

Page
The visitor-facing output produced in response to a request for a URI.

Parent
Element that directly contains another element.

Parse
The initial pass made by a user agent as it reads in HTML and CSS content, turning text into an internal structure that it may later use to render the content.

Property
In CSS, an aspect of presentation. Some properties, called shorthand properties, let you specify multiple related aspects in one pass.

Ragging
The practice of removing all extra letter and word spacing from a passage so that text does *not* justify to a margin. By default, web text that is left-justified is right-ragged, and vice versa.

Recommendation
Official documents of the W3C that provide stable specifications. Commonly referred to as "web standards."

Render
Creating a presentable view from the material parsed by a user agent.

Resource
A document or document fragment referenced by a discrete Uniform Resource Identifier (URI) over the Web.

Roman
When used to refer to a typeface, "Roman" is generally synonymous with *serif*.

Rule
A line placed to one side of a block of text. Usually controlled with the CSS border properties.

Sans-serif
A class of typefaces distinguished by reliance on obviously geometric shapes, evenly weighted strokes, and unadorned terminals.

Script

A class of typeface also referred to as *cursive* and designed to resemble continuous handwriting; usually decorative.

Selector

In CSS, a terse description which identifies structures in a page to which a specified presentation form should be applied.

Serif

Inspired by classical incised letters, serif typefaces are characterized by variable-weight strokes and the presence of *serifs*—slight feet or flanges—on terminals.

Server

The side of an HTTP transaction that responds to requests with content.

Sibling

Element that shares a common parent with the element at the focus of concern. Siblings are often described as prior, if they came earlier in the document, or following, if they came late.

String

An arbitrary sequence of characters of variable validity requirements (depending on the platform in use).

Stylesheets

Descriptions of how markup structures should be presented. Cascading Style Sheets (CSS) is the dominant stylesheet form on the Web.

Tags

Markup, enclosed by < and >, to define elements in an HTML, XHTML, or XML document.

Transmission character

A sequence of bits included for reasons of legacy support, indicating data stream status and meant to be sent from a terminal (usually a teletype) to a host computer, remote storage device, or remote output device such as a printer or cardpunch. The range of control and transmission characters is represented in *ASCII* by the 00–1F

(0–31 decimal) *code position* range, as well as code position 7F/127 (Delete). The inclusion of *control* and transmission characters in ASCII was a historically significant step toward the commoditization of user interface hardware.

Typeface

An entire family of letterforms with close commonalities of design; functionally synonymous with *font family*, though in application the latter refers primarily to the vector data used to describe a typeface.

Unicode

An encoding scheme devised by a broad consortium in the early 1990s, for the purpose of serving as a framework for supporting the electronic storage and transmission of all known writing systems in aggregate. Unicode fonts reference Unicode code positions, but rarely support the breadth of Unicode. Unicode code positions U+0000–U+007F (0–127 decimal) are identical to *ASCII*, and Unicode code positions U+0080–U+00FF (128–255 decimal) are identical to their counterparts in *ISO 8859-1*.

User agent

Any software which consumes content from the web. May be a browser, or some other kind of software process.

UTF-8

A popular encoding scheme for Unicode-supported text, especially for web content written in European languages. *ASCII* characters are encoded with one bit apiece, the *ISO 8859-x* characters outside of ASCII with two bits apiece, the remaining breadth of the *Basic Multilingual Plane* with three bits apiece, and all remaining Unicode characters with four bits apiece. *Cf. variable width encoding*.

Variable-width encoding

Character encoding schemes such as UTF-8 that can use a variable number of bytes to represent a single character. In the case of UTF-8, the byte width of a character is signaled by the number of initial bits that are

Weight

set on a given character: zero for 1-byte characters, otherwise *n* for the number of bytes used to represent the character.

Weight

The width of a rule, stroke, or font. When applied to entire passages of text, weight is controlled by the CSS `font-weight` property. Common font weights for print applications range from hairline (lightest) to extra black (heaviest); the typical body copy weight is sometimes assigned the appellation of "Medium" or "Book," but usually takes no special appellation at all.

Whitespace

Characters such as spaces and tabs that represent the absence of data and text. Among these, tabs and line feeds are included in the range of *control characters*, because when these characters were first included in *ASCII*, analog teleprinters were understood to be a primary output device for ASCII-encoded data. Additionally, the amount of literal whitespace to be inserted by these characters is dependent upon hardware-, software-, or operator-controlled configuration, rather than the underlying character set specification.

Windows-1252

The 8-bit character set originally used by Windows to represent the orthography of English and Western European languages, and used as the encoding for older Windows system fonts and Microsoft's older Core Fonts for the Web. Similar but not identical to ISO 8859-1. The lower half of both Windows-1252 and the *ISO 8859-x* character sets is identical to the ASCII character set.

World Wide Web Consortium (W3C)

An organization that serves as the primary forum for specifying open web-oriented technologies.

Index

Symbols

& (ampersand), 247
? (question mark), 247

A

a element, 279
abbr element, 140, 168
accesskey attribute, 261
acronym element, 140
action attribute, 247
:active pseudoclass, 137, 139
ActiveX platform, 269
additive color model, 144
adjacent selectors, 29
Adobe Photoshop
  applying multiple adjustments, 185
  background textures/patterns, 155
  color profiles, 186
  cropping images, 180
  downsampling images, 187
  Layers palette, 157
  matting images, 181
  optimizing photo contrast, 183
  preparing images, 178
  resampling images, 182
Adobe Shockwave Flash platform, 195, 197
:after pseudoelement, 142
Ajax (Asynchronous JavaScript And XML),
  xxv
aliasing, 210
align attribute, 287
all media type, 26
AlphaImageLoader filter, 270
alt attribute
  about, 15, 179
  captioning images, 191
  FIR considerations, 160
  form accessibility and, 260
  sizing type, 216
Amazon.com, 273
ampersand (&), 247
ancestors, 28
anti-aliasing, 210
article element, 72
ASCII standard
  about, 225
  choosing an encoding scheme, 225
  reserved characters, 248
aside element, 72
assistive technology, 163
atomic grids, 108
attribute selectors, 29, 173
attributes
  about, xxv, 8
  universal, 14–17
  XHTML rules, 8
audio element, 199–201

B

background images
  composing, 152–157
  drop shadows, 153, 157
  Faux Columns, 152, 154
  FIR and, 123, 139, 154, 157–160
  gel effects, 153, 157
  nonrepeating motifs, 153, 156
  properties supported, 150
  rounded corners, 154, 157
  setting values, 151

We'd like to hear your suggestions for improving our indexes. Send email to *index@oreilly.com*.

textures and patterns, 153, 155–157
background property, 144, 151, 152
background-attachment property
    about, 151
    nonrepeating motifs, 157
background-color property
    about, 151
    Faux Columns, 155
    file upload controls and, 249
    stylesheet rules, 144
background-image property
    about, 151
    lists and, 117
    negative margins and, 79
    sprites and, 161
background-position property
    about, 151
    Faux Columns, 155
    setting values, 151
    sizing type, 215
    sprites and, 160, 161
background-repeat property
    about, 151
    Faux Columns, 155
    lists and, 117
background-size property, 152
:before pseudoelement, 142
behavior
    forms and, 246–251
    JavaScript support, xxv
    separation considerations, 18–20
Bergevin, Holly, 268
biological classification, 68
blink element, 286
block element
    collapsed margins, 80
    flow behavior, 83
    increasing link footprint, 138
    layout properties and, 38
    positioning, 86–88
    stacking, 101
blockquote element, 142, 276
blowouts, 232, 268
body element
    assigning box properties, 82
    background images, 156
    location cues, 71
    multicolumned layouts, 92
    relationship examples, 28

selector support, 30
    sizing type, 217
border-bottom property, 133
border-collapse property, 169
border-left property, 153
border-radius property, 157
border-right property, 153
border-top property, 133
borders
    composing table cells, 168
    element size control, 73
    image, 179–180
    layout properties, 81
bottom property
    about, 38, 39
    positioning elements, 97, 99
box model (see CSS box model)
box-sizing property, 73, 250
br element, 281
braille media type, 27
breadcrumbs
    defined, 64
    orientation of, 65, 103
brightness values (color), 145
browsers
    box behavior of root elements, 82
    collapsed margins, 80
    defined, xxv
    disabling document links, 67
    graded support, 273
    list default styles, 115
    navigating forms, 261
    parsing content, 20
    pseudoclasses and, 138
    recent browser wars, 266
    rendering content, 20
    rounded corners, 157
    selector considerations, 173
    sizing type, 216, 235
    targeting with conditional comments, 24
    URI limitations, 247
    URI support, 2
    viewing recommendations, 272
    XHTML limitations, 11
bullets, inserting custom, 121

C

canvas element, 201
canvas grids

defining, 108
Fibonacci sequence, 110
flexible, 111–113
Golden Ratio, 110
Rule of Thirds, 110
CanvasRenderingContext2D API, 201
caption element
about, 166
sample table markup, 167
captioning images, 191
cascade
applying taxonomy via, 70–72
conflict resolution, 31
deviations in, 272
case sensitivity, HTML markup, 8
cathode ray tube (CRT), 145, 149
character encoding
about, 224
choosing encoding scheme, 225
inserting non-ASCII characters, 226–228
literal spaces, 248
reserved characters, 248
standards for, 225
charset attribute, 221
@charset declaration, 286
child elements
defined, 28
selecting, 30
child selectors, 29, 173
cite element, 140, 142
Clason, Steve, 269
class attribute
about, 14
aligning data, 171
captioning images, 192
consistency considerations, 56
definition lists, 127, 128
flexibility considerations, 53
form accessibility and, 260
form markup, 246
fouling values, 272
inline lists, 120
location cues, 70
multicolumned layouts, 93
navigation and, 117, 124
referencing links, 67
scope of content, 58
selector support, 29
simplicity considerations, 52

table composition, 173
clear property
about, 38, 39, 86
applying, 88
definition lists, 128
grids and, 108
multicolumned layouts, 90, 93
styling definition lists, 125
client-side environment
about, xxv
architecture, 291
layers supported, xxv
clients (see browsers)
clip property, 284
closing tags
defined, 8
failure to insert, 272
cm unit, 34, 36
CMS (Content Management System)
handling unpredictable, 78
publishing images, 188–190
URI support, 2
code element, 140, 280
col element
about, 165
aligning data, 171
sample table markup, 167
colgroup element
about, 165
aligning data, 171
sample table markup, 167
collapsed margins, 80
color blindness, 144
color profiles, 185
color property
about, 143
file upload controls and, 249
color theory
about, 143
additional information, 143
additive color model, 144
complementary colors, 146
contrast considerations, 146
design considerations, 146
display environments, 148–149
HSB color model, 145, 256
identifying colors, 147
RGB color model, 146
subtractive color model, 145, 146

vision conditions and, 144
color units, 34, 37
ColorZilla extension (Firefox), 147
colspan element
    aligning data, 171
    rollover effects, 175
    sample table markup, 168
column-span property, 96
comments, conditional, 24
complementary colors, 146
conditional comments, 24
conflict resolution, 31, 32
content
    assessing scope, 229
    creating effective link, 136–137
    defined, xxiv
    describing with attributes, 15
    element size control, 73
    markup support, xxv
    multidimensionality of, 62
    parsing, 20
    plug-in, 190–195
    progressive enhancement, 53
    rendering, 20
    replaced elements and, 177
    scenario without links, 1
    secondary, 230
    separation considerations, 18–20
Content Management System (CMS)
    handling unpredictable, 78
    publishing images, 188–190
    URI support, 2
content property
    definition lists, 126
    quotation markup and, 142
    usage considerations, 285
contenteditable attribute, 17
contrast
    color theory on, 146
    optimizing for photos, 183
    table header/footer, 173–175
controls (see form controls)
controls attribute, 200
counters, 284
CREATE statement (SQL), 239
CREATE TABLE statement (SQL), 237
cropping images, 180, 185
CRT (cathode ray tube), 145, 149
CRUD acronym, 238, 240

CSS box model
    determining, 12
    element size control, 73
CSS layout
    @-rules, 282
    advanced, 96
    auto values for properties, 74–78
    borders, 81
    boundaries on element dimensions, 77
    box property considerations, 82
    commonly supported properties, 37, 38
    content property and, 285
    counters, 284
    disadvantages of tables, 163–165
    element flow, 83–86, 285
    element size control, 73
    forms and, 252–254
    handling unpredictable, 77
    hiding stuff, 284
    inherit value, 283
    margins, 78–80
    multicolumned layouts, 88–96
    navigation considerations, 102–106
    overflow property, 75–77
    padding, 82
    popular approaches, 106–113
    positioning block elements, 86–88
    positioning properties, 96–99
    property prefixes, 283
    rendering modes, 73
    rounding differences, 282
    Unicode considerations, 285
    visibility property, 99
    z-index property, 99
CSS Zen
    about, 59
    achieving consistency, 55–57
    divisibility principle, 61
    functional principles, 60
    habits of effective stylists, 49–59
    interconnection principle, 61
    KISS principle, 50–52
    maintaining bearings, 57–59
    maintaining flexibility, 52–55
    mutability principle, 61
    separation principle, 61
CSS3 module, 96
cursor property, 67, 140

D

damnpersands, 247, 276
data tables (see tables)
dd element
    about, 124
    dictionary example, 126
    thumbnail images and, 192
def element, 141
definition lists
    defined, 124
    dialogue example, 127–128
    dictionary example, 125–127
    styling, 124
del element, 141, 278
DELETE statement (SQL), 239
deprecated elements, 12
descendant selectors, 29
descendants, 28
design considerations
    assessing content scope, 229
    color theory, 146
    distinguishing type, 230
    entering type treatments, 233
    for forms, 237, 239, 252–254
    hierarchy in, 228
    secondary content, 230
    setting type around blowouts, 232
    styling passages of similar priority, 232
Dhakar, Lokesh, 194
diacritics, 226
digital typesetting, 205
DigitalColor Meter application, 147
dir attribute, 14
DirectoryIndex directory, 247
disabled attribute, 257
display property
    about, 38
    changing element flow, 84–86
    creating lists, 116
    definition lists, 126
    element positioning and, 97
    FIR considerations, 158
    form accessibility and, 259
    form markup, 245, 252
    increasing link footprint, 138
    margin doubling and, 268
    multicolumned layouts, 92, 96
    navigation considerations, 66, 122, 123
    replaced elements and, 178

div element
    cautions using, 288
    collapsed margins, 80
    inline lists, 120
    navigation and, 117
dl element, 192
doctype declaration
    defined, 10
doctype declarations
    additional information, 13
    box models, 12
    choosing right type, 13
    defined, xxv
Document Object Model (see DOM)
document trees
    defined, 28
    working with, 19
documentation as compass, 59
documents
    box behavior of root elements, 82
    connecting stylesheets to, 23–39
    defined, xxiv
    disabling links, 67
    life cycle overview, 20
    links to specific passages, 135
    scenario without links, 2
    scope of content, 58
DOM (Document Object Model)
    about, xxv
    defined, 42
    SWFObject support, 195
Dominey, Todd, 194
downsampling, 187
Dreamhost Wiki, 198
drop shadows, 153, 157
DROP statement (SQL), 239
dt element
    about, 124
    dialogue example, 128
    thumbnail images and, 192
DTD (document type definition), xxv, 11
dyads, 149

E

ECMA-262 standard, 42
elements
    changing flow behavior, 84–86
    choosing to style, 27
    default flow behavior, 83

defined, xxv, 8
deprecated, 12
dimension boundaries, 77
flow rules, 285
nesting, 28
page structure, 10
parts of tables, 165–168
positioning, 96–99
replaced, 177
selector support, 29
size control, 73
stacking, 101, 275
structural, 72
styling for navigation, 121–124
styling heading, 131–133
universal hooks, 14
value inheritance, 33
em element, 140, 280
em unit
    about, 33, 34
    background-position property and, 151
    sizing type, 215, 216
embed element
    embedding multimedia, 196, 197, 198
    object element versus, 274
embedding multimedia, 196
embossed media type, 27
enctype attribute, 249
Eolas, 197
error messages, 240
event handler attributes, 288
expression function (JavaScript), 269

F

Facebook website, 123, 273
Fahrner Image Replacement
    about, 154
    bitmapped copy and, 157–160
    drawbacks, 159
    implementing, 123
    layout considerations, 139
    sprite considerations, 160–161
    stylesheet rules, 159
Fahrner, Todd, 158
Faux Columns, 152, 154
Fibonacci sequence, 107, 110, 112
fields
    form rules for, 239, 240
    identifying required, 255

fieldset element
    about, 243
    form layout and, 255
    identifying required fields, 255
    identifying user input errors, 256
figure element, 72
files
    defined, xxiv
    uploading, 249
Firebug extension (Firefox), 108, 147
Firefox browser
    ColorZilla extension, 147
    navigating forms, 261
    pseudoclasses and, 138
    rounded corners, 157
    selector considerations, 173
    Web Developer Toolbar extension, 108, 147
Fitts's Law, 85
fixed layouts, 106–108, 139
flexible layouts, 106–108, 139
float property
    about, 38, 39, 86
    applying, 88
    canceling values, 87
    converting two-column layout, 89
    FIR considerations, 159
    form markup, 252
    margin doubling and, 268
    multicolumned layouts, 90, 93, 95
    navigation and, 102, 105, 123
    styling navigation elements, 121
    thumbnail images and, 192
    usage rules, 86
:focus pseudoclass, 138
font element, 217
font property, 222–223
font-family property
    applying choices, 220–221
    character encoding, 224
    finding typeface names, 222
    system default types and, 222
font-size property
    about, 34
    form controls, 250, 253
    hasLayout property and, 268
    setting values, 132
    sizing type, 216
    system default types and, 222

values supported, 36, 217
font-variant property, 235
font-weight property, 125, 208
fonts (see Web typography)
footer element, 72
footer links, 121
form controls
    grouping by appearance, 254
    HTML5 supported, 262
    manipulating, 249–251
    name attribute, 279
    plug-ins and, 275
    rules for effective, 240
    value inheritance and, 33
form elements
    enctype attribute, 249
    links and, 133
formnovalidate attribute, 262
forms
    additional information, 241
    behavior and, 246–251
    building effective, 237–241
    creating accessible, 258–263
    establishing requirements, 241–243
    get requests, 247
    identifying required fields, 255
    keyboard navigation, 260
    layout and, 252–254
    markup and, 243–246
    organizing UI by function, 238
    presentation and, 246–251
    prototyping, 251–252
    rules for effective, 239–241
    structure and, 243–246–251
    submission constraints, 255–258
    URL encoding, 248
frame element, 277, 279
frameset element, 277
Frameset HTML subtype, 12

G

gallery, image
    Lightbox tool, 194
    working with previews, 192–193
gel effects, 153, 157
get method, 247
GetXMLHttpRequest API, xxv
GIF format, 186, 187
Git RCS, 189

Golden Ratio, 107, 110
grids (see canvas grids)
Gutenberg's press, 204
gutters, 82

H

handheld media type, 27, 34
hasLayout property, 268
HCI (human-computer interaction), 62, 85
header element, 72
Header function (PHP), 224
headers attribute, 168
headings
    creating rules, 133
    levels supported, 129
    normalizing dimensions, 132
    optimal insertion, 131
    size considerations, 132
    styling elements, 131–133
    type treatment, 132
    usage in print materials, 129
height property
    about, 38
    auto value, 74
    captioning images, 191
    form controls, 249
    grids and, 110
    image dimensions, 179
    link dimensions, 138, 139
    multicolumned layouts, 95
    navigation and, 104, 123
Hewlett-Packard, 185
hinting (typography), 211
Holly Hack, 268
:hover pseudoclass, 137, 139
hr element, 281
href attribute
    about, 134
    ampersand and, 247
    creating effective link content, 136–137
    image publication, 190
    linking to specific passages, 135
HSB color model, 145, 256
HTML documents (see documents)
html element, 82
HTML markup
    avoiding legacy attributes in tables, 168
    case sensitivity, 8
    failure to validate, 276

forms and, 243–246
frame considerations, 277
HTML variants, 11, 12–13
image dimensions, 179
KISS principle, 50
links and, 133
rendering modes, 10
separation considerations, 18–20
syntax overview, 7–10
typical selector interface, 29
universal attributes, 14–17
usage suggestions, 278–281
validation and implementation, 272
HTML5 specification
canvas element, 201
contenteditable attribute, 17
form features, 261–263
new structural elements, 72
video/audio elements, 199–201
HTMLMediaElement interface, 200
HTTP (Hypertext Transfer Protocol)
about, 41, 292
client-server architecture, 291
Content-Disposition header, 199
Content-Language header, 16, 221
Content-Type header, 199, 221, 271
controlling request volume, 294
MIME types, 293
REST support, 240
http-equiv attribute, 289
hue values (color), 145, 149
human-computer interaction (HCI), 62, 85
hyperlinks
contenteditable attribute, 17
creating effective content, 136–137
disabling for documents, 67
to document passages, 135
implementation challenges, 4
improving user experience via, 3
increasing footprint, 138
inline links, 64
managing, 3
markup considerations, 133
scenarios without links, 1
styling, 137–140
URIs in, 2
Hypertext Transfer Protocol (see HTTP)

I

ICC (International Color Consortium), 185
id attribute
about, 14
captioning images, 192
consistency considerations, 56
flexibility considerations, 54
form accessibility and, 260
form markup, 246
fouling values, 272
linking to specific passages, 135
location cues, 70
multicolumned layouts, 90, 93
navigation and, 104, 122, 124
sample table markup, 168
scope of content, 58
simplicity considerations, 52
table composition, 173
id attribute selector support, 29
iframe element
about, 12, 277
form controls and plug-ins, 275
name attribute, 279
value inheritance and, 33
ImageMagick, 192
images, 177
(see also background images)
additional information, 180
alt attribute, 179
applying multiple adjustments, 185
captioning, 191
cropping, 180, 185
dimensions and borders, 179–180
downsampling, 187
layouts within columns, 190
level changes, 183, 185
matting, 181, 185
optimizing, 186–188
optimizing contrast, 183
organizing, 188
preparing for production, 178–180
production process, 180–185
publishing, 188–190
replaced elements and, 178
resampling, 182, 185
styling, 190–195
thumbnail, 192–193
working with color profiles, 185
images directory, 188

img element
   about, 178
   embedding video, 200
   evolution of, 177
   image publication, 190
   replaced elements and, 178
@import declaration
   about, 25
   adding media values, 26
   connecting stylesheets, 23
   usage suggestions, 282
in unit, 34, 36
include function, 25
information architecture
   additional information, 62
   applying taxonomy through cascade, 70–72
   creating usable interfaces, 66–67
   defined, 61
   multidimensionality of content, 62
   scenarios and user testing, 67
   site navigation, 63
   taxonomy and nomenclature, 68
   visit strategies, 64
information, presentation and, 60
inheritance
   CSS considerations, 283
   value, 33
inline elements
   about, 83
   link markup and, 133
   table of supported, 140
   usage suggestions, 280
inline images, 190
inline links, 64
inline lists, 120
inline-block element
   flow behavior, 84, 85
   footer link layouts, 121
   increasing link footprint, 138
   layout properties and, 38
   thumbnail images and, 193
input element
   about, 242
   CSS interactions, 249
   form controls and, 249, 253, 255
   required attribute, 262
   SQL statements and, 239
   usage suggestions, 66

ins element, 141, 289
INSERT statement (SQL), 239
International Color Consortium (ICC), 185
Internet Explorer
   about, 265
   ActiveX filters/transitions, 269
   browser wars, 266
   expression function and, 269
   hasLayout property, 268
   margin doubling, 268
   navigating forms, 261
   PNG support, 270
   poor selector support, 267
   property support, 270
   pseudoclasses and, 138
   selector considerations, 173
   sizing type, 216
   targeting with conditional comments, 24
   thumbnail images and, 193
   URI limitations, 247
   user interface properties, 287
   XHMTL/XML issues, 271
ISO 8859 standard, 42, 225, 226

J

JavaScript
   about, xxv
   behavior support, xxv
   expression function, 269
   identifying user input errors, 256
   SWFObject support, 195
Jessey, Simon, 198
JPEG format, 186, 187, 270
jQuery framework, 96

K

kbd element, 140
KISS principle, 50–52

L

label element
   form markup, 240, 246, 253
   identifying required fields, 255
lang attribute, 14, 15
layout (see CSS layout)
LCD (liquid crystal diode), 145, 149
left property
   about, 38, 39

positioning elements, 97, 99
legend element
    about, 244
    form markup, 245, 255
Lehrer, Tom, 147
length attribute, 245, 249
letter-spacing property, 207, 236
letterforms
    aliasing and, 210
    history of, 203–205
li element
    creating lists, 116
    form markup, 244, 246
    identifying required fields, 255
    identifying user input errors, 256
    relationship examples, 28
    styling definition lists, 125
Lightbox tool, 194
line-height property
    about, 207
    form controls, 249
    secondary navigation, 124
    setting type around blowouts, 232
    sizing type, 216, 234
    styling headings, 132
    system default types and, 222
link element
    attributes supported, 134
    connecting stylesheets, 23
    media attribute, 26
    name attribute, 279
    referencing stylesheets, 23
    replacing with style element, 25
:link pseudoclass, 137
link rot, 3
liquid crystal diode (LCD), 145, 149
list-style-image property, 117, 121
list-style-type property, 116, 120, 124
lossless compression, 187
lossy compression, 187

M

map element, 279
margin doubling, 268
margin-bottom property, 80
margin-left property, 116, 124, 142
margin-right property, 90
margin-top property, 80
margins

collapsed, 80
element size control, 73
multicolumned layouts, 90
negative, 79
table cells, 170
markup, 7
    (see also HTML markup)
    content support, xxv
    defined, xxiv
    structure support, xxv, 7
marquee element, 286
matting images, 181, 185
max-* property, 77
maxlength attribute, 245
media attribute, 26
@media declaration
    style blocks, 26
    usage suggestions, 282
media types
    color management, 185
    targeting rules, 26
meta element, 224, 279
Meyer, Eric, 203
Microsoft Corporation, 185, 197, 205, 266
MIME types, 293
Model-View-Controller architecture, xxv
Morse Code, 224
Mosaic browser, 177
multicolumned layout module (CSS3), 96
multicolumned layouts
    advanced, 96
    converting two-column layout, 89
    empty containers and, 95
    Faux Columns, 155
    implementing, 88–96
    moving to three columns, 93–95
    stylesheets and, 92
    two-column overview, 90–92
multimedia
    adding motion/sound, 195
    embedding, 196–202
multiple selectors, 29

N

name attribute, 247, 279
name/value pairs, 247
nav element
    about, 72, 117
    accessibility/usability, 118

alternative navigation, 118
determining source order, 122
navigation
alternative means, 118
creating usable interfaces, 66–67
forcing into desired coordinates, 104–106
KISS principle, 52
orienting the list, 102–104
primary layout, 122
secondary, 123
sprites and, 160
styling elements, 121–124
supporting for forms, 260
typical approaches, 63
visit strategies, 65
negative margins, 79
nesting
elements, 28
ordered lists, 120
Netscape, 197, 266, 272
newspaper design, 213–215
noframes element, 279
noscript element, 279

O

object element
embed element versus, 274
embedding multimedia, 196, 197, 201
evolution of, 177
publishing multimedia content, 198
Odeo markup, 196
ol element
creating lists, 116
relationship examples, 28
opacity property, 269
opening tags, 8
OpenType format, 205
Opera Web Standards Curriculum, 245
optgroup element, 250
optimizing
images, 186–188
photo contrast, 183
option element, 250
ordered lists
changing ranges, 119
creating, 116
list-style-type property, 116
nav element, 117–119
nesting, 120

outline support, 120
selectors and, 30
thumbnail images and, 192
UA default styles, 115
outlines, 120
overbuilding, 53
overflow property
aligning data, 171
captioning images, 191
Faux Columns, 154
handling unpredictable, 77
heading dimensions, 132
multicolumned layouts, 90, 95
navigation and, 123
setting type around blowouts, 232
values supported, 75–77
overflow-x property, 78
overflow-y property, 78

P

p selector, 30
padding
about, 82
element size control, 73
navigation and, 123, 124
padding-bottom property, 157
padding-left property, 116, 121
padding-top property, 92, 106
Page Zoom functionality, 112
pages
above the fold, 214
defined, xxiv
grid considerations, 109
rendering, xxv
structure considerations, 10
palettes
creating, 149
grays in, 146
web-safe, 148–149
param element, 196, 197
parent elements, 28
parsing
about, xxv
content, 20
% unit
about, 33, 34
sizing type, 217
percentage value, 82
photographs, optimizing contrast, 183

platesetter, 205
plug-ins, 190–195, 275
PNG format, 186, 187, 269, 270
position property
    about, 38, 39, 96
    converting two-column layout, 89
    disadvantages of tables, 164
    file upload controls and, 249
    form layout and, 255
    multicolumned layouts, 96
    navigation and, 102, 106, 123
    positioning elements, 99
    simplicity considerations, 51
    stacking elements and, 101
    values supported, 96
post method, 247, 249
Postel's Law, 197, 272
pre element, 236, 281
presbyopia, 144
presentation
    CSS support, xxv
    forms and, 246–251
    information and, 60
    inline elements, 280
    separation considerations, 18–20
    style attribute cautions, 25
print media type, 27, 36
projection media type, 27, 34
property/value pairs
    canceling values, 87
    defined, xxiv
    Faux Columns, 155
    font-size keywords, 36, 217
    formatting inline images, 191
    inheritance considerations, 33
proportional layouts, 106–108
prototyping forms, 251–252
pseudoclasses, 137
pt unit, 33, 36
publishing images, 188–190
px unit
    about, 33, 34
    background-position property and, 151
    display pitch and, 34
    hasLayout property and, 268
    sizing type, 216

Q

q element, 141, 142

question mark (?), 247
quirks mode rendering, 73, 249
quotation marks, 9

R

ransom note effect, 228
RCS (Revision Control System), 189
readonly attribute, 257
Really Simple Syndication (RSS), 195
RealNetworks, 274
rel attribute, 134
rendering
    about, xxv
    content, 20
    modes supported, 10, 73
    tables, 170
replaced elements, 177
required attribute, 262
required fields, form rules for, 239
resampling images, 182, 185
reserved characters, 248
resources
    defined, xxiv
    scenario without links, 1
REST (REpresentational State Transfer), 240
Revision Control System (RCS), 189
RFC 2396, 134
RFC 3986, 248
RGB color model, 146
right property
    about, 38, 39
    positioning elements, 97, 99
rollover effects, 175
rounded corners, 154, 157
rounding differences, 282
rowspan element
    aligning data, 171
    rollover effects, 175
    sample table markup, 168
    selector considerations, 173
RSS (Really Simple Syndication), 195
Rule of Thirds, 107, 110
rules
    conflict resolution, 31, 32
    CSS layout, 282
    defined, xxiv
    effective web forms/applications, 239–241
    element flow, 285
    image dimensions/borders, 180

selector weight, 31
targeting to specific media, 26
XHTML, 8
Rundle, Mike, 159

S

Safari browser
ICC support, 185
navigating forms, 261
rounded corners, 157
Saint-Exupéry, Antoine de, 230
samp element, 140
saturation values (color), 145
Scalable Vector Graphics (SVG), 185, 187, 202
scope attribute, 168
screen media type
commonly used units, 34
defined, 27
px unit support, 34
screen readers, 119
search capability, navigation and, 64, 65
Search Engine Optimization (SEO), 93, 135, 159
Search Engine Result Page (SERP), 63
section element, 72
select element
about, 243
form controls and, 250, 254
plug-in content and, 198
SELECT statement (SQL), 239
selector weights, 31, 137
selectors
conflict resolution, 31, 32
CSS-supported types, 29
defined, xxiv
IE limitations, 267
pseudoclasses and, 137
rule priority, 31
table composition, 173
typical markup interface, 29
writing, 27
SEO (Search Engine Optimization), 93, 135, 159
SERP (Search Engine Result Page), 63
server-side environment
about, xxv
architecture, 291
Shea, Dave, 60, 160

sibling elements, 28
site maps, 64, 65
size attribute, 217
slideshow presentations
Lightbox tool, 194
SlideShowPro tool, 194
working with previews, 192–193
SlideShowPro tool, 194
source element, 200
span element
definition lists, 127, 128
FIR considerations, 158
form markup, 245
speech media type, 27
sprites, 160–161
SQL databases, 237–239
src attribute
ampersand and, 247
embedding video, 200
image publication, 189, 190
sRGB color space, 185, 270
stacking elements, 101, 275
standards (see web standards)
start attribute
changing list ranges, 119
creating lists, 116
Stearns, Geoff, 195
Strict HTML subtype, 12
strict mode rendering, 73
strike element, 278
strong element, 83, 140, 280
structure, 61
(see also information architecture)
forms and, 243–246–251
markup support, xxv, 7
new elements, 72
processing content, 10
scenario without links, 1
separation considerations, 18–20
style attribute
about, 14
cautions using, 25, 287
style element
connecting stylesheets, 23
media attribute, 26
replacing link element, 25
stylesheets
color property and, 144
commonly used units, 34

connecting to documents, 23–39
defined, xxiv
Fahrner Image Replacement rules, 159
image dimensions, 179
multicolumned layouts, 92
pseudoclasses and, 137
referencing with link element, 23
universal hooks, 14
sub element, 141
subtractive color model, 145, 146
Subversion RCS, 189
summary element, 167
sup element, 141
SVG (Scalable Vector Graphics), 185, 187, 202
SWFObject, 195, 198

T

tabindex attribute, 260
table element
composing cells, 168
form accessibility and, 260
multicolumned layouts, 92
sample markup, 167
tables
adding rollover accents, 175
aligning, 172–175
composing cells, 168–171
disadvantages, 163–165
parts of, 165–168
reducing header/footer contrast, 173–175
rendering, 170
sample markup, 166
tags
closing, 8
defined, xxv, 8
navigation and, 64, 65
opening, 8
target attribute, 134
taxonomy
applying through cascade, 70–72
defined, 68
tbody element
about, 166
invalid markup, 276
td element
about, 165
aligning data, 170
sample table markup, 168

template layout module (CSS3), 96
templates
achieving consistency with, 56, 57
disadvantages of tables, 164
flexibility considerations, 54
fragility of, 272
layout types supported, 106–108
testing
prototypes, 251–252
scenarios, 67
tetrads, 149
Text Zoom functionality, 112
text-align property
about, 207
secondary navigation, 123
table composition, 170, 172
text-decoration property, 139
text-indent property, 159
text-transform property, 125, 128, 235
textarea element
about, 242
form controls, 249
required attribute, 262
tfoot element
about, 166
invalid markup, 276
reducing contrast, 173–175
sample table markup, 168
selector considerations, 173
th element
about, 165
aligning data, 170
sample table markup, 168
selector considerations, 173
thead element
about, 166
aligning data, 171
invalid markup, 276
reducing contrast, 173–175
sample table markup, 168
selector considerations, 173
thumbnail images, 192–193
title attribute
about, 14, 15
captioning images, 191
creating effective content, 136–137
hyperlinks and, 134
title element
about, 130

rollover effects, 175
sample table markup, 167
tool tips, 15
top property
    about, 38, 39
    positioning elements, 97, 99
tr element, 165
Transitional HTML subtype, 12
triads, 149
TrueType format, 205
tty media type, 27
Turnbull, Angus, 270
tv media type, 27
type attribute
    about, 116
    changing list ranges, 120
    creating lists, 116
typography (see web typography)

U

ul element
    form markup, 244
    relationship examples, 28
underlines, gratuitous, 289
Unicode standard
    about, 225
    choosing an encoding scheme, 225
    CSS considerations, 285
    inserting non-ASCII characters, 227–228
Unicode Transformation Format (UTF), 42
Uniform Resource Identifiers (see URIs)
universal attributes
    contenteditable attribute, 17
    defined, 14
    describing content, 15
    stylesheet hooks, 14
universal selectors, 29
unordered lists
    creating, 116
    list-style-type property, 116
    nav element, 117–119
    thumbnail images and, 192
    UA default styles, 115
UPDATE statement (SQL), 239
uploading files, 249
URIs (Uniform Resource Identifiers)
    browser limitations, 247
    defined, 2
    href attribute and, 134

hyperlink implementation challenges, 4
    improving user experience via, 3
    managing links, 3
    reserved characters, 248
user agents
    alternative navigation, 118
    defined, xxv
    list default styles, 115
    stripping styles, 122
    styling definition lists, 124
user testing, 67
user-generated content (see forms)
UTF (Unicode Transformation Format), 42
UTF-8 encoding scheme, 225

V

value attribute
    changing list ranges, 119
    creating lists, 116
    form markup, 246, 250
values
    about, xxv, 8
    canceling for float property, 87
    common units, 33
    computed, 282
    inheriting, 33, 283
    percentage, 82
var element, 141
vertical-align property, 170, 172
video element, 199–201
Vimeo markup, 196
visibility property, 100, 259
vision conditions, 144, 258
:visited pseudoclass, 137

W

W3C Recommendations, xxv, 10
WAI-ARIA, 260
wayfinding (see navigation)
WCAG (Web Content Accessibility
        Guidelines), 41, 259
Weakley, Russ, 159
web application rules, 239–241
Web Content Accessibility Guidelines
        (WCAG), 41, 259
Web Developer Toolbar extension (Firefox),
        108, 147
web forms (see forms)

web standards
    accessibility, 43
    benefits of, 46
    best practices, 44
    debated issues, 42–45
    development rules, 46
    forward compatibility, 43
    interoperability, 42
    legacy asset inertia, 44
    listed, 41
    market forces, 43
    strict constructionism, 45
    vendor priorities, 44
web typography
    aliasing, 210
    anti-aliasing, 210
    applying choices, 220–221
    balanced type treatments, 228–234
    character encoding, 224–228
    good practices, 236
    hinting, 211
    history of letterforms, 203–205
    legibility, 213
    limited choices, 217–220
    readability, 212
    sizing type, 215–217
    type styles, 212–215
    typographical properties, 234–236
    visual glossary, 206–208
    working with typefaces/fonts, 217–223
web usability (see information architecture)
web-safe palettes, 148–149
weblogs, 123
websites
    simplicity and, 52
    typical navigation approaches, 63
Webstandards.org, 276
white-space property
    about, 77, 236
    secondary navigation, 124
    styling for legibility, 213
    usage suggestions, 281
width property
    about, 38
    aligning data, 171
    auto value, 74
    composing table cells, 169
    converting two-column layout, 89
    form markup, 245, 249, 252

    image dimensions, 179
    increasing link footprint, 138
    multicolumned layouts, 90
    navigation and, 104, 123
    percentage value, 82
    positioning elements, 99
    sample table markup, 168
    styling definition lists, 125
Windows Media Player, 197, 274
Windows-1252 standard, 226
word-spacing property, 207, 236

X

XHTML
    about, 11
    attribute rules, 8
    case sensitivity, 8
    Internet Explorer issues, 271
    quotation mark rules, 9
XML, IE issues, 271
xml:lang attribute, 14, 16
XMLHttpRequest object, 199, 277

Y

Yahoo!, 273
YouTube markup, 196

Z

z-index property
    CSS considerations, 284
    navigation and, 103
    simplicity considerations, 51
    stacking elements and, 101

About the Author

Ben Henick has been building websites since September 1995, when he took on his first web project as an academic volunteer. He has worked on nearly every aspect of site design and development, from foundation HTML to finicky CSS to larger-scale architecture and content management. He has written for A List Apart, the Web Standards Project, and most recently for Opera Software's Web Standards Curriculum.

Colophon

The animal on the cover of *HTML & CSS: The Good Parts* is a ring-tailed cat (*Bassariscus astutus*). Its Latin name means "cunning little fox," though it is neither a cat nor a fox; it's a mammal in the raccoon family. The ring-tailed cat is native to the southwestern United States and Mexico and prefers rocky, semiarid habitats, including deserts. It can also be found in woodland areas.

True to its name, the animal's tail—which is longer than the rest of its body—displays rings of black and white fur, contrasting with its body's dark brown color. It is nocturnal and omnivorous, foraging for fruits and berries and preying on small rodents, lizards, and birds after dusk. To help in these tasks, it boasts incredibly flexible ankle joints—capable of rotating over 180 degrees that allow it to climb and move along narrow ledges quickly.

Ringtails are easily tamed if found when young. Settlers in the American southwest often kept them as pets, using them to keep their homes free of rodents, earning them the nickname "miner's cat."

The cover image is from *The Riverside Natural History*. The cover font is Adobe ITC Garamond. The text font is Linotype Birka; the heading font is Adobe Myriad Condensed; and the code font is LucasFont's TheSansMonoCondensed.

Get even more for your money.

Join the O'Reilly Community, and register the O'Reilly books you own.It's free, and you'll get:

- 40% upgrade offer on O'Reilly books
- Membership discounts on books and events
- Free lifetime updates to electronic formats of books
- Multiple ebook formats, DRM FREE
- Participation in the O'Reilly community
- Newsletters
- Account management
- 100% Satisfaction Guarantee

Signing up is easy:

1. **Go to: oreilly.com/go/register**
2. **Create an O'Reilly login.**
3. **Provide your address.**
4. **Register your books.**

Note: English-language books only

To order books online:

oreilly.com/order_new

For questions about products or an order:

orders@oreilly.com

To sign up to get topic-specific email announcements and/or news about upcoming books, conferences, special offers, and new technologies:

elists@oreilly.com

For technical questions about book content:

booktech@oreilly.com

To submit new book proposals to our editors:

proposals@oreilly.com

Many O'Reilly books are available in PDF and several ebook formats. For more information:

oreilly.com/ebooks

O'REILLY®

Spreading the knowledge of innovators   www.oreilly.com

Buy this book and get access to the online edition for 45 days—for free!

Better Ways to Build Websites that Work

HTML & CSS: The Good Parts

O'REILLY®

Ben Henick

HTML & CSS: The Good Parts

By Ben Henick
February 2010, $34.99
ISBN 9780596157609

With Safari Books Online, you can:

Access the contents of thousands of technology and business books

- Quickly search over 7000 books and certification guides
- Download whole books or chapters in PDF format, at no extra cost, to print or read on the go
- Copy and paste code
- Save up to 35% on O'Reilly print books
- **New!** Access mobile-friendly books directly from cell phones and mobile devices

Stay up-to-date on emerging topics before the books are published

- Get on-demand access to evolving manuscripts.
- Interact directly with authors of upcoming books

Explore thousands of hours of video on technology and design topics

- Learn from expert video tutorials
- Watch and replay recorded conference sessions

To try out Safari and the online edition of this book FREE for 45 days, go to **www.oreilly.com/go/safarienabled** and enter the coupon code BFQCIWH. To see the complete Safari Library, visit safari.oreilly.com.

O'REILLY®

Spreading the knowledge of innovators

safari.oreilly.com